For years Roma and I have endeavored to be noisy Christians. Noisy, but thoughtful. Andy has captured both ideas with a single word, "irresistible." But as you are about to discover, he's done more than that. In *Irresistible*, Andy reacquaints us with the original version of our faith. The version that was irresistible indeed! We love this book!

—*Mark Burnett,* television and film producer

I've been a Christ follower for more than thirty years and perhaps no other book I've ever read has caused me to wrestle with the very foundations of my faith like this one. In *Irresistible*, Andy Stanley challenges us to rediscover the gospel and reclaim the version of faith that ultimately transformed our world. This provocative book could potentially disrupt the core of your theology. And when it does, it may very well change how you read the Bible and live out your faith forever more.

—*Tony Morgan,* founder and lead
strategist at The Unstuck Group

It's time for the church to rethink how it presents a timeless gospel to this generation. In *Irresistible*, Andy Stanley challenges us to make sure we handle the Scriptures with the kind of integrity that compels everyone to seriously consider following Jesus. Any Christian who reads this book will suddenly find themselves embracing the mission of Jesus with a new passion.

—*Reggie Joiner,* author; founder and CEO of Orange

People rarely reject Jesus as he truly is. Instead, they reject a distorted view of who they *think* he is. In his new book, *Irresistible*, pastor Andy Stanley takes you on a historic journey to rediscover the first-generation passion of what it means to faithfully follow Christ. This book will knock you off center, push you out of complacency, and reawaken an unshakable faith that cannot be ignored.

—*Craig Groeschel,* pastor of Life.Church and author of *Hope
in the Dark—Believing God Is Good When Life Is Not*

Irresistible is like a once-in-a-generation shot across the bow. Andy Stanley takes a lifetime of accumulated insight and wisdom about the Christian faith, history, and why the church isn't connecting with our current culture, and combines them together in a masterpiece work. Succinctly, powerfully, and convincingly, Andy shows us how so many Christians have misunderstood what Christianity is and helps us recapture what Christianity originally was. I pray we have the courage to live out the ethic of the early and accurate Christian faith Andy so capably describes. The world just might come running if we do.

—*Carey Nieuwhof,* author and founding
pastor, Connexus Church

Warning: This book will set you and your ministry back—back to the first century and the approach to advancing the gospel modeled by Jesus and the apostles. Andy reminds us that the resurrection was at the center of the first-century apologetic. Then he challenges twenty-first century believers to reclaim it as the center of ours as well. I agree with Andy—this approach changed the world once. I'm convinced it could do so again. Read and apply now!

—*Frank Turek,* Christian author, public speaker, and radio host

More than any other book I've read in years, *Irresistible* has stretched my view of Scripture. I can't hear or read a passage from the Old or New Testaments without thinking about Andy's provocative insights. If you and I take this book seriously, our lives and our churches will never be the same.

—*Kara Powell,* PhD, executive director of the Fuller
Youth Institute and coauthor of *Growing Young*

This book challenged me to rethink my thoughts about the Old Testament, discuss with fellow believers what I was learning, do more connecting and less correcting of others, and be salt and light, making things better and brighter. I love how Andy loves people . . . ALL of them.

—*John Maxwell,* author of *The 360 Degree Leader*

Andy Stanley believes that the gospel of grace is an irresistible message. So why do so many resist it, reject Jesus, and rebuff the church? Perhaps the fault lies not with Jesus but with a burdensome set of rules and regulations that have been added to the simple ethic he taught in the great commandment: love God and love others (Matthew 22:36–40). Biblical in its basis, provocative in some proposals, convicting in its challenges, this book makes an important contribution to the ongoing conversation about the mission of the church, as she seeks to reach a pluralistic culture with the good news of the gospel.

—*Glenn R. Kreider,* professor of theological
studies, Dallas Theological Seminary

Irresistible

Reclaiming the New that Jesus Unleashed for the World

ANDY STANLEY

ZONDERVAN REFLECTIVE

ZONDERVAN REFLECTIVE

Irresistible
Copyright © 2018, 2020 by Andy Stanley

ISBN 978-0-310-53702-1 (audio)

Requests for information should be addressed to:
Zondervan, *3900 Sparks Dr. SE, Grand Rapids, Michigan 49546*

This edition: ISBN 978-0-310-11406-2

Library of Congress Cataloging-in-Publication Data

Names: Stanley, Andy, author.
Title: Irresistible: reclaiming the new that Jesus unleashed for the world / Andy Stanley.
Description: Grand Rapids, Michigan: Zondervan, [2018] | Includes bibliographical references. |
Identifiers: LCCN 2018056411 (print) | LCCN 2019000415 (ebook) | ISBN 9780310536994 (ebook) | ISBN 9780310536970 (hardcover)
Subjects: LCSH: Christianity--Essence, genius, nature. | Apologetics.
Classification: LCC BT60 (ebook) | LCC BT60 .S695 2018 (print) | DDC 239--dc23 LC record available at https://lccn.loc.gov/2018056411

Cover design: Micah Kandros
Interior design: Kait Lamphere

Printed in the United States of America

21 22 23 24 25 /LSC/ 20 19 18 17 16 15 14 13 12 11 10 9 8 7 6 5 4 3 2

For Sandra

Thirty years later . . . still the finest woman I know

CONTENTS

SECTION 3
A NEW ETHIC

SECTION 4
A NEW APPROACH

Acknowledgments

No book is the product of individual effort. *Irresistible* is certainly no exception. To begin with, I want to thank our Atlanta congregations for the stewardship of trust they've extended to me for twenty-three years as I've endeavored to lead our churches to embrace the concepts presented in this book. It's not always been a comfortable journey. Churches gravitate toward the people who are already there. From day one I've insisted that reaching people far from God is more important than keeping folks who have already crossed the line of faith.

That's not always comfortable.

Thank you!

On the research side of the equation, I'm forever grateful to Thomas Horrocks. I met Thomas on Twitter. He'd written a well-thought-out piece defending my approach to ministry and preaching. I reached out to thank him and eventually invited him to help me on the research side of this project. Thanks, Thomas!

Once again, I'm grateful to my friends at Zondervan, John Raymond and Ryan Pazdur in particular. John, thank you for your enthusiasm for this project as well as your honest and pointed feedback. Your personal interest in the message of this book has been most encouraging. Ryan, thank you for reading, rereading, and then rereading again. And thank you for keeping me between the rails in my tone and messaging.

On the production side, this project would have never gotten off the starting blocks or to the finish line without the relentless focus, time, and energy of Suzy Gray. Suzy, your passion around this content was infectious and inspiring. Thank you for taking it personally!

Finally, I want to thank Sandra. Thanks for listening. Thanks for reading. Thank you for the multiple times you interrupted my studying to read a portion of this manuscript out loud because you loved it so much and you couldn't wait for others to read it as well. Thank you for reminding me over and over again that a "you" is always more important than a "view." You really are the finest woman I know.

SECTION 1

Simply Resistible

INTRODUCTION

In 2005, my son Andrew, who was thirteen at the time, accompanied me on a trip to China. During our visit we were invited to tour an American-owned leather goods factory. The owner was a friend of a friend. When we arrived, he graciously insisted on serving as our guide. Before we began the tour, he introduced us to a Chinese girl in her twenties who had worked her way from the factory floor into management. He asked if we would be okay if she shadowed us during the tour.

Two hours later, we were back in his office for a quick recap. As we wrapped up, he asked, "Does anyone have any questions?" To all our surprise, raising her hand to shoulder level, our shadow spoke up. "I have a question," she said. Turning to me, she asked, "Are you a pastor?"

I had no idea where this was going. I had not introduced myself as a pastor. I wasn't even sure if it was okay that I was a pastor. We were in China. For all I knew, she was a government plant assigned to follow us around all afternoon.

"Yes," I said. "I'm a pastor."

What she said next, in her beautiful broken English, caused the hair to stand up on the back of my neck.

"How good is good enough? I recognize your voice."

I was stunned. *How Good Is Good Enough?* is the title of a little book I had recently published. The manuscript was based on a message I had preached years earlier. She continued.

"Two years ago, someone gave me a CD of your sermon, 'How Good Is Good Enough?' I listened to it over and over. Then I asked Jesus to save me and live inside me. Before, I was empty. Now, I am full."

If you think I made this up, I don't blame you.

I have witnesses.

She went on. "I wanted to go to church, but there are no churches in my city. I began attending a Bible study in an apartment close to where I live. Sometimes I ride the bus to church, but it is two hours and I'm always late. The bus ticket is expensive and I don't know anyone at the church."

I was both honored and humbled. But she wasn't finished. Looking to her boss, she said, "Can I ask the pastor another question?"

He nodded.

"Pastor," she said, "why doesn't everyone in America go to church?"

I still haven't recovered from her question.

I had no idea how to respond. I still don't.

How do you explain thousands of empty churches to a young lady who would ride two hours to attend a church in another town? A young lady who would be there every time the door was opened, if there was a door to open? The Bible study she attended was part of a network of *underground churches*, what the Chinese government refers to as unregistered churches. Her participation put her at risk. Owning a Bible put her at risk. Talking about attending church in front of her boss put her at risk.

Imagine her shock if she were to discover that not only do most American Christians not read the Bible, in most churches there is a closetful of Bibles that have been *left behind*.

I don't remember how I responded. I said something entirely forgettable. But I haven't forgotten her question. It's bothered me ever since. Her question is one of the reasons I've written this book.

So, why doesn't everybody in America go to church?

Why is the church so *resistible*?

Jesus wasn't.

Once upon a time, his church wasn't either.

Chapter 1

THE NEW STANDARD AMERICAN VERSION

Much of what makes American Christianity so resistible to those outside the faith are things we should have been resisting all along. While many of us have been working hard to make church more interesting, it turns out that fewer people are actually interested. And while most people outside the church continue to have a favorable view of Jesus, they don't necessarily have a favorable view of his body, the *church*.

That's a problem.

It would be like me saying, *I like you; I just don't want to be around your body.*

The decline of Christianity in America, the popularity of the New Atheists, and the meteoric rise of the *nones* underscore something that's been true for generations but didn't matter much until now. Modern, mainstream Christianity is fatally flawed. These flaws make it fragile and indefensible in the public square. The populist version of cultural Christianity we see today is anchored to two assumptions that create a straw-man version of our faith. Sadly, this straw man passes for actual faith in many evangelical churches.

This version of Christianity is simplistic and easily discredited. For decades, college professors with biases against religion have found Christian freshmen easy targets. I've talked to, listened to, and read interviews, blogs, and books by dozens of folks who've left the Christian faith. I've yet to hear a story from anyone who abandoned Christianity based on anything directly related to Christianity—at least the original version, anyway.

I recently read a blog by a former worship leader who left the faith after she read a book "proving" contradictions in the Bible. Apparently, she grew up believing the foundation of our faith is a non-contradicting book.

It's not.

A renowned New Testament scholar recently acknowledged he lost his faith and embraced atheism because of suffering in the world. But the foundation of our faith is not a world without suffering. Pain and suffering don't disprove the existence of God. It only disproves the existence of a god who doesn't allow pain and suffering.

Whose god is that?

Not ours.

Ours promised it.

People leave the faith because they had a bad church experience.

Me too.

So what?

Quantum physics doesn't undermine the claims of Jesus. Neither does natural selection. Unverifiable Old Testament miracles don't cause our house to come tumbling down.

By the way, if something in the previous paragraphs made you wince, I can't tell you how happy I am you're reading this book. Keep reading and you'll be introduced to a better, more robust, version of *your* faith.

In all my years of ministry, I've only had one conversation with an unbeliever—a Jewish friend—who had an objection to Christianity based on anything to do with the claims of Jesus. "Andy," he said, "I just don't believe someone can pay for someone else's sins. I believe each of us is responsible for our own sins." I smiled and said, "Well, congratulations, you're standing on the threshold. That *is* the issue."

THE WAY FORWARD

The way forward is not complicated, though some will find it controversial. It's not original with me. It's hidden in plain sight in the Gospels and the epistles of Paul. We know it *works* because it already worked. Once upon a time, members of a Jewish cult called *The Way*, against all odds, captured the attention and, ultimately, the dedication of the pagan world, both inside and outside the Roman Empire. So perhaps we need to hit pause on much of what we're doing today—which isn't working all that well anyway—and take notes from the men and women credited with turning the world upside down.

What did first-century Christians know that we don't?

What made their faith so compelling, resilient, and, in the end, irresistible?

How did a religious cult birthed in the armpit of the empire, whose leader had been rejected by his own people and crucified as a wannabe king by Rome, survive in the face of overwhelming resistance? How is it that this same upstart religion would eventually be embraced by the very empire that sought to extinguish it?

I'm not the first to ask these questions. Scholars and historians have pondered these mysteries for generations. For the most part, they've all arrived at the same conclusion. British author Karen Armstrong, no friend to evangelical Christianity, sums it up this way:

> Yet against all odds, by the third century, Christianity had become a force to be reckoned with. We still do not really understand how this came about.[1]

Historically speaking, she is correct. It's virtually impossible to explain. Anthropologists, historians, and even skeptics with agendas have reached the same conclusion. Namely, something *happened* in the first century that resulted in Christianity spreading like an airborne disease. There was something about the faith of these first- and second-century believers that made it attractive, compelling, and seemingly irresistible.

The role of scholars and historians, like medical doctors diagnosing a disease, is to look for natural causes. We seek rational explanations as to why things happened the way they did. So when it comes to the seemingly unexplainable meteoric rise of the church, I'm convinced we should accept the explanation offered by those closest to the actual events. The testimonies of Peter, Luke, James, Paul, and others provide ample explanation for why the Jesus movement not only survived the first century but eventually overcame the very political and religious machines intent on destroying it.

Sandwiched between the Jewish temple and the Roman Empire, the Jesus movement should have been buried right alongside its founder. But it wasn't. At this very moment, Christians from all over the world are visiting the ruins of the Roman Forum, while fifteen hundred miles away, tourists are snapping pictures of the temple mount. Rome is adorned with crosses. Jerusalem is filled with Christian tourists.

Rome and Jerusalem are connected at the hip by the church. Two thousand years ago, the cross symbolized the power of empire. Today it symbolizes the power of God.

How did that happen?

What can we learn?

And, most importantly, could it happen again?

I believe so.

NEW, NOT IMPROVED

Jesus stepped into history to introduce something new.

He didn't come to Jerusalem offering a new version of an old thing or an update to an existing thing. He didn't come to make something better. Jesus was sent by the Father to introduce something *entirely new*. People gathered by the thousands to listen. To see. To experience. Read the Gospel of Mark and circle the word *crowd*. There's a crowd in practically every chapter.

But it wasn't just his *new* message that made Jesus irresistible. It was Jesus himself. People who were nothing *like* him *liked* him. And Jesus *liked* people who were nothing *like* him. Jesus invited unbelieving, misbehaving, troublemaking men and women to follow him and to embrace something *new*—and they accepted his invitation.

As followers of Jesus, we should be known as people who like people who are nothing like us. When we invite unbelieving, misbehaving troublemakers to join us, they should be intrigued—if not inclined—to accept our invitation.

"Pastor Stanley, why doesn't everybody in America go to church?"

THE RESISTERS

In the Gospels, we discover two groups that considered Jesus a threat—the self-righteous and those whose political and financial fortunes were secured by the fragile peace between temple and empire.

For the most part, Jesus' critics did not target his character. No one accused him of being immoral, dishonest, or cruel. They were threatened most by his teaching and his popularity. Religious leaders around Jerusalem were jealous of the favor he found with the populace. When you read the transcripts from his trials, you can't help but agree with Pilate when he announced to Jesus' accusers: "I find no *basis* for a charge against this man."[2]

He found none because there was none.

Pilate knew why temple leaders were insistent that Jesus be crucified. It had nothing to do with their law or their exclusivist religion. They wanted to be rid of Jesus purely out of "self-interest."[3]

The tipping point for those opposed to Jesus was not a *scandal*. It was a *miracle*. An extraordinary act of compassion. Jesus raised a well-known citizen from the dead. When news of this particular miracle circulated, the chief priests and Pharisees called a meeting of the Sanhedrin. That may not mean much to us, but it was unusual in first-century Judea.

These groups disagreed on just about everything. But in Jesus they found common ground. A common threat. A common enemy.

After multiple attempts, neither group had succeeded in diminishing Jesus' influence with the crowds. So in a moment of desperation, they joined forces. All they needed was a . . . how did Pilate put it? A *basis* for a charge. The apostle John knew or later met someone in attendance. At one point, someone's emotions got control of their mouth and they blurted out what everyone in the room was thinking:

> What are we accomplishing? Here is this man performing many signs. If we let him go on like this, everyone will believe in him, and then the Romans will come and take away both our temple and our nation.[4]

Forty years later, that's exactly what happened.

More on that in a bit.

In the end, religious leaders were able to manufacture a *basis* for a charge. Jesus was found guilty of bad theology and terroristic threats against the temple. Pilate joined the charade to keep the people who kept the people happy, happy. This was never about justice. No crime had been committed. When we step back from the chaos and the rapid-fire string of events leading to his crucifixion, it's abundantly clear Jesus was arrested and crucified because he was *too popular*. He was crucified for drawing too large of a crowd. People who were nothing like him liked him. And he liked them back. He was hard to resist. Impossible to dismiss. Why? He offered something new. Something brand-new.

But new brands rarely sit well with those whose fortunes are tied to the old ones. Those who profit most from the status quo are least inclined to let it go.

The plot twist was that Jesus' crucifixion was more beginning than end. His death initiated the *new* he had spoken of throughout his public ministry—the *new* predicted by Old Testament prophets and foreshadowed in Genesis. What Jesus' enemies did not know—could not have known—was that while ending Jesus' life brought about an end, it was not the end they had envisioned. His death and resurrection initiated a chain of events that would eventually bring an end to ancient Judaism, as well as the Roman Empire in its current form, the empire directly responsible for his death.

THE JESUS MOVEMENT

It was after the resurrection that Jesus' reengaged followers began to understand he had not come to simply add an additional chapter to the story of Israel. Jesus had not come to introduce a new version of Judaism. His movement was not regional. The Jesus movement was an all-skate. It was for all nations. His followers claimed he was the final sacrifice for sin, eliminating the need for the Jewish temple. But not just the Jewish temple. Twenty years or so after the resurrection, the apostle Paul would stare down the idol-worshipping civic leaders in Athens and declare their temples were unnecessary as well.[5] In that same speech, Paul labeled idol worship ignorant. Like a parent, waiting for a child to outgrow her childish ways, God had overlooked idol worship for a season.[6] But now it was time for the world to grow up and acknowledge the living, portable, for-all-nations God.

Needless to say, the Jesus movement was immediately at odds with both Jewish and non-Jewish culture. Understandably so. Jesus claimed to be the *fulfillment* of Judaism and a *replacement* for paganism.

Jesus was new wine. Judaism and paganism were old wineskins. The *new* Jesus offered was a departure from the traditions of both. Jesus, along with his early followers, argued that Judaism and paganism both pointed to a day when God would unleash something *new* in the world, for the world. Those with eyes to see would recognize it. Those with ears to hear would listen and follow.

Specifically, Jesus came to establish a new covenant, a new command, and a new movement. His new *movement* would be international. The new *covenant* would fulfill and replace the behavioral, sacrifice-based systems reflected in just about every religion of the ancient world.

His new *command* would serve as the governing behavioral ethic for members of his new movement.

The *new* Jesus introduced stood in stark contrast to the values and tempo of both empire and temple. The empire assumed *might made right*. And while Rome claimed the right to make the rules, those who maintained the temple were committed to protecting their rules at all costs. While the Roman Empire and the Jewish temple were worlds apart, imbedded within each were values and assumptions that knit them together, creating a formidable obstacle to first-century Christianity. That the church survived both is a testament to the power of the gospel and the courage of first- and second-century Christians.

The first-century church withstood the pressure to adopt and integrate the familiar streams of empire and temple into their new faith. This is a testament to how incompatible they understood the two to be. The *new* Jesus introduced stood in stark, blatant, and unambiguous contrast to the values and assumptions of both empire and temple. Those closest to Jesus understood this contrast. The gospel accounts underscore and illustrate the differences. The apostle Paul leveled his harshest criticisms at those who attempted to integrate empire and temple thinking into the *new* Jesus introduced.

For almost three hundred years, the church fended off pressure to integrate and incorporate the old ways. But with the conversion of Constantine the Great and the signing of the Edict of Milan, the church transitioned quickly from persecuted minority to empowered majority. Almost immediately, resistance to the old ways was replaced by adoption, integration, and incorporation.

REFORM

Fast-forward to the sixteenth century and reformers would dedicate, and on occasion forfeit, their lives to free the church of the values, culture, and tone of empire and temple. For many, the birth of Protestantism signaled a revival of the *new* Jesus introduced. But the struggle would not end there. The temptation to pour the new wine Jesus offers into the old wineskins of temple and empire is with us today. Every generation needs imperfect reformers—men and women who, like the apostle Paul, become apoplectic when they see a trace of the old ways creeping into the *new* Jesus introduced. I'm convinced it's the mixing, blending, and integration of the old with the new that makes the modern church so resistible. It's the mixing, blending, and integration of the old with the new that make our faith indefensible in this misinformation age. Jesus warned us two thousand years ago against pouring new wine into old wineskins. In the end, both the wine and the wineskins are ruined.[7] The result is a mess.

"Pastor Stanley, why doesn't everybody in America go to church?"

To understand the uniqueness of Jesus' message, movement, and ethic, we must first understand the *old* with which these were contrasted. To punctuate this contrast, it's necessary for us to journey back through a stretch of familiar biblical history.

Chapter 2

GOING GLOBAL

Ancient Israel was a means to an end.

That's not a slight.

Being a *means* to an end is what gives things meaning. Purpose. If you refuse to become a means to an end, your life will never have meaning. That's the meaning of *meaning*. Live for yourself and you'll only have yourself to show for yourself. Become a means to an end and your life takes on . . . meaning. Funerals teach us this. Funerals remind us that the value of a life is always measured by how much of it was given away.

Back to Israel.

God created the nation of Israel as a means to a divine end. He created the nation for a global purpose. God's global plan for the nation was first announced long before there was a nation. Around 2067 BC, God promised ninety-nine-year-old Abraham a son who would become a nation that would bless the world.

The entire world.

Here's the original wording:

> I will make you into a *great nation*,
>   and I will bless you;
> I will make your name great,
>   and you will be a blessing.

God promised Abraham he would make his "name great." That's Bible speak for "I'll make you famous."[1] I'm guessing this isn't the first time you've heard of Abraham.

So there you go.

Promise kept.

But here's the real news:

> and *all* peoples on earth will be blessed *through* you.[2]

We can't imagine how ridiculous that sounded to a man with *no* people standing in the middle of *no*where. But that promise initiated a chain of events that would roll out over the course of about two thousand years. In addition to the unimaginable scope of this promise, there was something historically peculiar about it as well.

God promised to "bless" the world through Abraham's descendants.

That didn't make any sense.

Ancient people didn't *bless* one another.

Ancient tribes conquered, plundered, and enslaved one another. Let's face it; modern nations don't *bless* one another. We spy, negotiate, and impose sanctions. Again, we can't begin to imagine how ridiculous this sounded to Abraham.

Moving on.

Abraham eventually had some *people* who eventually migrated to Egypt, where they eventually multiplied themselves to nation status, which made their host nation terribly uncomfortable. Instead of kicking 'em out, Pharaoh put 'em to work.

As slaves.

So much for all those promises. It's difficult to *bless* all the nations of the earth when you're making bricks for a king who considers himself master of the universe. But unlike Egypt's gods, Abraham's God was mobile. So when Abraham's God was good and ready, he showed up. He tapped Moses as his representative and sent him to Pharaoh with that unforgettable line.

Let's all say it together.

"Let my people go!"

After a bit of arm-twisting, Pharaoh did just that.

The reason I feel the freedom to summarize four hundred-plus years of Israel's history in four-plus sentences is our familiarity with the story line. But while many modern readers (and moviegoers) know the story, it's next to impossible for us not to miss its significance. In the most extraordinary, drawn-out, spectacle-filled, worthy-of Hollywood's-attention manner imaginable, Israel's God demonstrated his *mobility* and *authority*. Clearly, his authority was not constrained by geography. The earth was his jurisdiction. His message to Pharaoh was unequivocal:

> You've got something that belongs to me and I'm not leaving here without it!

One by one, Israel's invisible God king humiliated Egypt's pantheon of gods. In the end, he worked it out for his people to plunder what was arguably the wealthiest nation on the planet. All this without holding anyone at the point of a sword. By the time Israel put Egypt in the rear-view mirror, Egypt's economy was decimated. Clearly, Israel's one God was mightier than all Egypt's gods combined. And all that without home field advantage. Israel's God was the visiting team. He was mobile. Mobile gods were not a thing in the BCs.

Fast-forward four months and we find the people of Israel camping at the foot of Mount Sinai watching Moses descend with God's instructions for the nation. We call it the *Ten Commandments*. But before it was over, it was more like the *600 Commandments*. Those famous first ten functioned a bit like a table of contents—the CliffNotes version. If you grew up in church, you may remember how this most ancient of ancient constitutions began:

> I am the LORD your God, who brought you out of Egypt, out
> of the land of slavery.[3]

Translated: That was me who did that.

He continued,

> You shall have no other gods before me.[4]

To which they thought, *Correct! We shall not. We saw what you're capable of.*[5] And then the statement that set Israel apart from everybody else in the neighborhood:

> You shall not make for yourself an image in the *form* of any-
> thing in heaven above or on the earth beneath or in the waters
> below. You shall not bow down to them or worship them.[6]

When Moses finished reading the summary points of all God required of the nation, they responded with a hearty:

> Everything the LORD has said we will do.[7]

But of course they didn't.

And we shouldn't be surprised.

They were at camp.

Does anybody keep their camp commitments?

I didn't. You probably didn't either. If you didn't grow up going to church camp . . . perhaps it's for the best.

The movies and bedtime versions of this narrative don't accurately reflect how Moses made several trips up and down Mount Sinai. Each time Moses returned with even more detailed instructions for the nation. One of these mountain-climbing excursions lasted forty days. While he was gone, the natives grew restless. You may remember this part from Sunday school:

> When the people saw that Moses was so long in coming down from the mountain, they gathered around Aaron and said, "Come, make us gods who will go before us. As for this fellow Moses who brought us up out of Egypt, we don't know what has happened to him."[8]

Seriously?

God is still dictating the fine print and his people are already abandoning the first and most important commandment. How could that be?

> Aaron answered them, "Take off the gold earrings that your wives, your sons and your daughters are wearing, and bring them to me." So all the people took off their earrings and brought them to Aaron. He took what they handed him and made it into an idol cast in the shape of a calf, fashioning it with a tool. Then they said, "These are your gods, Israel, who brought you up out of Egypt."[9]

What? Those cows we just watched you make out of our plundered Egyptian gold were what delivered us from Egypt?

This is where most of us get confused. Why would recently freed slaves abandon the God who had recently freed them? How could they adopt something they saw created before their very eyes as an object of worship? It's confusing for us because we grew up believing in an invisible, everywhere-at-the-same-time God. But this was new territory for the people of Israel. Not having an object to worship was as confusing to them as their insistence on having one is to us. They *needed* something tangible. Visible. Stationary. That episode didn't end well. In the end it meant Moses had to make another trip up Mount Sinai to fetch yet another set of tablets.

So began Israel's formal relationship with the invisible, mobile God of Abraham. Freed from their Egyptian taskmasters and equipped with rules to live by, they prepared to break camp and begin their journey north to the promised land. But before they put Sinai in the rear-view mirror, Moses commissioned the construction of a portable tent called the tabernacle to house and transport the sacred law tablets. When the construction of this tent was complete and the stone tablets were resting safely in the wooden box constructed for that purpose, something extraordinary happened. Moses describes it this way:

> Then the cloud covered the tent of meeting, and the *glory* of the LORD *filled* the tabernacle. Moses could not enter the tent of meeting because the cloud had settled on it, and the *glory* of the LORD *filled* the tabernacle.[10]

God took up residence.

Nobody carried a portable statue-god into the tabernacle and set it on a pedestal, as was the custom in pagan nations. When Israel's God was satisfied that everything was as it should be, he chose to inhabit the tabernacle. He filled it with his glory. His presence. On his terms.

But even with the presence of God in their midst, Israel was still in no position to "bless" all the nations of the earth.

Just ask Pharaoh.

Nobody in Egypt was feeling "blessed" at that particular moment.

ONE LAST THING

In addition to Moses' multiple trips up and down Mount Sinai, there's something else we modern Bible readers miss as well. The content, wording, and arrangement of God's instructions to Israel are in the form of a legal contract. Scholars refer to this template as a *suzerainty treaty* or a *bilateral suzerainty treaty*. This form of agreement was used by non-equal parties when defining the terms and conditions of their relationship. In a suzerainty treaty, the greater power, the suzerain, dictates terms to the lesser power, the vassal.

Think curfew.

The point being, the Ten+ Commandments were more than commandments. They were just one part of a comprehensive legal contract or covenant between God (the Suzerain) and the nation. Here's some original wording:

> Then the LORD said to Moses, "Write down these words, for in accordance with these words I have made a *covenant* with you and with Israel."[11]

The events at Mount Sinai signaled the inauguration of a covenant relationship between God and the nation of Israel. As we will discover, this covenant would define and govern God's relationship with the nation of Israel for the next thousand-plus years. The primary terms and conditions are found in Exodus 19–24. They are repeated, expanded, and in some cases clarified in Leviticus, Numbers, and Deuteronomy. But the following three verses pretty much summarize the deal points:

> You yourselves have seen what I did to Egypt, and how I carried you on eagles' wings and brought you to myself. Now if you obey me fully and keep my *covenant*, then out of all nations you will be my treasured possession. Although the whole earth is mine, you will be for me a kingdom of priests and a holy nation.[12]

This was a classic, *I will* as long as *you do* suzerain treaty. *Keep my commands and I'll keep you safe.* The agreement was bilateral and conditional. If the nation of Israel didn't uphold their end of the deal, God was under no obligation to uphold his.

Got it?

Let's keep moving.

FAST-FORWARD

Israel eventually arrived safely in the promised land. Once they arrived, however, they didn't do much in the way of blessing the inhabiting nations. Instead, they conquered and on occasion plundered their way to dominance in the region.[13] After several generations operating as a loosely organized theocracy ruled by judges, the elders of the nation decided it was time for something new. It was time for Israel to grow up and start acting like "all the other nations."[14] That would require a king. A visible king.[15]

KINGS AND THINGS

It was never God's intention for Israel to have a king *other than himself.* But all the cool kids had kings. So the elders and leaders of the nation confronted the prophet Samuel and insisted he appoint a king. Samuel checked with God and received this response in return:

> Listen to all that the people are saying to you; it is not you they have *rejected*, but *they have rejected me* as their king.

Ouch!

> As they have done from the day I brought them up out of Egypt until this day, *forsaking me* and serving other gods, so they are doing to you. Now listen to them; but warn them solemnly and let them know what the king who will reign over them will claim as his rights.[16]

Samuel returned to the elders and did as God had instructed. He did his best to scare the king out of 'em, but to no avail.

But the people refused to listen to Samuel. "No!" they said. "We want a king over us.[17]

What they said next set the stage for what happened next.

> Then we will be *like all the other nations*, with a king to lead us and to go out before us and fight our battles.[18]

The problem, of course, was God did not intend for Israel to be *like all the other nations.* God intended for Israel to stand out from *all the other nations* because he was planning to do something through Israel on behalf of *all the other nations*.

They were a means to a global end.

In the end, they caved to peer pressure and got what they asked for. A king. Several actually. For decades they had more than one at a time. As predicted, most of Israel's kings were disasters. The nation paid for this decision in treasure and blood. In this way they did become *like all the other nations*. In spite of this, God kept his promise to Abraham. He did not abandon his global purposes for the nation. All the nations on the earth would indeed be blessed through a nation that insisted on being like all the other nations of the earth.

Chapter 3

TEMPLE TANTRUM

I need you to imagine for just a moment what would *not* have happened and who we would *never have met* if Israel had listened to Samuel and abandoned the idea of a royal family.

There would have been no King Saul. No King David or King Solomon. Solomon's parents would have never met. Not only would there have been no Psalms of David, there would be no Proverbs, Ecclesiastes, or Song of Solomon. There would be no record of the activities of the kings and there would be no documents documenting what the prophets prophesied in response to the decisions of the kings. Why? Because there would have been no kings.

The story line would be different. A lot different.

But here's the real kicker:

If there had been no king, there would have been no temple.

All the cool kids with kings had temples too. So Israel eventually got herself one of those. Just as Israel's kings brought with them all the problems associated with kings, the temple led to the challenges associated with temples. Israel didn't need a king. And Israel didn't need a temple. Both of these were attempts to be *like all the other nations*.

Let me explain.

TAKING STOCK

After taking over from the disaster that was King Saul, King David spent years expanding, settling, and fortifying the nation of Israel.

Eventually there was a break in the action. During the lull, it dawned on David that while everybody else had moved indoors, God was still living in a tent.

Like a boy scout.

Like a shepherd.

So David made an appointment with the prophet in residence, Nathan, and here's what he said:

> Look at this: Here I am, comfortable in a luxurious house of cedar, and the Chest of God sits in a plain tent.[1]

Nathan smiled and suggested David do something about it. He went so far as to suggest that whatever David had in mind, God would support it.[2] Turns out Nathan was wrong. He spoke out of turn. What happens next is often overlooked.

On the evening following Nathan's *whatever suits you* conversation with David, God spoke to Nathan. He explicitly tells him to go back and give David a different answer:

> I have not dwelt in a house from the day I brought the Israelites up out of Egypt to this day. I have been *moving* from place to place with a tent as my dwelling.

This is my favorite part.

> Wherever I have moved with all the Israelites, did I ever say to any of their rulers whom I commanded to shepherd my people Israel, "Why have you not built me a house of cedar?"[3]

God was fine living in a tent.

He seemed to prefer it.

Besides, he wasn't home most of the time anyway.

But there was something else in play here. Unlike David's fine house of stone, everything about the tabernacle was temporary. It was constructed of linen curtains, goat's hair curtains, and wood. It was in constant need of repair. But the *portable* and *temporary* nature of the tabernacle underscored the *point* of the tabernacle. Everything about the tabernacle and everything connected to the tabernacle were merely context for something greater and grander. The tabernacle was a means to an end. And in the end, the need for a tabernacle would end as well.

To put words in God's mouth . . . a dangerous thing to do . . . it was as if God was saying, "I'm fine with my temporary digs. This entire system is temporary anyway. There's no point building me something fancy that I won't use for very long."

From there, the conversation takes a hard right turn. After assuring David he was fine living in a tent, God changes the subject completely. Paraphrasing, God says to David:

> Enough about building me a new house; let's talk about your family, David. Enough about what's temporary, let's talk about the endgame. You want to *build* me a house. But I'm going to *establish* your house! I'm going to do something through your family that has *forever* written all over it.[4]

Similar to his promise to Abraham, God tells David he will make his name great, like "the names of the greatest men on earth."[5]

I'm guessing you'd already heard of David too.

God tells David he has too much blood on his hands to build a temple. David doesn't argue, but he doesn't give up on his idea. He forges ahead to ensure that when his son Solomon becomes king, everything will be in place for construction of a permanent structure. David envisions a temple to beat all temples. The ultimate temple.

David raised the money. He had plans drawn. He hired stonecutters. He did everything right up to cutting the ribbon and sticking a shovel in the ground. And according to plan, when Solomon took the throne, the grand construction project began.

Twenty years later it was completed.

At the end of those twenty years, Solomon invited God to leave his tent and move indoors. So to speak. Eventually, he did. So to speak. But before he did, he said something to Solomon that should have sent chills down his spine. It didn't. But it should have.

God gave Solomon the *before I hand you the car keys* talk. Remember that? Either the one your parents had with you or the one you've had with your own kids? With my kids it went something like this:

> I'm so happy I was able to purchase a car for you to drive. I hope you enjoy it. But understand . . . if you abuse this freedom, I'll sell it.

God's version to Solomon is found in 1 Kings. It goes something like this:

> Solomon, I really appreciate all that's gone into creating this fabulous piece of architecture. I accept your gift. I'll move in immediately. But Solomon, if I catch you or my people misbehaving out there because you think I'm tucked away safely in here, I will tear this place apart!
>
> This piece of real estate will always reflect my power and my glory. But I can accomplish that with or without a building on it. In its current form, it reflects my presence. But if you abandon me to worship other gods, this piece of land will stand vacant as a testimony to my absence.

All that before he'd even moved in! Think I'm making that up? Read 1 Kings 9. Here's a taste:

> This *temple* will become a heap of rubble. All who pass by will be appalled and will scoff and say, "Why has the LORD done such a thing to this land and to this *temple*?"[6]

God moved in, but he wasn't committed to staying there under just any conditions. Why?

This is important.

Because the temple was linked to God's conditional, I-will-as-long-as-you-do covenant with the nation. The one established on Mount Sinai.

God would see to the demolition of his own home if the people abandoned him for other gods. The temple was a "nice to have." But it wasn't necessary. It wasn't his idea. The temple was more *beautiful* than it was *important*. And if Solomon thought the permanent nature of their temple somehow altered the temporary and conditional nature of God's covenant with the nation, he was wrong. God had made it clear from the founding of the nation that Israel was a divine means to a divine end.

CONSPICUOUSLY MISSING

You may not know this, but Solomon's temple embodied design features similar to pagan temples found throughout the ancient world. If you take the Old Testament seriously, it's hard to imagine this to be the case. The Jewish Scriptures include extraordinary detail of how the temple was to look, operate, and who had permission to operate it. But despite a few unique features, the Jewish temple shared much in common with pagan temples in the ancient world, including porches, chambers, courts, living quarters, and an altar used for animal sacrifice. Pagan temples of that era always included a sacred space designed specifically for the image of the god for whom the temple was built and to whom the temple was dedicated. A god-vault. It was this most sacred of sacred chambers that set the Jewish temple apart from all the competition. In fact, it could be argued that this chamber, often referred to as *the holy of holies,* was the *only* thing that set the Jewish temple apart from the competition.

The distinguishing characteristic of the Jewish temple was not something it included that the competition lacked. Quite the opposite. The differentiating characteristic of the Jewish temple was something it lacked that everybody else had.

An image.

The holy of holies was like a beautiful, ornately designed frame without a picture. This was why Israel didn't need a temple to begin with. The distinguishing characteristic of Judaism was not the design of their temple. It was the lack of an image representing their God. Images were strictly forbidden in Judaism. As we discovered earlier, this particular prohibition was one of the Big Ten.

The notion of worshipping an image or idol is so foreign to us that an empty idol chamber doesn't strike us as odd. But in ancient times, the very opposite was true. A religion without an image was . . . absurd. When Roman general Pompey entered Jerusalem in 63 BC, he conducted a self-guided tour of the temple. He was curious to see this Jewish God he'd heard so much about—the one so easily offended and who considered himself too good to join any pantheon of gods. He brushed aside the priests and boldly went where only the high priests had gone before, the holy of holies. As he pulled aside the over-engineered curtain separating the god chamber from the outer court, he was dismayed to find there was no god! No idol. Only a golden table, a candlestick, and about two thousand talents of gold.[7]

All of which he left undisturbed.

Perhaps he thought, *These crazy Jews. They built this elaborate physical structure for a God who has no physical representation. Whoever heard of a god without an image?*

Exactly.

Who *would hear* of this strange God who could not be contained within, reduced to, or defined by any created thing?

Everybody.

How?

Through the nation of Israel.

Back to Solomon.

While the temple may not have been God's original idea, it served a purpose. It highlighted, accentuated, and underscored the principle difference between Israel's God and those of her neighbors. Israel served a living God. Unlike the pagan gods in Solomon's day or those worshipped centuries later by citizens of Rome, Israel's God did not need to be carted into his temple and hoisted onto a pedestal. Israel's God never needed to be wheeled out by priests on festival days. Israel's God didn't need to be locked up at night so no one would steal him or chip off a piece for good luck. Israel's God didn't need bodyguards. He didn't need to be protected from the elements. Israel's God was Spirit.

A Holy Spirit.

Israel's God wasn't *put* in his temple.

Israel's God *inhabited* his temple.

Just as he had inhabited the tabernacle all those years ago, he inhabited Solomon's temple on his own terms. Here's how it happened.

> The priests then brought the ark of the LORD's covenant to its place in the inner sanctuary of the temple, the Most Holy Place, and put it beneath the wings of the cherubim.[8]

But the presence of the ark did not equate to the presence of God. The ark containing God's law was not created as an object of worship. What happened next gave the temple its significance:

> When the priests withdrew from the Holy Place, the cloud *filled* the temple of the LORD. And the priests could not perform their service because of the cloud, for the *glory of the* LORD *filled his temple.*[9]

The *on-his-own-terms* presence of the Spirit God was the distinguishing characteristic of the Jewish temple. Every nation had laws. Every nation had religious rituals and priests. Most ancient religions mandated animal sacrifice. The Jews had all that minus the one thing everybody else had. Their temple served as an awe-inspiring frame to draw attention to something that wasn't there. But the purpose behind this magnificent edifice, built to the glory of the invisible God, extended beyond Israel.

The Jewish temple, with its intricate sacrificial system, would serve as *context*. The temple in Jerusalem would serve as ground zero for a series of events that would later reshape the world. And not just the ancient world. Unlike pagan gods, Israel's God was not a regional god with a regional scope. Israel's God was the living God whose power and presence was not limited to a particular piece of real estate. The temple would play an *important* but *temporary* role in God's revelatory plan. Its similarities with other temples in the region punctuated, highlighted, accentuated, and underscored the one significant difference, which set the stage for God's next great activity in the world. "Image-free, idol-free" was more than a differentiating detail. It pointed to *God's global purpose for the nation*.

TEMPLES OF DOOM

When Solomon was anointed king, there was peace in the land. Some refer to this season as Israel's *golden age*. At last, it looked as if there was an opportunity for Israel to be a blessing to other nations. But God wasn't ready. Turns out, Israel wasn't either. Solomon got a bit distracted. By women. Foreign women and their foreign gods. The temple talk didn't stick.

Here's something often overlooked. Along with building his God a temple, Solomon built a host of gods their own miniature temples. Why? To keep his foreign wives happy. How many miniature temples, you ask?

Ready for this?

About seven hundred.

The author of 1 Kings tells us Solomon had seven hundred wives of royal birth.[10] He built altars, shrines, and houses of worship for each god worshipped by his—let's say it together—*seven hundred wives of royal birth*. One of these wives was, can you believe it, Pharaoh's daughter! Even worse, we learn that toward the end of his life, Solomon was worshipping these foreign gods right along with his wives.[11] Not to the exclusion of the God of his father, David. It was worse than that. He worshipped them *along with* the God of his father, David.

While this is confusing to us, it made all the sense in the world to Solomon. Once Solomon *moved God*, so to speak, into his very own temple, he reduced God to the level of all the other pagan deities of *all the nations of the earth*. God had a location. A location similar to the locations Israel's neighbors created for their gods. With the construction of the temple, Israel's mobile God looked a bit more domesticated. Regional. Gone was the tent, the visual reminder that Israel's God was a traveling God. Gone was the reminder that he could pick up and go without notice. And with peace in the land, gone was the need to call upon God to protect Israel from her enemies.

Under Solomon, Israel was in no position to bless the nations of the earth. By the end of Solomon's reign, Israel looked a lot *like all the other nations of the earth*. But whereas Solomon forgot or just straight-up abandoned his promise to God, God did not forget nor abandon his promise to Solomon. His agreement with Solomon mirrored the conditional nature of his agreement with the nation.

> This *temple* will become a heap of rubble. All who pass by will
> be appalled and will scoff and say, "Why has the LORD done
> such a thing to this land and to this *temple*?"[12]

True to his word, in 587 BC, after a bloody siege, Nebuchadnezzar's soldiers poured through a breach in Jerusalem's walls, murdered thousands of citizens, enslaved thousands more, and tore Solomon's temple down to its foundation.

Fortunately, God wasn't home that afternoon.

He'd moved out long before.

Chapter 4

SPLITTIN' UP

After Solomon's death, his son Rehoboam became king. Rehoboam made a foolish decision that resulted in the nation being divided into a northern and a southern kingdom. By 700 BC, the Northern Kingdom (Israel) had abandoned God completely and embraced the idol-worshipping cults of her neighbors. The Southern Kingdom (Judah) was on the verge of the same apostasy. The notion of Israel being a blessing to other nations was unimaginable. After all, the nation couldn't solve her own internal disputes. The divided nation suffered from a divided military and divided economy. Both Assyria and Syria were looking for an excuse to invade. These were harsh times for folks in both kingdoms.

God sent a series of prophets to exhort, chastise, and warn the revolving door of kings. One of those prophets was Isaiah. Isaiah's prophecy is not easy to follow, especially without historical context. Actually, it's difficult to follow his train of thought *with* historical context. The reason I bring him up is that in the midst of what was perhaps the lowest point to that time in Israel's history, Isaiah resurrects and puts his own spin on God's promise to Abraham. If it sounded strange to Abraham, it sounded even stranger to the inhabitants of Judah in those troubled times. Isaiah writes:

> It is too small a thing for you to be my servant
>> to restore the tribes of Jacob
>> and bring back those of Israel I have kept.
> I will also make you a *light for the Gentiles*,
>> that my salvation may reach to the *ends of the earth*.[1]

Not gonna happen.

Once again, this was an era of conquest, plunder, and enslavement. Nobody was trying to be a "light" to anybody. Nobody was trying to save anybody other than themselves. After Isaiah died, Judah, the Southern Kingdom, was invaded by Babylon. It was in the aftermath of this siege that Solomon's magnificent temple was destroyed. But before it was razed, as was his habit, King Nebuchadnezzar ordered the image of the conquered god extradited to Babylon to be placed in his god collection.

No lie. Nebuchadnezzar had a god collection.

But, of course, when his soldiers entered the Jewish god-vault, there was no image to be found. So they took the flatware and dishes and headed home . . . with a significant portion of the significant population in tow. Including the Fab Four: Shadrach, Meshach, Abednego, and Daniel.

> I will also make you a *light for the Gentiles*,
>   that my salvation may reach to the *ends of the earth*.[2]

Hmmm.

Lucky for Israel, their God was mobile. Unbeknownst to Nebuchadnezzar, God managed to smuggle himself out of Judea and into Babylon. The book of Daniel chronicles his mischief.

Moving on.

THE LAST WORD

When Babylon fell to the Persians around 538 BC, Emperor Cyrus the Great allowed the Jews to return to their homeland and even encouraged them to rebuild their temple. Actually, he ordered them to rebuild it and he told them how big to build it.[3]

Smaller.

A lot smaller.

So they did. When the foundation was complete and folks could see just how *not big* and *ungrand* their new temple would be, the older folks in the crowd, the ones who remembered Solomon's temple, "wept aloud."[4] The newer, smaller temple was a visible reminder of how low a nation could go.

The fact that a foreign king dictated how large they could build their own temple stung as well. But the older folks weren't the only ones who were less than thrilled with econo-temple. Apparently, God wasn't either. Best we can tell, he never moved in. He never "inhabited" the renovated temple. Spoiler alert: God never inhabited Herod's renovated edition either.

Apparently, God was done with temples.

Wasn't his idea to begin with.

He was the mobile, inhabiting, Spirit God. He was fine in his tent. Besides, by this time, the ark of the covenant was missing along with several other important articles. It wasn't like the old days. But God understood what the temple represented to these precious people so recently returned from exile. So he spoke to them through the prophet Haggai.

> Who of you is left who saw this house in its former glory? How does it look to you now? Does it not seem to you like nothing?

To which they thought, *Yes. It is "nothing" compared to Solomon's temple.*

He continued:

> "Be strong, all you people of the land," declares the LORD, "and work. For I am *with* you," declares the LORD Almighty.
> "This is what I covenanted *with* you when you came out of Egypt.
> And my Spirit remains *among* you. Do not fear."
> This is what the LORD Almighty says:

Ready for this?

> "In a little while I will once more shake the heavens and the earth, the sea and the dry land. I will shake *all nations*,

There's that "all nations" thing again. And again, it seemed highly unlikely Israel would do anything that would affect "all nations." He continued:

> "I will shake *all nations*, and what is desired by *all nations* will come, and I *will* fill this house with glory," says the LORD Almighty.[5]

If you read those verses carefully (which, let's be honest, you didn't), you'll notice God pretty much told them he wasn't moving in. At least not then. He would be "with" the nation and "among" the people of the nation. He would keep his all-nations oriented promise (whatever that meant). But he would not "fill" that temple with his glory until a future date. Then he ends with one final nod to the future:

> "The glory of this present house *will* be *greater* than the glory of the former house," says the LORD Almighty. "And in this place I *will* grant *peace*," declares the LORD Almighty.[6]

Restated: Something big is coming.

LIGHTS OUT

Not too long after the scaled-down temple was completed, things in Judea spiraled once again. The newly reconstructed temple revived hope that perhaps the glory days of David and Solomon were returning. But nothing on that order transpired. The temple and everything associated with it served as painful reminders of a bygone era that in all likelihood would never return. The economy continued to decline. Interest in temple worship waned. Political and temple leaders bickered among themselves and leveraged their power to the detriment of the people, which only deepened the cynicism and distrust.

Into the melee stepped the prophet Malachi. His prophecy served as a bookend to what we refer to as the Old Testament.[7] While he was last, he was certainly not least. Like prophets before him, Malachi berated the people for their apathy, faithlessness, immorality, and selfishness. He reminded the nation of God's unending love, as well as his unavoidable judgment. Standard prophetic fare.

But early in his remarks, Malachi reiterates Israel's divine destiny, God's global intent.

In spite of everything they had done to dishonor his name, God was committed to fulfilling his covenant with Abraham. Israel would be a means to his end. The world would, in fact, be blessed through them.

> "My name will be great *among the nations* . . .

There it is again.

> "My name will be great *among the nations* from where the sun rises to where it sets. In every place incense and pure offerings will be brought to me, because *my name will be great among the nations*," says the LORD Almighty.[8]

Then later . . .

> "I will send my messenger, who will prepare the way before me. Then *suddenly* the Lord you are seeking will come to his *temple*;

So, he wasn't there after all.

> ". . . the messenger of the *covenant*, whom you desire, will come," says the LORD Almighty.[9]

The end.

Malachi turned off the lights, locked the door, and disappeared into the desert.

Not really. But it must have felt that way.

For the next four hundred years or so, there were no prophets. None the people took seriously anyway. Judea remained under foreign control. After the Persians came the Ptolemies, followed by the Seleucids. Around 167 BC, a faint glimmer of hope appeared. A group of zealous Jews known as the Maccabees launched a revolt. Under the leadership of Judah Maccabee, they overthrew and ousted their Greek invaders. They cleansed, rededicated, and opened the temple for business. For the first time in centuries, the Jews were free from foreign control. Many believed Judah Maccabee was the Promised One, the Savior sent by God to restore the nation to its former glory. But it was not to be. Following Judah's death, the nation once again spiraled into economic and military instability. Then, in 63 BC, general Pompey made his famous visit to the Jewish temple and annexed Judea to the Roman Republic.

SILENT BUT NOT STILL

While it could be argued God was silent in the years of Israel's occupation and oppression, he certainly wasn't still. The apostle Paul captured the tension perfectly when he wrote:

> But when the set time had fully come . . .

Once God had *everything* and *everyone* in place . . .

> God sent his Son, born of a woman, born under the law, to redeem those under the law, that we might receive adoption to sonship.[10]

When no one expected it.

When most had given up hope.

As the Roman Republic transitioned to empire . . .

God moved.

A carpenter discovered his fiancée was pregnant and while trying to decide what to do, an angel spoke to him in a dream:

> "Joseph *son of David*, do not be afraid to take Mary home as your wife, because what is conceived in her is from the Holy Spirit. She will give birth to a son, and you are to give him the name Jesus, because he will save his people from their sins."
>
> All this took place to fulfill what the Lord had said through the prophet: "The virgin will conceive and give birth to a son, and they will call him Immanuel."[11]

This was it.

The wait was over.

God's promise to Abraham would be fulfilled. The nations of the earth were on the verge of being blessed. As part of the process, God would visit the temple one last time.

But not as a cloud.

This time he would show up as a Galilean day laborer turned rabbi. A rabbi who would start a fire neither empire nor temple would extinguish. And in the end, as promised, all the nations of the world would be blessed.

Chapter 5

RECENTERING THE UNIVERSE

Perhaps the most prominent narrative theme in the Gospels, the four accounts of Jesus' life, is the incessant conflict between Jesus and religious leaders. While it's easy to identify where they differed in perspective and interpretation of the law, it's not as easy to wrap our minds around why these differences caused the Pharisees, Sadducees, and teachers of the law to *hate* Jesus. They couldn't agree to disagree with him. They hated him. They didn't just wish him dead; they orchestrated his arrest and execution. While that seems a bit over the top to us, as it did to Pilate, they actually had good reason to despise him.

They saw what we miss.

Temple leaders did not view Jesus as Judaism 2.0. They rightly understood Jesus to be a threat to *everything* they valued. Everything. If what he claimed was true, it signaled the end of, not a new version of, the world as they knew it.

Modern Bible readers see Jesus as an extension of the Jewish Scriptures, our Old Testament. Jewish leaders in Jesus' day didn't see him as an extension or fulfillment of anything. We see Jesus as an *and*. His first-century detractors saw him as an *instead of*.

On this point, they were correct. Jesus was introducing something new.

One of Jesus' most offensive statements is recorded in Matthew's Gospel. If you've read it before, chances are you kept right on reading. Few of us even notice it. During one of his many squabbles with religious leaders over what entailed a violation of the Sabbath, Jesus, referring to himself, stated:

I tell you that something greater than the *temple* is here.[1]

Infuriating, right?

No?

Never noticed that statement before?

Didn't think so.

For first-century Jews, nothing and no one was *greater* than the temple. If there was something *greater* than the temple, the temple was pointless. Useless. While there are places we consider *special*, perhaps *sacred*, our emotional connection with those places pales in comparison to how Jews felt, and in some cases still feel, about their temple. For first-century Jews, the temple was everything. It was the center of the world. Not just their world. The world.

The temple was the epicenter of Jewish religious life. It was the official home of the official law. The temple was the presence of God on earth. To compare oneself to the temple or to suggest anything was greater than the temple reflected extraordinary arrogance, ignorance, or insanity. For someone to claim to *be* greater than the temple was blasphemy worthy of death. A threat to the temple was a threat to the nation. The Jewish populace would *die* before allowing this sacred real estate to be desecrated or threatened.

Die.

That's not hyperbole.

Case in point.

IDOL TALK

Around year AD 40, citizens of Jerusalem were notified that a statue of Emperor Gaius Caligula was to be erected within the temple walls. Petronius, governor of Syria, was given responsibility for transporting the statue from the port city of Ptolemais to Jerusalem. He was accompanied by two legions (approximately 10,000 soldiers). When he arrived to take possession of the statue, he was shocked to discover thousands of Jews from the region had gathered in protest.[2] When threatened with violence, instead of organizing to defend themselves, the protesters knelt and exposed their necks to Roman blades. The message was clear. They would die before they witnessed their temple defiled. Petronius was outmaneuvered.

Armed conflict was one thing. Slaughtering unarmed citizens was something else entirely. Ignoring the crowds, Petronius and his legions made their way inland to Tiberius. According to Josephus, upon reaching Tiberius, he was met with an even larger contingency of protesters. He was still over a hundred miles from Jerusalem. Josephus described the scene outside Tiberius this way:

> So they threw themselves down upon their faces, and stretched out their throats and said they were ready to be slain; and they did this for forty days together and in the meantime left the tilling of their ground, and that while the season of the year required them to sow it. Thus they continued firm in their resolution and proposed to themselves to die willingly rather than to see the dedication of the statue.[3]

Farmers throughout the region went on strike, putting the economy of the region in jeopardy. Once again, Petronius found himself at an impasse. To fulfill the emperor's wishes would require something far worse than armed conflict. It would require something closer to genocide. Reluctantly, he wrote the emperor asking for further instruction, fully aware his failure to carry out his orders would be interpreted as incompetence and would no doubt result in his removal or worse. In an extraordinary twist of fate, or providence, officers of the Praetorian Guard conspired with a handful of Roman senators to have the emperor assassinated before Petronius' letter reached the capital.

Crisis averted.

So yeah, the temple was a big deal.

Jesus claimed to be greater than the temple.

That was a problem.

MODEL FLAWS

By the time Jesus reached adulthood, the Jewish temple system was completely corrupt. He thought so anyway. While we're introduced to a smattering of sincere priests, lawyers, and Pharisees in the Gospels, they are the exception. Jesus' trial alone is enough to remove any doubt about the state of the state.

The widespread corruption in the religious community is not simply inferred and illustrated in the Gospels. Jesus addressed it directly. In Matthew's Gospel, we find Jesus' description of the men in charge.[4] Here's a sampling:

- Everything they do is done for people to see.
- They love the place of honor at banquets.
- They love their titles.
- They love to be greeted with respect in the marketplaces.
- They neglect justice, mercy, and faithfulness.
- They are hypocrites.
- They are full of greed and self-indulgence.
- On the outside they appear righteous, but on the inside they are full of wickedness.

Lovely fellows.

Jesus concludes his remarks by calling them snakes and asking them how they plan to escape hell.[5] On the positive side of the ledger . . . Well, there wasn't a positive side. Jesus considered the entire enterprise corrupt. By the time Jesus stepped out of the Jordan River to begin his ministry, temple leaders had created a sophisticated and convoluted system of loop-holes that enabled them to avoid the most inconvenient demands of the law. They were especially adept at reinterpreting and dumbing down those portions of Moses' law that would cost them financially. Consequently, those in the upper echelon of temple authority lived like kings. In Jesus' day, it was profitable to be a priest in Jerusalem. Most people don't know this, but in Jesus' day, the temple was an enormously profitable enterprise.

Enormously.

Here's why.

PASSING THE PLATE

The temple benefited from several sources of revenue, not least of which was the temple tax. Jewish men over twenty were required to pay an annual temple tax of one half shekel, equal to approximately one and a half day's wages. This was not an enormous amount of money, but it was not limited to men living within the vicinity of the temple.

The tax was required of every Jewish man regardless of where he lived. In the first century, there were millions of Jews scattered throughout the Roman Empire and beyond.[6] An elaborate system existed for col-lecting, guarding, and transporting the temple tax to Jerusalem. Jewish men could pay the tax at treasury centers located in major cities in and around the Roman Empire, or they could pay it at the temple directly. Josephus references one such treasury city, Nisibis, located in modern-day Turkey. The following quote gives us some idea of how much wealth was collected and transferred to Jerusalem from treasury cities:

> . . . for they made use of these cities as a treasury, whence, at a proper time, they were transmitted to Jerusalem; and many ten thousand men undertook the carriage of those donations, out of fear of the ravages of the Parthians . . .[7]

Josephus is famous for his hyperbole. But even if a single thousand Babylonian Jews were assigned to protect the tax convoy, that would be a medium-size army. All this to support the activity taking place on thirty-seven acres in the middle of Jerusalem. The amount of wealth exported out of Roman provinces and shipped to Jerusalem was so large it caused Roman governors to propose laws banning Jews in their cities from paying the tax. At one point, the Roman senate, in an effort to keep Jewish wealth in the capital, passed a law forbidding the export of silver. But Jews in and around Rome continued to pay the tax.

That was just the beginning.

By the first century, Jews were forbidden from minting their own coinage. Rabbis in charge of the temple treasury were forced to look for a foreign coin that approximated the value of a shekel or half shekel. They chose silver coins minted in the city of Tyre.[8] The Tyrian didrachmas and tetradrachmas closely approximated the value of the ancient Jewish half shekel and shekel. In Jesus' day, the temple would *only* accept Tyrian coinage.

That created a problem for taxpayers and an opportunity for tax collectors. Jews traveled from all over the world to visit the temple. Few of them would be carrying Tyrian coins. To remedy this "problem," tables were set up in the temple courtyard where moneychangers exchanged whatever currency a worshipper happened to be carrying for a Tyrian shekel. And who do you suppose determined the exchange rate? Temple authorities, of course. Worshippers had little choice but to submit to the posted rate.

So in addition to taxes flowing in from all over the civilized world, the temple staff had discovered yet another way to raise revenue. It was this practice, along with the sale of second-rate, overpriced, sacrificial animals that drove Jesus to exercise his messianic authority in that most unforgettable manner. In a strange twist, it was undoubtedly thirty pieces of Tyrian silver pilfered from the treasury that the chief priest used to pay off Judas.

The power, politics, and profit associated with the first-century Jewish temple was the perfect storm. It was a recipe for corruption. Add religion to the mix and it was a recipe for extraordinary hypocrisy as well—something John the Baptist and Jesus consistently pointed out and condemned. In spite of all that, the temple was still a big deal in first-century Jewish culture. A *really* big deal. And Jesus claimed to be greater than the temple.

That was an even bigger deal.

UNIMAGINABLE

One afternoon as Jesus and his crew were exiting the temple, somebody commented on the massive stones and magnificent buildings that were part of the temple complex.[9] Jesus stopped, looked back, and said:

> Truly I tell you, not one stone here will be left on another; every one will be thrown down.[10]

Translated: Don't be too impressed; *it's a teardown*.

They were stunned.

Hoping there was a punch line.

But Jesus turned and made his way down into the city.

"Thrown down?" Did he really say, "Thrown down"? Every single stone "thrown down"? As in thrown down off the thirty-seven-acre plaza into the valley below? How could this be? More to the point, how could this even be accomplished? Earthquakes were common in the region. But Herod the Great had rebuilt the temple in such a way as to make it virtually earthquake proof. The entire structure was constructed from cut stone. The foundation stones weighed as much as five hundred tons. An earthquake may at best crack a ceiling, topple over a parapet, or create a fissure in a wall. But even an earthquake wouldn't do what Jesus described. That would require an army. And the only army capable of such a feat would involve Roman Legions. But Rome wouldn't destroy the temple. It was Rome's client king, Herod, who was responsible for rebuilding it to begin with.

Perhaps they misunderstood.

Later that day they gathered outside the city on the Mount of Olives, a location providing them with a panoramic view of the city, including the temple. The suspense was killing them. Jesus' statement regarding the future of the temple was . . . well, it was apocalyptic. The end of the temple signaled the end of the world as they knew it. And nobody felt fine. Finally, someone spoke up and asked what everyone was dying to know:

> . . . when will this happen . . .[11]

The Gospels of Matthew, Mark, and Luke record Jesus' answer. What followed is the most remarkable and verifiable prophecy given by anyone, anywhere, at any time. Christians are fond of leveraging Old Testament prophecies to "prove" Jesus is who he claimed to be. But this epic prediction is far more convincing than anything we find in the Old Testament. Here's a taste of Jesus' answer from Luke's Gospel:

> When you see Jerusalem being surrounded by armies, you will know that its desolation is near. Then let those who are in Judea flee to the mountains, let those in the city get out, and let those in the country not enter the city.[12]

Chances are you've read that before. Chances are you've heard a sermon or two that included those verses. And chances are whoever delivered those sermons associated those verses with the last days . . . the book of Revelation . . . the second coming . . . etc. That's unfortunate.

Here's why.

Jesus wasn't predicting the end of the world as depicted in the final book of our Bibles. He was predicting something local. Something that would occur during the lifetimes of many in his audience. And sure enough, forty years after Jesus made this disturbing prediction, the soon-to-be-elected emperor of Rome, General Vespasian, trapped thousands of Jewish rebels inside the city of Jerusalem. This was the culmination of a four-year campaign between Jewish rebels and the empire. Historians refer to this as the Jewish War or the Judean War. It was unimaginable when Jesus spoke of it, but Vespasian's army literally surrounded Jerusalem and sealed both the rebel forces as well as the citizenry inside the city walls—city walls that would eventually become prison walls for the terrified citizens of Jerusalem. With that bit of history as a backdrop, let's look at Jesus' statement one more time:

> When you see Jerusalem being surrounded by armies, you will know that its desolation is near. Then let those who are in Judea flee to the mountains, let those in the city get out, and let those in the country not enter the city.[13]

As Vespasian's army approached Jerusalem, thousands of Jewish pilgrims were making their way to the Holy City to celebrate a religious festival. Initially, Roman commanders blocked the travelers from entering the city. Vespasian countermanded that order and instructed his legions to protect and escort the pilgrims as far as the city gates. This went on for days. Once everyone was safely inside the walls, Vespasian had the city sealed off. It was both a brilliant and cruel move on the part of the Roman general. The more mouths to feed, the shorter the siege. By the time the Tenth Legion finally punched through the interior wall of the city, the population was literally starving to death.

... and let those in the country not enter the city.[14]

Jesus continued:

> How dreadful it will be in those days for pregnant women and nursing mothers! There will be great distress in the land and wrath against this people.[15]

"Wrath" was an understatement. The siege went on for so long that by the time Roman infantry poured through the breach, their pent-up anger made them merciless. Thousands of Jews were butchered. Jewish historian Josephus writes:

The slaughter within was even more dreadful than the spectacle from without. Men and women, old and young, insurgents and priests, those who fought and those who entreated mercy, were hewn down in indiscriminate carnage . . . The legionaries had to clamber over heaps of dead to carry on the work of extermination.[16]

Those who were spared were not spared out of mercy but out of greed. Survivors, including children, were sold to slavers, who waited impatiently for their payday. Josephus puts the number of Jews sold as slaves in the hundreds of thousands. Jesus predicted this as well.

They will fall by the sword and will be taken as prisoners to all the nations.[17]

This extraordinarily detailed prediction of what would transpire in Jerusalem is one reason secular scholars insist Matthew, Mark, and Luke were written more than a generation after the events recorded in the Gospels. In their view, by the time the Gospels were written, the supposed eyewitnesses of the resurrection were all dead. Anyone who actually knew Jesus or heard him teach was dead. In this view, the Gospels were written by Gentile Christians who put words in Jesus' mouth based on legend and hearsay. There are countless problems with this hypothesis. Books and articles have been written to demonstrate the absurdity of these claims. But I sympathize with those who insist on this view.

Why?

Because, if the Gospels were written before AD 70, before the events described by Jesus occurred, it is impossible to avoid the conclusion that Jesus predicted, in extraordinary detail, the end of ancient Judaism. If he did, one would be a fool not to give careful consideration to everything else he had to say as well.

And we haven't even gotten to the main event.

The destruction of the temple.

NOT ONE STONE

When Roman legions entered Jerusalem, they discovered the temple district well defended. While desperate rebels fought to defend their most sacred site, priests stood on the roof and pleaded with God for a miracle. In the end, the legions prevailed, but not before someone set fire to the interior of the temple. Everything that could burn was destroyed. The priests were slaughtered and everything of value that survived the flames was carted off. Standard military fare. But what happened next was unprecedented and unexpected.

Titus, who was now in command in his father's absence, ordered that every stone used in the construction of the temple be torn down, dragged to the edge of the plaza, and pushed off into the valley below. Some of those massive stones remain to this day where they landed almost two thousand years ago.

> Truly I tell you, not one stone here will be left on another; every one will be thrown down.[18]

When you read Jesus' description of what would transpire within view of where he was seated, it's easy to imagine the pain in his voice. It was as if he could see the carnage, hear the screams, and feel the panic of mothers clinging to their children.

These were his people. This was his nation. The nation God had raised up from one man for one purpose—to bless the world. But that chapter was drawing to a close. The temple era was coming to an end. God's covenant with the nation had served its purpose. It was no longer needed.

Why?

Because something *greater* than the temple had come.

Something that would make the temple and everything associated with it obsolete. Something new. Something better. Something for the whole world. Ancient Israel was a means to an end.

The end had come.

The new was just beginning.

SECTION 2

All Things New

INTRODUCTION

One thing should be abundantly clear from our sprint through the Old Testament. God had an agenda. His agenda had implications for all nations, not *a* nation. If the previous chapters didn't convince you, then perhaps this will:

> For God so loved the . . .

Anyone?

"World."

That's right, the entire world. As in everybody, in every nation, in every generation. The Creator of the World revealed himself to a man with no people who would become a nation with a divine purpose. Along that harrowing journey, he would use a variety of things to move the story along. Road trips, plagues, fire, brimstone, man-eating earthquakes, stone tablets, an ancient constitution, a portable altar, kings, and, eventually, with some reservation, a temple. Actually, several temples.

But these were all means to a specific end.

And they were all designed to *end*.

Everything on that list had a shelf life.

I'm not discounting the importance of anything on the list. I'm not discounting the importance of the Jewish Scriptures. When it comes to Jewish sacred texts, I'm with Jesus. His view is my view. And what does he say about the Jewish Scriptures? We'll talk more about that later in this section.

In many ways, the adventures and misadventures of the Jewish people as recorded in the first half of our English Bibles can be compared to a divinely engineered cocoon that "when the set time had fully come" gave birth to the fulfillment of God's promise to Abraham. When Jesus stepped into the Jordan River to be baptized, something brand-new was being unleashed on the world. It was so new, so totally *other*, so unlike anything that had been before, even John acknowledged his moment in the sun had come to an end. From that time on, it was all about the *new* guy.

Remember this?

> The next day John saw Jesus coming toward him and said, "Look, the Lamb of God, who takes away the sin of the . . .

There it is again.

> . . . world!"

John gets so excited he has a hard time getting his words out.

> This is the one I meant when I said, "A man who comes after me has surpassed me because he was before me."

Got to love that. But listen to . . . actually read . . . what he says next:

> I myself did not know him, but the reason I came baptizing with water . . .

Tell us John, why did you come baptizing with water?

> . . . was that he might be revealed to Israel.[1]

Implication: Now that he's been revealed, my small part in the story is complete. I'm simply one man in a long list of people God used to tee up what he is about to do. John the Baptist—like Abraham, Isaac, Jacob, Joseph, Moses, David, Solomon, Nehemiah, along with all the prophets—was a means to an end.

Like the road trips, plagues, fire, brimstone, stone tablets, portable altars, kings, and temples, he was *necessary* but *temporary*. He was so temporary, the Gospel writers tell us that when Jesus heard John had been arrested, not only did he not rescue him, he went to the lake.[2]

Seriously. He went to the lake.

But even after John's dramatic introduction, no one expected Jesus to architect something *new*. Just the opposite. If he was indeed Messiah, his role was to extend something old. If he were a prophet, his task would be to shepherd the nation back to the old ways. If he had been satisfied with the mantle of rabbi or teacher, his role would have been to clarify and apply the ancient words of Moses. Whichever role he chose, *new* wasn't part of the script. Improved? Perhaps. But not new.

In the following sections we will explore three facets of the *new* that Jesus unleashed in the world. We will begin with his *new* movement, the church. Then we will listen in as he explains to his disciples the terms and conditions of a *new* covenant, a new arrangement between God and humankind. And, finally, we will try to wrap our minds around the significance of Jesus' *new* command—a single command that was to serve as the overarching ethic for his new movement.

My hunch is the *new* Jesus inaugurated won't be news to you. It certainly won't bother you. What you may find disturbing are the implications for the *old*. Jesus came to fulfill and *re*place much of what was in place. New things don't generally bother us until we realize it means letting go of old, comfortable things. This explains why you kept your old couch after you purchased a new one. All that stuff in your attic, basement, or storage closet . . . you just can't seem to part with it, can you? That's human nature. And in the case of your closet, basement, or attic, it's harmless. The old couch in your basement in no way diminishes the enjoyment you get from the new one in your living room. But as we are about to discover, as long as we cling to the *old* Jesus came to replace, we will never fully appreciate, experience, or even recognize the *new* he came to put in place.

So yeah, what follows may be a bit disturbing.

But I hope you'll be more than disturbed. By the time we've finished our journey together, I hope you'll be ready to unhitch your faith, your theology, and your lifestyle once and for all from the *old* that Jesus came to replace. And I hope you will fully embrace the *new* Jesus came to unleash in the world, for the world.

Chapter 6

Brand-New Movement

Not only were Jesus' first-century followers not expecting something new, they associated him with someone old.

Really old.

Like dead old.

Here's what happened.

Jesus and his band of merry men were traveling through the region of Caesarea Philippi when Jesus asked them a pivotal question. Perhaps it was the backstory of this region with two names that prompted Jesus to ask,

> Who do people say the Son of Man is?[1]

What's the word on the street? What's my rep?

Turns out some believed he was John the Baptizer reincarnated. Others suggested he was Elijah or Jeremiah or some other dead Jewish prophet.[2] Implication? More of the same. Nothing new. Then Jesus asked a second question.

> Who do *you* say that I am?

Simon Peter spoke up. Of course.

> You are the Messiah, the Son of the living God.[3]

To which Jesus responded,

> Blessed are you, Simon son of Jonah, for this was not revealed to you by man, but by my Father in heaven. And I tell you that you are Peter . . .

And then the big announcement:

> . . . and on this rock *I will build my church*, and the gates of Hades will not overcome it.[4]

That is my favorite Bible prophecy.

Jesus predicted *us*.

More to the point, Jesus predicted something *new*. He spoke in the future tense. "I will build . . ." As in, it hasn't happened yet. Something new is on the horizon.

What was this *new* nobody *knew* was coming?

His "church."

FIRST TIME

This is the first time the term *church* appears in our English New Testaments. Turns out, it shouldn't have appeared at all. Whereas the majority of your English New Testament is a word-for-word *translation* from Greek, the term *church* is an exception. The term *church* is not a *translation*. It's a *substitution*. And a misleading one at that.

The term *church* is a derivative of the German term *kirche* meaning: *house of the Lord* or temple. This term of German origin was used to *interpret*, rather than *translate*, the Greek term *ekklesia* throughout most of the New Testament. There are five notable and important exceptions. Notable and important because they clarify for us English readers the point Jesus was making that afternoon. He certainly wasn't predicting a new house of the Lord. Just the opposite. As we've already seen, God was pretty much through with houses by this point.

A quick look at one of the notable exceptions in the translation of *ekklesia* dispels any confusion regarding what Jesus was and wasn't predicting that afternoon in Caesarea Philippi. The one I've chosen is found in the context of one of Paul's missionary journeys.

THE IDOL GUILD

While visiting the city of Ephesus, the apostle Paul found himself at the center of a local controversy caused primarily by his success in converting a significant number of idol-worshipping locals. They were abandoning their idol-worshipping ways in such large numbers, it threatened the idol-manufacturing business. In response, a silversmith named Demetrius called a meeting of the idol-manufacturing guild, along with other related trades, and shared his concerns. Next thing you know, there was a riot.

Luke, who was there, claims the entire city was in an uproar.[5] The following is his description of what ensued. The Greek term *ekklesia,* translated *church* over one hundred times in your English New Testament, is translated differently in this passage. Let's see if you can find it:

> So then, some were shouting one thing and some another, for the assembly was in confusion and the majority did not know for what reason they had come together.[6]

Spot it? Here's how the passage would read if *ekklesia* had been translated *church.*

> So then, some were shouting one thing and some another, for the *church* was in confusion and the majority did not know for what reason they had come together.[7]

That's actually an accurate description of a church meeting I sat through in the eighth grade. Before it was over, someone actually slugged my dad. But that's a story for another day.

As you probably guessed, *ekklesia* is translated *assembly* in the passage above. Why? That's what the term means. *Ekklesia* was not, is not, a religious term. It does not mean *church* or *house of the Lord*. It certainly shouldn't be associated with a *temple*. The term was used widely to describe a *gathering* or *assembly*, civic gatherings, or an assembly of soldiers. Or as we just saw, an assembly of rioting idol manufacturers. An *ekklesia* was a gathering of people for a specific purpose. Any specific purpose.[8]

And the point is . . .

LIKE NO OTHER

This mistranslation of what Jesus *said* detracts from what Jesus *meant*.[9] Jesus announced the formation of a *new assembly* in his name: "my *ekklesia*." This was blasphemy. Jesus was setting himself against the temple and all it represented. In doing so, he made his point offensively clear. He was not just another rabbi trailed by another ragtag group of followers who would eventually disband once their teacher moved on, passed away, or worse.

Jesus was not just another in a long line of prophets that had come to castigate and correct the nation. He was certainly no zealot. Roman rule didn't seem to bother him in the least . . . which bothered his followers . . . a lot. Jesus was none of these. He was a category of one. Peter got it right. He was *the* Christ, *the* Son of *the* living God. Unlike everyone who had come before, nothing, not even his own death, would stop the *new* he would introduce into the world.

THE WAY

Standing in that scorching Galilean sun, Jesus did not predict a place. He predicted a people, a new assembly signaling a new movement. As Luke documented later, Jesus' promise eventually materialized. Weeks after the resurrection, his followers took to the streets of Jerusalem and the movement started moving. Filled with the Spirit of the mobile God, they were mobile. No sacred facility was required. No facility could contain them. The Jesus movement was airborne.

Before long, the movement had a name. But it wasn't *church*. His post-resurrection followers weren't called Christians. That would come later. In the beginning, the Jesus movement had a dynamic name. A name that spoke of direction, intention, and passion. In the beginning, the Jesus movement was called *The Way*.

Before his conversion, the apostle Paul referred to Jesus followers as those belonging to *The Way*. After his conversion he admitted to Governor Felix that he was, in fact, a follower of *The Way*.[10] The Greek term translated *way* can also be translated *road*, *path*, or *street*. Jesus' followers viewed themselves as stewards of *the way* forward for all humankind. Unlike ancient Judaism or the various pagan religions, *The Way* was not regional. It was not national. It was not tied to a sacred spot. This was a movement offering a way forward to every people group, tribe, and tongue. This moniker underscored yet again the newness of the Jesus movement. It was not a continuation of something old but the beginning of something new. Jesus had come to put *in place* something designed to fulfill and *replace* all that had been *in place* before.

As stated earlier, the term *church* should have never been incorporated into Christian Scripture or Christian culture. It's more than a mistranslation. It represents a misdirection. If you've never heard any of this before, you may be asking, "Why haven't I heard any of this before? If the Greek word meant *gathering*, why don't our English Bibles say 'gathering'? Why do our English Bibles use a German derivative, *church*, instead of a direct translation?"

The short answer is, somebody tried that once and it didn't turn out well.

MEET WILLIAM

In 1522, William Tyndale began translating the Greek New Testament into English. Tyndale had the audacity to actually translate the term *ekklesia* rather than superimpose the widely accepted German term *kirche*. Instead of *church*, he used the term *congregation*. If that wasn't offensive enough, the Greek text led him to use *elder* instead of *priest* and *repent* instead of *do penance*.[11]

Tyndale was branded an outlaw and, after successfully eluding authorities for ten years, was betrayed by a friend and arrested. A tribunal of the Holy Roman Church condemned him as a heretic and turned him over to civil authorities, who bound him to a beam, strangled him with a rope, burned his body, and scattered his remains.

All that to say, you should think twice before changing your church marquee.

But seriously, think about that.

"Church" officials executed a man for translating and distributing the words of Jesus in a language adults and children could read and understand.

How could that be?

It could be because by this time in church history much of what Jesus came to *replace* had been put back *in place*. As we will discover throughout our journey together, whenever the church opts to mix old with new, bad things happen. People get hurt.

By the time William Tyndale came along, church officials had abandoned Jesus' new model of leadership. They had replaced it with the top-down, imperial model. Officials knew if commoners had access to the Scriptures, they would discover the church of their generation was nothing like the church described in the New Testament. They would encounter a Savior who was nothing like the fire-breathing deity depicted in the sermons of that era. They would search in vain for terms such as *purgatory*, *indulgence*, and *excommunication*. Access to the text would have removed the primary currency of the official church: fear. Something Jesus refused to leverage. Something he repeatedly instructed his followers not to do.

Thanks to the courage of men like Tyndale, Huss, Luther, and others, the *ekklesia* of Jesus was liberated in part from the tyranny of hierarchical ecclesiastic manipulation. The Protestant Reformation breathed new life into the *ekklesia* of Jesus. The gospel was unchained from the pulpit and made accessible beyond mass to the masses.

It's unfortunate Tyndale's bold but accurate translation of the term *ekklesia* didn't stick. By the time of the reformers, the term *church* had become so deeply entrenched in culture and conversation, there was no going back. So while much of Tyndale's translation made its way into the modern and postmodern world, the term *ekklesia* remains a casualty of translation tradition.

The term, but not the movement.

From the first century through the twenty-first century, there has always been a remnant, a group who has refused to define church in terms of location or hierarchy. There have always been, and will always be, men and women who view the church as a movement with a divinely inspired mission and mandate.

Back to Jesus.

SOMETHING NEW

Walking with his disciples in the region of Caesarea Philippi, the Twelve had no idea they were at the precipice of a new era. They had no way of knowing how significant that particular conversation would turn out to be. They certainly had no idea how significant their role would be in the events that would transpire. They were thinking *kingdom*. Their vision was no larger than the ancient borders of Israel. But Jesus had something bigger in mind.

Something new.

His *ekklesia*.

His new movement would eventually carry his new message beyond the borders of Judea and Galilee. In an astonishingly short span of time, against unimaginable odds, the message of Jesus made its way to the heart of the Roman Empire. By the beginning of the second century, it had captured the attention of pagans both inside and outside that empire. One of those pagans was a lawyer turned Christian theologian and apologist named Quintus Septimius Florens Tertullianus, better known as

Tertullian. Tertullian was both a product of as well as an eyewitness to the spread of Christianity in the late second and early third centuries. When Tertullian penned the following words, crosses in Rome still had bodies hanging from them. Yet the *ekklesia* of Jesus flourished:

> What shall I say of the Romans themselves, who fortify their own empire with garrisons of their own legions, nor can extend the might of their kingdom beyond these nations?
>
> But Christ's name is extending everywhere, believed everywhere, worshipped by all the above enumerated nations, reigning everywhere, adored everywhere, conferred equally everywhere upon all. No king, with Him, finds greater favor, no barbarian lesser joy; no dignities or pedigrees enjoy distinctions of merit; to all He is equal, to all King, to all Judge, to all God and Lord.[12]

"But Christ's name is extending everywhere, believed everywhere..."

This would have been impossible for the twelve young men traipsing along behind Jesus to comprehend.

"Everywhere"?

But following his resurrection, Jesus' first-century followers oversaw the launch of a movement that would in fact extend "everywhere." The centerpiece of this movement would be Peter's inspired declaration concerning the identity of his teacher and friend. Jesus was, in fact, the Messiah, the Son of the living God.

Chapter 7

BRAND-NEW AGREEMENT

For devout first-century Jews, much of what Jesus taught was scandalous, blasphemous, or at best uninformed. On a couple of occasions, religious leaders picked up stones to stone him.[1] Folks he grew up with tried to push him off a cliff. Following a sermon in which he referenced eating his flesh and drinking his blood, some of his most ardent followers deserted him. So, from a first-century religious point of view, Jesus was not a status quo kind of guy. But the common folk? They loved him.

His closest followers were convinced that in the end he would make nice with the movers and shakers in the Jewish community and that together they would usher out the Romans and usher in a new era of temple-centered Judaism. Right up to the end, they were convinced Jesus had come to extend something old rather than introduce something new. This may explain why the most offensive thing Jesus said didn't create a ripple.

CHRISTMAS SURPRISE

To put this *most offensive statement ever* in perspective, imagine next December your pastor announcing the following on the first Sunday of the month:

> *I want to take a minute to announce a permanent change in the way our church will celebrate Christmas. Beginning this year, rather than celebrating the birth of Jesus, we will celebrate my birthday instead.*

Once it dawned on you that he (or she) was serious, my hunch is you would slip out during the offering, never to return. That is, unless you're a deacon or elder in your church. In which case you would call an emergency meeting of the leadership followed by a call to a local psychiatrist.

Can you think of anything more absurd?

No?

I can.

Something Jesus said. Everybody should have gotten up and excused themselves. But they were still in it to win it. So nobody left.

Well, actually, one guy did. The one we don't name our sons after.

Here's what happened.

PASSING OVER

On the evening prior to his crucifixion, which nobody in the room saw coming, Jesus met with the Twelve for the Passover meal. Passover was one of the most, if not *the* most, important celebrations for ancient Jews. Passover was the annual commemoration and celebration of the nation's liberation from Egypt. No doubt first-century Jews had mixed emotions celebrating their liberation from Egypt while occupied by Rome. For many it was an annual reminder of what God could do if only he would . . . namely, send another Joshua to expel the invaders. The folks who gathered with Jesus that evening were hoping he was in fact Joshua 2.0.

During this most sacred occasion, Jesus made what was perhaps his most outlandish and offensive statement to date. You've read it or heard it dozens of times and my guess is it elicited low to no emotion.

> When the hour came, Jesus and his apostles reclined at the table. And he said to them, "I have eagerly desired to eat this Passover with you before I suffer."

His reference to suffering may be the reason the boys weren't offended by what came next. After all, if Jesus suffered, chances were high they would suffer as well. Suffering is distracting.

After taking the cup, he gave thanks and said, "Take this and divide it among you. For I tell you I will not drink again from the fruit of the vine until the kingdom of God comes."

At which point they may have thought, *You're kind of making this all about you. Perhaps we should take a few moments to remember what we're here to remember. Moses. Egypt. Let my people go.*

And he took bread, gave thanks and broke it, and gave it to them, saying,

Here we go.

"This is *my* body given for you; *do this in remembrance of me.*"[2]

To which they must have thought, *What? You want us to celebrate Passover in remembrance of you? That's worse than claiming to be greater than the temple!*

Jesus reframed and reinterpreted a meal pointing back to perhaps the most pivotal moment in Israel's history. Put yourself in the disciples' sandals and imagine how ridiculous, how blasphemous, this must have sounded. We don't mess with Christmas or Easter, and Jesus didn't have any business messing with Passover.

Unless.

Unless something bigger than Israel's deliverance from Egypt was about to transpire. But what could possibly be bigger than that? Perhaps he would explain later. Besides, it was time for the main course. So they settled into dinnertime banter while mulling over Jesus' strange and treasonous declaration.

But just about the time they thought things were getting back to normal, he did it again.

In the same way, after the supper he took the cup, saying, "This cup is the *new covenant* in my blood, which is poured out for you."[3]

"The new covenant."

Did he really say *the* new covenant? As in the one predicted by Jeremiah six hundred years earlier? If that was the case, then this really *was* big. Maybe not as epic as the nation's exodus out of Egypt, but big nonetheless. The Old Testament prophet Jeremiah warned that the covenant between God and the nation would eventually be fulfilled and replaced.

> "The days are coming," declares the LORD, "when I will make
> a *new covenant* with the people of Israel and with the people
> of Judah. It will not be like the covenant I made with their
> ancestors when I took them by the hand to lead them out of
> Egypt..."[4]

This new, replacement covenant would be different from the original covenant in several respects. According to Jeremiah, the new covenant would be a covenant of conscience.

> "I will put my law in their minds and write it on their hearts.
> I will be their God, and they will be my people."

The inauguration of this new covenant would eliminate the need for ceremonial animal sacrifice.

> "For I will forgive their wickedness and will remember their
> sins no more."[5]

LOST IN TRANSITION

The full implications of Jesus' declaration were lost on the boys in the room. Understandably so. There was a lot going on that night. And the night was just getting started. His earlier reference to suffering and leaving combined with the commotion created by Judas' unexplained disappearance distracted from the magnitude of his words. In a few hours the witnesses to this momentous declaration would run for their lives while their master was dragged to Caiaphas' house for questioning and worse. There was no time to digest the significance of what Jesus said.

They would remember later, however.

Somebody in the room would eventually pass it along to Luke, who may have been the one who passed it along to the apostle Paul, who passed it along to every major port city along the Mediterranean. However it happened, once the dust settled and the tomb was found empty, the significance of Jesus' words took center stage. Two thousand years later, in churches, homes, camps, in public, and in secret, Christians all over the world celebrate some version of that sacred meal in remembrance of him.

Jesus used his final Passover meal to announce the end of Passover as they knew it and to signal the inauguration of a new covenant. Not a new covenant between God and an individual, as was the case with Abraham. Not a covenant between God and a particular nation, as was the case with Israel. This was the big one.

The final one.

The everlasting one.

This was a covenant between God and the human race. Every nation for every generation. The inauguration of a new covenant signaled the *fulfillment* of God's promise to Abraham. Finally, something for everybody. With the inauguration of the new covenant, every nation would be blessed.

But while the new covenant signaled the *fulfillment* of God's promise to Abraham, it signaled the *finale* of the covenant God established with ancient Israel at Mount Sinai. First-century Jews had an extremely difficult time wrapping their minds around this. But as we are about to discover, first-century Jews were not the only ones who had a difficult time recognizing the temporary nature of that divinely instituted arrangement between God and ancient Israel.

LOST IN TRANSMISSION

The inauguration of the new covenant explains why most Christians don't mind a little bacon with their eggs. It explains why you can't get either at Chick-fil-A on Sunday. If we were still taking our marching orders from Moses, they would be closed on Saturday.

Perish the thought.

Thanks to the new covenant, we aren't required to kill anything to stay on speaking terms with God. Skim through Leviticus and you'll discover a whole lot of things we aren't required to do. But the church has an uncomfortable history and habit of selectively rebranding aspects of God's covenant with Israel and smuggling them into the *ekklesia* of Jesus. This habit explains how sixteenth-century church leaders justified and sanctioned the execution of William Tyndale for attempting to make the Bible accessible to the common folk. But the rebranding and smuggling began much earlier than that.

In the years following the death of the apostles, Gentile church leaders claimed the Jewish Scriptures as their own and insisted they were binding on the church. We will discuss this in greater detail in chapter twelve. Suffice it to say here, these non-Jewish church leaders viewed and thus interpreted the ancient Jewish texts through the lens of their developing Christian theology. At this point in history, the church had no official text of its own. Consequently, Gentile church leaders leaned heavily on the Jewish Scriptures. More specifically, they leaned heavily on their interpretation of the Jewish Scriptures. It wasn't long before old covenant values and imperatives began to inform the teaching of the church.

For example.

Not long after Christianity was legalized in the fourth century, the church began doing unto pagans as pagans had done unto the church. They persecuted and, in some cases, executed unrepentant, idol-worshipping, animal-sacrificing pagans. How did church leaders justify this un-Christlike violence? It was simple, really. The Scriptures required that idol worshippers be put to death.

Which Scriptures?

The recently incorporated Jewish Scriptures.

Julius Firmicus Maternus was a fourth-century pagan astrologer who converted to Christianity and eventually became a respected and outspoken Christian apologist. Around 346, he wrote a letter to the sons of Emperor Constantine, Constans and Constantius II, co-regents of the empire at the time. The letter is entitled *De errore profanarum religionum* [*Concerning the Error of Profane Religions*]. Idol worship and animal sacrifice had been banned in the empire by this time, but the laws prohibiting these expressions of pagan worship were not being enforced. This concerned Firmicus, and thus his letter.

In it Firmicus reminds the royal brothers that they are God's servants and as such it was their responsibility to eradicate paganism from the empire. This included the destruction and confiscation of pagan temples as well as the destruction of the pagans themselves if they refused to convert. Firmicus was a fan of forced conversion. He was convinced the forced converts would thank their enforcers later. Even if later was the afterlife. And how did this pagan-turned-Christian justify this violent and potentially bloody campaign?

With Scripture.

The Scripture he chose to support his appeal for violence against the pagans came from the lips of Moses. The original context was irrelevant because, after all, Scripture is Scripture. And all Scripture is equally inspired and equally binding. Here is the text he chose:

> If your very own brother, or your son or daughter, or the wife you love, or your closest friend secretly entices you, saying, "Let us go and worship other gods" (gods that neither you nor your ancestors have known, gods of the peoples around you, whether near or far, from one end of the land to the other), do not yield to them or listen to them.
>
> Show them no pity. Do not spare them or shield them. You must certainly put them to death. Your hand must be the first

in putting them to death, and then the hands of all the people. Stone them to death, because they tried to turn you away from the LORD your God.[6]

Hard to argue with that.

So they didn't.

Before long it was open season on the pagans.

In Jesus' name.

The eleventh century was host to the first crusade. Modern historians have made a compelling case that the crusades were justified in light of their geopolitical context. What no one attempts to justify is the way church leaders leveraged Scripture to inspire the wealthy and poor alike to make the perilous journey east to expel the Saracens from the Holy City. Church leaders weaponized Christianity by offering a "get out of hell free" card to anyone who joined the crusade. The duplicity of this combination of old and new covenant concepts is easy to miss. The church leveraged old covenant texts to sanction violence in God's name while promising the new covenant version of heaven for those who participated. In the end, Muslim infidels were not the only group to suffer. Thousands of Jews were murdered and their property confiscated as well. Why? Again, it was simple. Jews were responsible for crucifying Jesus. This made them enemies of God and thus enemies of the church. And the Scripture was clear. Enemies of God must be punished. In the end, church leaders found in the Jewish Scriptures justification to mistreat Jews. Granted, their interpretation and contextualization of the Jewish Scriptures was horrendous.

But that's my point.

REFORMERS TO THE RESCUE

By the fourteenth century, the church had drifted so far from the tenets of the new covenant that there was an internal demand for reform. When reform from the inside failed, reformers stepped away from the authority of the church, and the result was Protestantism—a term originating from a letter *protesting* an edict *protesting* the teachings of Martin Luther in 1529.

The theological underpinnings of the Protestant movement are best summarized in the *Five Solas*:

Sola Scriptura

Sola Gratia

Sola Fide

Solus Christus

Soli Deo Gloria

The five solas were a response to specific distortions of the new covenant. The reformers were primarily concerned with the way the church distorted doctrines related to salvation and authority. Borrowing from both pagan and Jewish traditions, the church had established its own priesthood. As was the case in all ancient religions, priests served as mediators between God and the people. This imbued them with extraordinary power and influence in a world where literacy rates were low and access to Scripture was limited. Church leaders claimed their authority was derived from a combination of Scripture, tradition, and the word of the Pope. To this the reformers responded with "Sola scriptura!" Scripture alone! And while reformers debated *which* documents should be considered "Scripture," they never debated the *authority* of the Scriptures.

Regarding salvation, the church concocted a rather convoluted approach. Salvation was acquired through a combination of new and old covenant concepts along with ... well ... along with stuff they made up. Essentially salvation came by way of God's grace, good works, and penance for the not-so-good works, along with the merits accumulated by the saints who preceded us.

Certainly made for a confusing last night at church camp.

To all this the reformers responded with, "Sola Gratia! Sola Fide! Solus Christus! Soli Deo Gloria!" Salvation comes by way of faith alone, through grace alone in Christ alone, to the glory of God alone!

Thanks to the reformers, we Protestants are pretty much people of the book. Thanks to the Reformation, we pretty much have salvation by faith through grace alone down pat. We all know John 3:16. We've all prayed the sinner's prayer.

Several times.

Most of us are convinced we can't lose our salvation. So on the question of who we are ultimately accountable to and how we gain access to our Father in heaven, we're good to go. But it's a mistake to assume our brand of Christianity is free of all old covenant leftovers.

It's not.

NOT IMMUNE

The modern church suffers from its own version of mix-and-match theology and orthopraxy. By mix-and-match I'm referring to our incessant habit of reaching back into old covenant concepts, teachings, sayings, and narratives to support our own teachings, sayings, and narratives. Here is a sampling of some of the "old covenant leftovers" just to whet your appetite.

- Why are Christians behind the movement to post the Ten Commandments in classrooms and courthouses? Why not portions of the Sermon on the Mount?

- Why do we give children a copy of the old covenant bound with the new without teaching them the difference?

- Why do some churches have priests?

- Why do Christians sometimes describe their pastors as "anointed" by God?

- Why do some Christian leaders constantly warn of God's impending judgment?

- Why would a Christian believe God judges nations at all? New Testament authors along with Jesus spoke of a once-for-all final judgment.

- Why would a Christian kick their son or daughter out of the house for being pregnant or gay?

- Why would Christian leaders declare a tsunami God's judgment on a predominantly Muslim region of the world?

- Why do Christians judge non-Christians for not behaving like Christians?

- Why do pastors leverage phrases like, "The Bible says . . ." and "The Bible teaches . . . ," inadvertently giving equal authority to everything in the Bible?

- Why do we take marriage and dating advice from a pagan king with seven hundred wives?

- Why would I blow up my career by writing this book?

THE REBRAND

Now, to be clear, none of this is a big deal as long as we are content creating closed church cultures designed by and for church people. For those churches, the blending of old with new simply creates unique religious expressions, theological differentiators, and a broad range of song lyrics. No harm done.

But . . .

But if you . . . if I . . . if we . . . desire to participate in the *ekklesia* of Jesus, there is no room for rebranded, repurposed, and retrofitted old. What some may be inclined to adopt as a *distinctive,* we must reject as *error.* The reformers refused to accept salvation via penance as a theological distinctive. They held it up against the new covenant and put a label on it. Error.

What's at stake goes beyond theological correctness. This is about the Great Commission. It's about evangelism. This is about the *ekklesia* of Jesus functioning as salt and unfiltered light. This is about ensuring that the life-changing *new* Jesus unleashed in the world doesn't get retrofitted with something old. Retro is fine for your middle school daughter's bedroom. It's not fine for the church. To paraphrase James, the brother of Jesus, this is about not making it unnecessarily difficult for those who are turning to God.[7] To paraphrase the apostle Paul, this is about winning some and saving some.[8] For Christians with their backs to the culture waiting for Jesus to return, or worse, waiting for revival to break out so they don't have to do the hard stuff, what follows won't feel urgent. It may even feel threatening.

I'm convinced our current versions of the Christian faith need to be stripped of a variety of old covenant leftovers. This has nothing to do with expressions of worship or style. Old is blended with new in modern, traditional, and liturgical churches. We are dragging along a litany of old covenant concepts and assumptions that slow us down, divide us up, and confuse those standing on the outside peering in.

So if your heart is broken by the brokenness of our world, you'll be encouraged by what follows. If you grieve over how easily culture dismisses Christianity and the church, I hope you will see this as more than theological wrangling. If you're a parent concerned about the durability of your children's faith, this is critical. And if you're interested in a version of our faith free of what makes us unnecessarily resistible . . . here we go!

Chapter 8

YOUR FIRST LOOK AT THE GOOD BOOK

My first Bible had my name printed on the cover.

In gold.

I still have it.

As a child I was told the Bible was God's Word, that it was all true, and not to set anything on top of it. If you grew up in church, you were probably told something similar.

And you believed 'em.

You believed what they told you about the Bible even though you hadn't read the Bible. If you're like most Christians, you still haven't read the whole thing. Chances are the folks who told you it was all true hadn't read it all either.

Think about that for a moment.

If you grew up attending a conservative Bible-believing church, the *entire* Bible was authoritative, not just the New Testament—all sixty-six books. Consequently, from day one, many of us were unintentionally encouraged to mix, match, and blend Old Testament concepts and values with New. It's unlikely anyone explained to you that the Bible is organized around several covenants or contracts between God and a variety of people and people groups. Odds are, nobody explained why the Old Testament was called old and the New, new. The entire book seemed old, didn't it?

What you *were* told, or figured out on your own, was that the New Testament was about Jesus. Mostly, anyway. And thus your relationship with the Bible began.

THE BLENDED APPROACH

If you were encouraged to read the Bible on your own, you may have adopted *The Sound of Music* approach and started at the very beginning. Generally speaking, a very good place to start. If you took that approach, and stuck with it, it took a while before you got to Jesus. When you finally arrived, it was like stepping into an entirely different world. If you were paying attention, you realized something was missing. Namely, about four hundred years of the story line. The narrative jumps from God setting people on fire while his followers trample the wicked under the soles of their feet straight to Christmas![1]

That's quite a jump.

Perhaps someone gave you a reading plan or devotional book that included portions of both testaments. A little bit of Old, a little bit of New, a little bit of Old, a little bit of New. That's how most of Protestant Christianity operates today. Put the Old and the New in a blender and serve it up as a single dish. Most preachers mix and match Old with New. Most Sunday school teachers do as well. Most reading plans are organized around the blended approach, as are most Christian books, calendars, greeting cards, and, of course, Christian music.

Decades of mixing and matching have resulted in a version of faith filled with leftovers from the covenant Jesus fulfilled and replaced. Old covenant leftovers explain why religious leaders feel it's their responsibility to rail against the evils in society like an Old Testament prophet. It's why our song lyrics are filled with invitations for God to fill our buildings. Bad church experiences are almost always related to old covenant remnants. Most bad church experiences are the result of somebody prioritizing a *view* over a *you*, something Jesus never did and instructed us not to do either. Self-righteousness and legalism usually stem from an imported approach to holiness. The prosperity gospel is rooted in God's covenant with Israel rather than the teaching of Jesus. The list goes on and on.

The justifications Christians have used since the fourth century to mistreat people find their roots in old covenant practices and values. As I mentioned in the introduction, imagine trying to leverage the Sermon on the Mount to start an inquisition, launch a crusade, or incite a pogrom against Jews. But reach back into the old covenant, and there's plenty to work with.

BRILLIANT

But to be clear, I'm not saying there is plenty to work with because God's covenant with Israel was flawed. Just the opposite. When understood in its ancient context, it was brilliant! The civil and religious law detailed in God's arrangement with Israel was superior in every way to the civil and religious law of the surrounding nations. The Torah may strike us as unsophisticated or perhaps barbaric, but the protections afforded to the most vulnerable were nothing short of revolutionary in their original context. Women, servants, foreigners, and children all fared better under Jewish law than did their counterparts in the surrounding nations. The Sinai covenant was a perfect arrangement within a specific cultural setting in light of God's purpose for the nation and for the world.

The challenges we face in mixing and matching covenants are not the result of the Mosaic covenant being flawed. Our challenges stem from our unwillingness to accept two undeniable historical realities. First, God's covenant with ancient Israel was . . . with ancient Israel. Second, God's covenant with Israel was temporary. Important, strategic, divinely ordained, but temporary.

Careless mixing and matching of old and new covenant values and imperatives make the current version of our faith unnecessarily resistible. This is why I insist that *most of what makes us resistible are things we should have been resisting all along.*

It was twenty years after the resurrection before Jewish church leaders officially and publicly acknowledged that Gentiles were not obligated to follow the law of Moses. This is entirely understandable. They were Jewish. The old covenant was more than a religious framework. It had been a way of life from childhood. But thanks to the clarity of Paul, the experience of Peter, and the leadership of James, the church eventually saw the light, so to speak. These early church leaders understood something we've forgotten—or have missed entirely.

Namely.

While Jesus was *foreshadowed* in the old covenant, he did not come to *extend* it. He came to fulfill it, put a bow on it, and establish something new. The *new* Jesus unleashed made the faith of first-century believers formidable. Their apologetic was irrefutable. Their courage, unquestionable. And the results were remarkable.

Back to us.

COVENANTS AND TESTAMENTS

The terms "Old Testament" and "New Testament" are common church vernacular, but many Bible readers have no idea where they came from. Most Christians are unaware of how the Old Testament got *old* and how something written two thousand years ago can be referred to as *new*. Many assume the Old Testament is labeled *old* because the events in the first half were older than the events in the second half. That's assuming they've ever stopped to think about it.

In Jesus' day, Jews had a collection of writings considered sacred. This collection of texts would eventually be taken over by the church and retitled the *Old Testament*. Jews have never referred to their Scriptures as the *old* anything for the same reason we don't call our Bibles *the old Bible*. While the arrangement of the Jewish Scriptures is different than what we find in our English Old Testaments, the documents included are pretty much the same. In other words, our Old Testament would have been Jesus' Bible. But it's important to note . . . actually, it's very important to note ... the term *Bible* wasn't applied to anyone's scriptures until two hundred-plus years *after* Jesus' farewell address. So, in the first part of the first century, there was no Old or New Testament. There was just Jewish Scriptures and some crazy folks who claimed a man had risen from the dead.

TESTAMENT

If you have a good study Bible (or if you read my earlier footnote), you know the term *testament* comes from a Latin term used to translate a Greek term that reflects an English term that lived in the house that Jack built.

Testament means *covenant*.

The common language outside of Palestine in Jesus' day was Greek. This explains why the documents that make up our New Testament were originally written in Greek. With the passing of time, Latin replaced Greek as the primary language of Western culture. The Latin phrase for new covenant is *novum testamentum*. *Novum* is Latin for *new* and *testamentum* is Latin for *covenant*. When the Bible was translated into English, editors chose to stick with the familiar Latin term *testament* rather than use the English term *covenant*. If they had stuck with a straight-up Greek-to-English translation, we would use the terms *old covenant* and *new covenant* rather than Old Testament and New Testament.

Bottom line: "covenant" and "testament" are interchangeable.

In your English New Testament, the word *covenant* is a translation of a Greek term used in ancient times to refer to wills and contracts, agreements or pacts.[2] Similarly, in your English Old Testament, the term *covenant* is a translation of the Hebrew term used in reference to treaties and contracts.[3] In ancient times, as in modern times, nations entered into treaties with one another. These treaties, or covenants, were created to define roles, expectations, and consequences of unmet expectations between tribes, regions, and eventually kingdoms.

BYE-BYE SINAI

As we discussed earlier, the nation of Israel entered into a formal covenant with God at Mount Sinai. The terms and conditions were etched in stone. It was a classic *bilateral suzerainty treaty*, a covenant between non-equals.

This was a conditional covenant. As long as the nation kept God's commands, God would keep the nation safe. But if the nation didn't uphold their end of the deal, God was under no obligation to uphold his. And while we're discussing the covenant made at Mount Sinai, I need to point out one other important facet of this covenant. This distinctive is overlooked in all our mixing and matching of Old and New Testaments.

The covenant God made with the nation of Israel at Mount Sinai was between God and the *nation*, not God and *individuals* in the nation. This was a national covenant. Individuals within the nation could cut themselves off from the covenant through personal unfaithfulness, but the covenant itself was with the nation.

When God punished the nation, everybody suffered, not just the guilty. When the nation was invaded, the righteous and the unrighteous were slaughtered and enslaved. When God blessed the nation, the wicked prospered right along with all the not-so-wicked. God judged the health and devotion of the nation by the behavior of the leaders, judges, and prophets. The point being, God's conditional promises to Israel were promises to the nation of Israel, not individuals in the nation and . . . and not *you*. You were not, are not, and should be glad you're not included in that covenant.

The way we present the Bible to children and the way we talk about the Bible in church leaves the impression that it's an all-skate. It's *all* God's Word for *all* God's people for *all* God's time. Hopefully you know better. Most folks don't.

Most non-Christians *really* don't.

Much confusion, not to mention bad theology, stems from our proclivity to cherry-pick, edit, and apply portions of God's covenant with

Israel (or texts referencing God's covenant with Israel). Walk into any Christian bookstore around graduation time and you'll see a plethora of graduation cards and gifts printed or engraved with Jeremiah 29:11.

> "For I know the plans I have for you," declares the LORD, "plans to prosper you and not to harm you, plans to give you hope and a future."

How encouraging. God-fearing graduates can step confidently into the next chapter of their lives assured of prosperity, divine protection, and, hopefully, a job.

Maybe.

But who is "you"? "For I know the plans I have for *you*." You who?

Certainly not you, that's who.

Here's the entire passage.

> This is what the LORD says: "When seventy years are completed for Babylon, I will come to you and fulfill my good promise to bring you back to this place. For I know the plans I have for you," declares the LORD, "plans to prosper you and not to harm you, plans to give you hope and a future. Then you will call on me and come and pray to me, and I will listen to you."

If this is indeed applicable to graduates, they will have to wait seventy years for God to prosper and protect them. But if they can hang on until age eighty-eight, the best is yet to come!

Fortunately, these verses don't apply to graduates. Graduates are covered under a different covenant. A better covenant. A covenant that doesn't require animal sacrifice to stay current. Here's another passage frequently ripped out of its old covenant context:

> If my people, who are called by my name, will humble them-selves and pray and seek my face and turn from their wicked

ways, then I will hear from heaven, and I will forgive their sin and will heal their land.[4]

This was part of God's message to King Solomon after he completed the construction of the temple in Jerusalem. Here God reiterates his commitment to the existing cause-and-effect covenant he established with the nation of Israel. To apply these verses to, or claim this promise for, any other group is dishonest and dangerous.

The new covenant established by Jesus stands in stark contrast to the assumptions and implications reflected in the verses cited above. To put it in broad terms, under the old covenant when you obeyed, you were blessed. When you disobeyed, you were punished. Under the new covenant, when you obey, you may suffer. If you disobey, the world may applaud you and you may even prosper.

That's what Jesus said, anyway.

He should know.

The old covenant, God's covenant with Israel, was a package deal. It was all or nothing. The fact that someone chose to publish the old covenant with the new covenant in a genuine leather binding doesn't mean we should treat them or apply them the same way. The Bible is all God's Word . . . to *somebody*. But it's not all God's word to *everybody*. And you should be happy about that. Most of us wouldn't have made it past adolescence had the old covenant been given equal status with the new covenant.[5]

But here's the real kicker.

The new covenant Jesus announced at Passover was not only new, it was a completely different kind of covenant than the one God established with the nation at Mount Sinai. The covenant Jesus inaugurated was more akin to the covenant God established with Abraham when he promised to bless the world through him. In ancient times this arrangement was sometimes referred to as a *promissory covenant*. Unlike the bilateral suzerain treaty discussed earlier, a promissory covenant was unilateral and unconditional. In a promissory covenant, one party made a pledge to another party and took full responsibility for fulfilling that promise.

Think middle school crush.

Remember that note where you promised unwavering love no matter what? That's how a *promissory* covenant starts. Fortunately for you, you never ratified the covenant by cutting the neighbor's cat into two equal parts and . . .

Oh yeah . . . I left out something important.

The root of the Hebrew term for covenant means *to cut*. We cut deals. In the old days, folks *cut covenants*. They would literally slice an animal into two equal parts and a representative of each party would walk between the eviscerated carcasses.

Why?

I'll let an expert explain:

> The one who passes between the divided halves of the slain animals invokes death upon himself should he break the word by which he has bound himself in the oath.[6]

In other words, *May it be unto me as it is with this unfortunate animal if I violate the terms of this covenant.* When God ratified his covenant with Abraham, he had instructed Abraham to bring a goat and a ram and to cut them in two and arrange the halves opposite each other.[7] In a traditional covenant ceremony, both parties would then pass between the eviscerated carcasses. But this was an unconditional covenant. The text says that as the sun set, Abraham fell into a deep sleep. And then something extraordinary happened:

> When the sun had set and darkness had fallen, a smoking firepot with a blazing torch appeared and passed between the pieces.[8]

God did not require Abraham to pass between the divided carcasses. Instead, the blazing torch, representing God's presence, did all the passing. This was God's way of saying, "Abraham, this is on me! I take full responsibility for fulfilling my promises to you."

Unilateral. Unconditional.

Now, with all that as a backdrop, let's revisit Jesus' reference to the new covenant during his final Passover. On that very night, he would surrender his own body to be flayed to the bone by a Roman cat–o'–nine–tails. Minutes later he would be forced to shoulder a wooden beam weighing upwards of a hundred pounds. Then his hands and feet would literally be torn in two by his own weight as he hung and bled to death on a Roman cross:

> This cup is the new covenant in my blood which is poured out for you.[9]

"Poured out for *you*."

Like Abraham, we would not be required to participate in the covenant ceremony. This was unilateral. Unconditional. It was Jesus' way of saying to the world:

> This is on me!
> This is on me, for you!

Dear Christian reader: Why? Why? Why would you even be tempted to reach back beyond the cross to borrow from a covenant that was temporary and inferior to the covenant established for us at Calvary? The author of Hebrews says it best. Jesus was the "guarantor of a *better* covenant."[10] Later he writes, "the new covenant is established on *better* promises."[11] Besides, you weren't included in the old covenant to begin with!

THE GREAT DIVIDE

I'm guessing when you received your first Bible no one told you any of this.

No one explained that your Bible was organized around two covenants. One between God and ancient Israel, and one between God and everybody who wants to participate. Perhaps what we should have been told, and perhaps what we should begin telling our children, is something along the lines of:

> The Bible is a book organized around two covenants: one between God and ancient Israel and one between God and you! Focus on the second one. The covenant between God and Israel is obsolete. Read it for historical context and inspiration. But don't try any of that stuff at home!

Our pithy bottom line could be:

> Take your *cue* from the covenant God made with *you*.

If you want to call the children's director at your church, I'll wait here.

Speaking of waiting, you may be thinking, *Wait a minute. You just called part of the Bible obsolete!* Actually, it wasn't me. One of the authors of our Bible calls part of our Bible obsolete.

Isn't this fun?

START IN THE MIDDLE

When we give a new or non-believer their first Bible, we usually tell them Julie Andrews was wrong. The very beginning is not a very good place to start. We generally point new and non-believers to the Gospels. Oftentimes, the Gospel of John. Why? Because we know the *new covenant* is *their covenant*. As our habit of pointing new believers to the New Testament implies, God's covenant with Israel is not as important for followers of Jesus as his *new* covenant with the church. I'm not suggesting the two testaments are not equally inspired. My point is they aren't equally *applicable*.

As heretical as that may sound, consider this. Folks with no church background and no biblical training have put their faith in Christ after reading the Gospel of John alone. Not the entire New Testament. Not the entire Bible. Just John. You may be one of those people. That one

Gospel reveals enough about the new covenant promises for a person to make an informed, faith-filled decision to follow Jesus.

That is not the case with the book of Genesis.

Or Exodus.

Certainly not Leviticus.

Granted, there are people who spot Jesus in every book of the Bible. But no one has spotted Jesus of Nazareth in the Old Testament until they were first introduced to him by way of the New Testament. The Old Testament anticipated him. The New Testament introduced him.

I realize I'm stating the obvious. But it's obvious what's obvious may not be all that obvious. One could read through the entire Old Testament every year and never know Jesus ever existed.

Obviously.

As we will discover later, our tradition of equating, mixing, and matching the two halves of our Bible has created an Achilles' heel for our post-reformation, *sola scriptura* version of faith. For now, it is enough to reaffirm what I will affirm throughout our journey together: *Jesus came to launch something new.* And as long as we blend the old with the new, we will miss the beauty and power of what Jesus gave his life to unleash in the world.

Chapter 9

THE BIBLE ACCORDING TO JESUS

As the hinge between the old and new covenants, Jesus was in the unenviable position of playing by an old set of rules while laying the groundwork for what was to come. He showed respect and deference to the old but was uncomfortably clear that something new was on the horizon. While he affirmed the goodness and divine origin of the Jewish Scriptures, he made claims that elevated him above those very same texts. And that's understandable. Jesus was born under God's covenant with Israel with the purpose of bringing that covenant to its sovereignly ordained end.[1]

TRADITION DEFYING AND REAPPLYING

One example of this foreshadowing is found in his most famous sermon. Somebody titled it the Sermon on the Mount. But over the course of his approximately three-year ministry, Jesus probably repeated this message, or some version of it, numerous times. My guess is he wasn't always standing on a mountain.

Anyway.

In Matthew's account, after getting everybody's attention with a unique take on how to be happy, Jesus put a new spin on several familiar commandments and traditions, commandments and traditions his audience had been taught since childhood.

You have heard that . . .

As in: *Your entire life the people you trust and respect have told you . . .*

You have heard that it was said, "Eye for eye, and tooth for tooth."[2]

Yes, they had. The Jewish Scriptures stated:

Show no pity: life for life, eye for eye, tooth for tooth, hand for hand, foot for foot.[3]

Instead of explaining what that bit of Scripture meant, Jesus surprised everyone with this:

But . . .

If he had paused after "But . . ." they would have thought, *But? Jesus, you don't respond to Moses with but unless it's, "But of course." You can't but something handed down by Moses!*

But he did.

Because Jesus was greater than Moses. Greater than the temple. Greater than the law. So he butted his way through.

But I tell you do not resist an evil person. If anyone slaps you on the right cheek, turn to them the other cheek also. And if anyone wants to sue you and take your shirt, hand over your coat as well. If anyone forces you to go one mile, go with them two miles.[4]

We can't begin to imagine how ridiculous this sounded to first-century Jews struggling to survive under the hobnailed sandals of Rome. But more to the point of our discussion, we can't begin to imagine how *unbiblical* this sounded to first-century Jews whose entire Scriptures were built on an ethic to the contrary.

You're familiar enough with Old Testament stories to know Israel never, ever, turned the other cheek. Joshua, the messiah figure for first-century Jews, was certainly not a cheek turner. He was a warrior. David, in whose line the Messiah was to come, had so much blood on his hands God wouldn't let him build the temple. Jesus wasn't simply contradicting their Scriptures. His teaching stood in stark contrast to their entire history! Many in his audience wanted *more* blood on their hands. Roman blood.

But that wasn't the only *but*. The next one was worse.

> You have heard that it was said, "Love your neighbor and hate your enemy." But I tell you, love your enemies and pray for those who persecute you, that you may be children of your Father in heaven.[5]

You won't find "hate your enemy" explicitly stated in the Jewish Scriptures. But the sentiment was certainly modeled and illustrated throughout Israel's history as documented in their Scriptures. The psalmists expressed a great deal of unmitigated animosity toward their enemies. Ancient Israel did not love her enemies. Ancient Israel took every opportunity to destroy her enemies, often with God's blessing and intervention. If the ancient Jews prayed for their enemies, they prayed for their enemies' destruction. Against the backdrop of their messianic militaristic aspirations, Jesus was a poor excuse for a messiah. Instead of fulfilling messianic expectations, he was dissing them.

One more.

> You have heard that it was said, "You shall not commit adultery."

Hang on, they must have thought. *Surely you are not about to tell us it's okay to commit adultery?*

> But I tell you that anyone who looks at a woman lustfully has already committed adultery with her in his heart.[6]

This time Jesus doesn't point his followers in the opposite direction of the old covenant. This time he insists they do *more* than the old covenant required.

He raised the bar. He does the same regarding the permanency of marriage. In fact, Jesus' teaching was so misaligned with the typical first-century Jews' take on their own Scriptures that in the end, the guardians of orthodoxy had more than ample evidence to convince the populace his teaching was in direct conflict with Moses'.

As they listened in stunned silence, some in his audience must have wondered: *Who does he think he is? What gives him the right to amend, expand, and reverse a thousand-plus years of teaching and tradition?* Others in Jesus' audience, the ones paying closest attention, knew exactly who he thought he was. He'd made that clear in his introduction.

> Do not think that I have come to *abolish* the Law or the Prophets; I have not come to *abolish* them but to *fulfill* them.[7]

Why did he feel the need to say he had not come to *abolish the law*? Because he knew it would sound to many as if he had come to do exactly that. Especially in light of all the *"You've heard it said . . . but I say"* rhetoric. So what exactly *had* Jesus come to do to the Law and the Prophets? What did he mean when he said he came to *fulfill them*?

The answer to that question has significant implications for how we read and understand the Old Testament. Here's what he said next:

> For truly I tell you, until heaven and earth disappear, not the smallest letter, not the least stroke of a pen, will by any means disappear from the Law until *everything* is *accomplished*.[8]

What did he mean by *everything*? And what happens to the law after "everything is accomplished"? The implication is that the law might "disappear" once everything is accomplished. And clearly Jesus was planning to be involved in the accomplishing. To put what he said in uncomfortable contemporary terms, *Exodus, Leviticus, Numbers, and Deuteronomy* may start disappearing once everything is accomplished.

FULLY FILLED

So what did Jesus mean when he said he came to *fulfill* the law? The Greek term translated *fulfill* is used by both Matthew in the Sermon on the Mount as well as Luke in his recitation of Jesus' synagogue message.[9] In both instances the term means *to bring to a designated end.*[10] Jesus did not come to abolish—as in destroy—the validity of, or undermine the credibility of, the law. Jesus came to *bring it to a designated end.*

If the law were a homework assignment, he was completing it.

If the law were a speech, he was concluding it.

If the law were a plane, he was landing it.

This was his way of saying God's *conditional, temporary* covenant with Israel was coming to an end, the intended-from-the-beginning end. When God established his covenant with Israel, he set a timer. According to Jesus, the time had run out. But the law wasn't just ending. The law was being fulfilled through him. Dr. John Piper puts it this way:

> Jesus was not just another member in the long line of wise men and prophets. He was the end of the line.[11]

I love that. "The end of the line."

> To be sure, many instructions and rules and religious practices and rituals from the Old Testament are no longer to be practiced. But this is not because these practices and rules were wrong but because they were temporary and were pointing forward to the day when Jesus Christ would fulfill them, and thus end them. The coming of Christ did not abolish them, but it did make them *obsolete.*[12]

"Obsolete." There's that word again. Perhaps an illustration will help.

If you had an overwhelming amount of debt that you wanted to rid yourself of, one option would be to declare bankruptcy. In that case, your obligation would not be *fulfilled*, just removed. But if someone came along and paid off your debt, the obligation would be *fulfilled* and the burden of fulfilling that obligation would be removed as well. Jesus fulfilled—as in ended—the necessity of the Jewish law. Just as you don't abolish a home by completing its construction, just as you don't abolish a flight plan by landing a plane, just as you don't abolish a homework assignment by completing the assignment, Jesus did not abolish the law when he fulfilled it. But in fulfilling it, he made it . . . obsolete. Again, that's not my term. Heck, John Piper used it as well.

My point?

I'm as smart as John Piper.

No.

My point?

Why do we insist on equating Jesus' new covenant with the fulfilled-and-now-obsolete old covenant? Doing so makes our apologetic, our approach to sharing and defending our faith, far more complicated than it needs to be.

Most evangelicals feel the need to defend the entire Bible, including God's temporary covenant with Israel, in order to defend Christianity.

Why?

Because of our time-honored tradition of mixing, matching, and equating what God clearly separated.

It doesn't help that both covenants are bound together for our convenience. The majority of people I've talked to who've abandoned their faith have lost faith in Jesus because they lost confidence in the Bible. Which part of the Bible? You guessed it—the part that doesn't apply to or include us—the Old Testament. Once they could no longer defend the historicity or inerrancy of the entire Bible, they found their entire faith to be indefensible as well. That's tragic.

It's tragic because, as we'll discuss later, Christianity predated *the Bible* by hundreds of years. There were thousands of Christians long before there was a Bible. The Bible did not create Christianity. It's the other way around.

FINISHED

According to Jesus, nothing in the law would "disappear" until everything was "accomplished." Once it was accomplished, however, the law would begin to disappear. Which is exactly what happened.

For the next forty years, religious Israel would wrestle with the internal tension created by *The Way*. The harder they tried to stamp it out, the faster it grew. Thanks to the tireless efforts of the apostle Paul and others, Jews throughout the Roman world began abandoning strict adherence to the rules of the local synagogue to follow the resurrected teacher from Nazareth.

Then, on August 6 in the year AD 70, the transition came to an abrupt end. It was on that day that the four-year conflict between Jewish rebels and Rome came to a bloody and violent end. As we discussed earlier, the Jewish temple was looted, burned, and razed. The destruction of the temple signaled the end of ancient Judaism. While the words of the covenant were preserved, Israel's ability to live in accordance with those words vanished in a day.

Judaism, as prescribed by Moses at Mount Sinai, ceased to exist. To use Jesus' term, it "disappeared."

As Jesus predicted.[13]

God's covenant with Israel was no longer needed. It had been fulfilled and replaced with a better covenant.

A new covenant.

New Testament scholars have long debated the significance of Jesus' famous last words from the cross: "It is finished."[14] As his disheartened followers would soon discover, Jesus wasn't finished. But something was. Perhaps, in his final moments, he was announcing to those gathered that the covenant he came to fulfill was at last fulfilled. And through the shedding of his blood, a new covenant, a better covenant, a broader covenant was being established between God and all who would choose to participate.

Chapter 10

HOMEBODIES

When Jesus announced the inauguration of his *new covenant*, it marked the beginning of the end of the old one. While his short ministry served as a transition between the two, it was clear that he didn't intend for his followers to blend the two.

Jesus left no room for a blended covenant model. Not only had he explained this several times before his death, he restated it in his final farewell address. You've read or perhaps heard these words read dozens of times. As you read them this time, count the number of references to Moses or the law:

> Then Jesus came to them and said, "All authority in heaven and on earth has been given to me. Therefore, go and make disciples of all nations, baptizing them in the name of the Father and of the Son and of the Holy Spirit, and teaching them to obey everything I have commanded you. And surely I am with you always, to the very end of the age."[1]

That would be *none*.

Jesus claimed "all" authority. If someone has "all" authority, they are the only authority to whom one need appeal. Implication: In the old days, Moses was your guy. Those days are over. Something new has come. Someone new has come.

No doubt, the Jews in his audience noticed who was conspicuously missing from the "Father, Son, and Holy Spirit" list. Again, Moses. Jesus wrapped up his final words by instructing his followers to center their teaching on *his* commandments, not those other ones.

No room for confusion.

Yet despite his consistency and insistency, many of his first-century followers still opted for a blended covenant model.

A BEAUTIFUL DAY IN THE NEIGHBORHOOD

The first-century blended model stemmed partially from the fact that Jesus' disciples didn't go into *all the world* like he instructed them to. They stayed in Jerusalem in the shadow of the temple. They surrounded themselves with Jewish converts for whom the blended, Jewish version of Christianity worked just fine.

Thousands of Jews living in and visiting Jerusalem embraced Jesus as Messiah. There was plenty to do right there in their own backyard. The world could wait. Besides, they were under the impression Jesus was coming back soon. As in, maybe Thursday. So what was the point of leaving town?

If they'd paid closer attention to what Jesus said in those closing moments, they would have known he wouldn't be showing up anytime soon. That "all nations" thing would take a while. To their credit, Jesus was leaving them. Again. That had to have been an extraordinarily emotional gathering.

Besides, they had expectations.

It was difficult for Jesus' first-century Jewish followers to hear what he was *actually* saying because of what they *wanted* him to say. Luke tells us they were hoping Jesus was ready to restore the nation to kingdom status. They were still hoping for a political or military solution. Whatever the reason, they left assuming he would return soon. So the disciples remained in the predominantly Jewish populated regions of Judea and Galilee. Consequently, the gospel intended for *all nations* took on a uniquely *Jewish* flavor.

The old began infringing on the new.

Something needed to be done.

Here's what happened.

(I may have made this up.)

HIGH ABOVE THE HEAVENS

As God the Father watched his Son's new movement struggling to gain traction outside Judea, it dawned on him what the problem was.

"Son," he said, "come here and have a seat. We need to chat."

"What's up?" asked the Son.

"It's your movement. It isn't moving. It's stalled."

"Yes, sir," said the Son, "I've been meaning to bring that up."

"Well," said the Father, "I think I know what the problem is."

"What's that?" asked the Son.

"You chose the wrong folks to lead it. Don't get me wrong. They're nice guys. But they lack vision. Drive. Motivation. If you intend to roll this out to all nations, I'm afraid you'll need to go back and great-commission somebody else. Someone who won't take no for an answer. Somebody who's not afraid to leave home. While you're at it, look for someone who's connected and respected. Someone with credentials."

As Father and Son stood looking over the world, suddenly the Father grabbed the Son by the shoulder and pointed with his right hand. "Hey, what about that guy! That's who you should recruit!"

"Saul of Tarsus?" the Son replied. "Are you kidding?"

"You know I don't kid, Son," said the Father.

"But, Dad, Saul is singlehandedly dismantling everything I worked so hard to create. Besides, he's a Pharisee! And not just any Pharisee. He's an all-star Pharisee."

"Perfect," said the Father. "What a coup. Imagine the talk around Jerusalem if we recruited Saul for our team!"

"Dad," said the Son, "he already thinks he's working for our team."

"Well," said the Father, "that should make your job even easier. And I suggest you get busy. He's on his way to Damascus with a pocketful of arrest warrants."

You probably know the rest of the story. While traveling to Damascus on his way to arrest followers of *The Way*, Saul of Tarsus was intercepted and recruited. Jesus gave him specific instructions: "You are to proclaim the gospel to the *Gentiles* and to their *kings*."[2] *All nations*. In exchange for his service, Jesus promised . . . suffering. Oddly enough, Saul accepted and wasted no time getting down to business. Luke tells us that immediately upon regaining his sight, Saul:

> Began to preach in the synagogues that Jesus is the Son of God. All those who heard him were astonished and asked, "Isn't he the man who raised havoc in Jerusalem among those who call on this name? And hasn't he come here to take them as prisoners to the chief priests?" Yet Saul grew more and more powerful and baffled the Jews living in Damascus by proving that Jesus is the Messiah.[3]

MEANWHILE

Meanwhile, back on their home turf, neither Father nor Son was quite ready to give up on the original gang of eleven. But it required a divine intervention to get them moving. So a few years following Saul's conversion, Peter had a conversion of his own.[4] He was in Joppa at the time and, while praying, he fell into a trance in which he saw a collection of animals that included animals Jews were forbidden to eat. Then Peter hears a voice commanding him to kill 'em, cook 'em, and eat 'em!

It's important to note that apart from circumcision, nothing embodied the old covenant more than the dietary restrictions. In the minds of faithful Jews, to break the dietary laws was to break the covenant. A Jewish legend describes a Jewish mother and her seven sons who willingly endured torture and execution for their refusal to eat pork.[5] So Peter's response is understandable.

"Surely not, Lord!" he said.

That's pretty strong.

"I have never eaten anything impure or unclean."[6]

Implication: And I ain't about to start now! Lord, sir . . .

The dream is repeated twice when suddenly Peter is awakened by someone in the front yard shouting his name. When he opens the door, he's greeted by two men and a soldier. These strangers invite him to Caesarea to be the overnight guest of Cornelius, a Roman centurion. A *Gentile* centurion—what could be worse! Peter may have pinched himself in the hope this was still part of his bad dream. But with a bit of divine prompting, he accepted their invitation.

Reluctantly.

How reluctantly, you ask?

Well, here's his opening line to a living room full of Cornelius' non-Jewish friends and family. Don't rush. Imagine the tension created by Peter's opening statement. Remember, this was ten or more years *after* the resurrection. Peter begins:

> You are *well aware* that it is against our law for a Jew to associate with or visit a Gentile.

Translated: Everybody knows Jews don't *associate* with, much less visit, the homes of Gentiles. Even Christian Jews. He continues:

> But God has shown me that I should not call anyone *impure or unclean.*[7]

To which I'm sure somebody in the house was tempted to respond, "Well that's mighty big of you!"

Don't miss this. Peter *admitted* he considered non-Jews *impure* and *unclean*. That's what he'd been taught since childhood. That summed up the first-century Jewish attitude toward non-Jews. This is the same Peter who heard everything Jesus taught firsthand. Peter, who was instructed by Jesus, in first person, to go into all the world. He continued.

> I *now* realize . . .

Translated: It's taken me awhile.

> I *now* realize how true it is that God does not show favoritism
> but accepts from *every nation* the one who fears him and does
> what is right.[8]

This was Peter's John 3:16 moment. He finally got it. Turns out Jesus did love all the little children of the world. Even Gentile children. After his awkward introduction, Peter preached the gospel to this living room full of Gentiles. Before he could hum the first verse of an invitation hymn, the Holy Spirit interrupted and filled his Gentile audience. The response of Peter's traveling companions further illustrates the racism that existed between Jews and Gentiles in the first century.

> The circumcised believers who had come with Peter were *aston-ished* that the gift of the Holy Spirit had been poured out even on Gentiles.[9]

"Astonished."

The Jewish Christians traveling with Peter were "astonished" God would do for Gentiles what he'd done for believing Jews. In spite of everything Jesus taught, his followers were still clinging to old covenant thinking. To this point, the church was exclusive and excluding. So while the message of faith was appealing to Gentiles, the community of faith was not. People who were nothing like Jesus liked the message of Jesus. But they didn't necessarily like the community charged with stewarding that message.

Sound familiar?

When word of Peter's escapades made it back to headquarters in Jerusalem, it caused quite a stir. When Peter made it back to Jerusalem, well, here's what happened:

> The circumcised believers rejoiced, recognizing this had been what Jesus intended from the beginning. Together they vowed to abandon the blended covenant model once and for all to fully embrace the new covenant.

Hardly.

Here's what really happened.

> So when Peter went up to Jerusalem, the circumcised believers *criticized* him and said, "You went into the house of uncircumcised men and ate with them!"[10]

There it is again. Christians—Jesus followers—were appalled Peter would enter the home of a Gentile. This is years after the resurrection. They couldn't get it through their hearts and heads that Jesus had completely—once and for all, stick a fork in it, put down your pencil, exit the plane, tip the waiter—fulfilled the old covenant. It was over.

So starting from the beginning, Peter told them his entire story. He described his trance, his invitation to Cornelius' home, but most importantly, he described how the Holy Spirit had fallen on the Gentiles just as he had fallen on Peter and his friends years before. He concluded with this:

> So if God gave them the same gift he gave us who believed in the Lord Jesus Christ, who was I to think that I could stand in God's way?[11]

Hard to argue with that. Luke tells us they "had no more objections" and exclaimed:

> So then, *even* to Gentiles God has granted repentance that leads
> to life.[12]

Yep, *even* to Gentiles. Even to people outside God's covenant with Israel. They were so surprised, which is surprising.

Shocked, which is shocking.

Astonished, which is astonishing.

Why?

It was the very thing God promised Abraham hundreds of years before Moses uttered his first "Let my people go." They should have seen it coming. They should have welcomed it. Instead, they resisted.

So do we.

MORE TROUBLE

A few years following Peter's visit with Cornelius, Saul (a.k.a. Paul) and his traveling companion, Barnabas, embarked on a missionary journey through modern-day Syria and Turkey. Their habit was to visit synagogues in port cities and interior cities that served as crossroads for commerce. As a Pharisee from the motherland, Paul was usually invited to address the local Jewish citizenry. But halfway into his message, it would become apparent something was amiss. Once he got to the Jesus section of his outline, things would get tense. A crucified Messiah was an oxymoron.

But when Paul described how Jesus' death negated the need for Moses' law . . . well. It wasn't unusual for Paul's synagogue sermons to end with him being branded a blasphemer and sent packing. While he rarely won the crowd, he almost always won a convert or two. Having given the home team an opportunity to embrace *The Way*, he would turn his attention to the local Gentile population.

Eventually Jewish Christians in Jerusalem caught wind of what Paul and Barnabas were up to. It was bad enough they were inviting Gentiles into the family. But that Paul was discounting the need for the law? Them were fighting words. So the Christian Jews in Jerusalem took it upon themselves to do a bit of missionary work of their own. They sent blended-model reps to the cities Paul and Barnabas visited to correct the errant, anti-Moses theology left in their wake.

It's important to note there were virtually no missionary efforts focused on Gentiles until Paul took it upon himself to take the *all nations* thing seriously. The first organized missionary initiative sponsored by the Jerusalem church was designed to undermine the credibility of the first bona fide Christian missionary.

Think about that.

This cauldron of confusion eventually came to a boiling point three hundred miles north of Jerusalem in the predominantly Greek city of Antioch. Once again Luke gives us the scoop:

> Certain people came down from Judea to Antioch and were teaching the believers: "Unless you are circumcised, according to the custom taught by Moses, you cannot be saved."[13]

For the men, that meant salvation by surgery—circumcision. To which they must have thought, *Somebody should have told us about this before we signed up!* Imagine how that would play out in the twenty-first century church. "Honey, you and the kids go on into the service. I'll wait in the car."

Besides, how would we know?

Sorry.

Notice whose name suddenly pops up in the discussion. Moses. These men were arguing for the blended model. The Moses *and* Jesus model. The mix-and-match model. Unfortunately for the "missionaries" from Jerusalem, before they could get their circumcision blades cleaned and sharpened, the devils themselves, Paul and Barnabas, showed up.

And once they arrived, things got contentious. So the first-century Christians in Antioch did what Christians have been doing ever since. They called a business meeting. A synod. An ecclesiastical court.

> So Paul and Barnabas were appointed, along with some other believers, to go up to Jerusalem to see the apostles and elders about this question.[14]

DON'T MAKE IT DIFFICULT

The meeting took place in Jerusalem. It's commonly referred to in theological circles as *the Jerusalem Council*. It's impossible to overstate the significance of what took place at that gathering. Fortunately, Luke provides us with the minutes. The first and only item on the agenda was *whether or not Gentiles who embraced Jesus should be required to embrace the law of Moses as well*.[15] The pro-Moses faction, led by converted Pharisees, was adamant. Gentile believers must be required to keep the law of Moses and the men must be circumcised. The Jesus-only group, led by Paul and Barnabas, responded with stories to support their conviction that God was accepting Gentiles apart from the law. Paul confirmed the reports trickling in from Gentile communities outside Judea. Gentiles were, in fact, embracing *The Way* and God was confirming his approval with tangible manifestations.[16] After a lengthy debate, Peter stood to address the gathering.

> Brothers, you know that some time ago God made a choice among you that the Gentiles might hear from my lips the message of the gospel and believe. God, who knows the heart, showed that he accepted them by giving the Holy Spirit to them, just as he did to us.[17]

To which he could have added, *and it was astonishing!* Again, it's impossible for us to comprehend the significance—the seismic shift—associated with those last six words: "just as he did to us." Standing at what everyone in that room considered to be the epicenter of the world, the city Jews had bled and died for, and perhaps a stone's throw from the holy of holies, Peter declared that God had thrown open the doors of the Jesus movement to outsiders. Divine approval once reserved for the Jewish race was now available to *everyone*.

Then he acknowledged something every man in the room had thought a thousand times but dared not express aloud:

> Now then, why do you try to test God by putting on the necks of Gentiles a yoke that neither we nor our ancestors have been able to bear?[18]

Keeping the law was difficult. This was true for Jews raised in it, on it, and around it. How much more difficult would it be for adult Gentiles? Every man in the room realized how unrealistic it was to expect adults raised in pagan households with a pagan worldview and pagan customs to instantly adopt all that came with being a devout Jew. Circumcision was nothing compared to the burden of reorienting every facet of life around the Jewish civil, moral, and religious code. Apparently, nobody responded to Peter's question so he answered it himself.

> No! We believe it is through the grace of our Lord Jesus that we are saved, just as they are.[19]

It took about twenty years, but Peter had finally come to terms with the uncomfortable but undeniable reality that the *ekklesia* of Jesus was not the continuation of or version 2.0 of Judaism. It was stand-alone new. There was no need to mix and match. No need to blend old and new. The old way had passed away and something brand-new had come. The new covenant Peter witnessed Jesus inaugurate at Passover years earlier served as an end and a beginning.

As Peter was returning to his seat, James, the brother of Jesus, stood and made his way to the center of the room.

The brother of Jesus.

Imagine that.

What would your brother have to do to convince you he was the Son of God? James' recognition of his brother as his Lord may be *the* best argument for the deity of Jesus. According to Josephus, James was eventually arrested and executed for his unwavering faith in his big brother.

By the time of the Jerusalem Council, James had risen to a place of prominence in the church. His opinion mattered a great deal. Like the former Pharisees in the room, James did not become a believer until after the resurrection. But unlike the Pharisees in the room, he *was* convinced Gentile believers should be included in the community of faith without first converting to Judaism. After quoting a short passage from the prophet Amos, he concluded his remarks with what has become one of my favorite statements in the New Testament:

> It is my judgment, therefore, that we should not make it difficult for the Gentiles who are turning to God.[20]

I love that.

Imagine where the church would be today if we had kept that simple idea front and center. Years ago, I printed that verse and hung it in my office. Before long it started showing up on walls and plaques in all our churches. I look at it every day. Perhaps James' statement should be the benchmark by which all decisions are made in the local church. The brother of Jesus said we shouldn't do anything that makes it unnecessarily difficult for people who are turning to God. The fact that we've ignored James' advice serves as a partial answer to my Chinese friend's discomforting question.

Remember her?

EVEN MORE ASTONISHING

When James finished, he smacked his gavel on the table and decreed that Gentiles would not be required to follow Moses as a prerequisite to following Jesus. But what he said next was . . . well . . . what he said next is so astonishing and disruptive, it has been pretty much ignored throughout the history of the church.

Do you know what he said next?

Without looking?

No?

It must not have been all that important.

Actually, outside the teaching of Jesus, what James said next may be the most instructive statement in the New Testament. What came next defines your relationship to about half of your English Bible.

Ready?

CLEAN BREAK

The Jerusalem Council began with the question of how Jewish a non-Jew had to be to be "saved" and included in the church. Circumcision was not the only thing at stake. The entire law and everything associated with it was at stake. The Ten Commandments were up for grabs along with hundreds of supporting commandments. And don't forget that three hundred miles north of Jerusalem a group of Gentile believers are waiting to learn how much if any of the Jewish law they would be responsible for keeping.

Immediately following his decision to "not make it difficult" for Gentiles to turn to God, James says:

> Instead we should write to them . . .

"Them" being the Gentile believers in Antioch. If you are a Gentile, them is you!

> Instead we should write to them telling them to abstain from food polluted by idols, from sexual immorality, from the meat of strangled animals and from blood.[21]

Do what?

He explains.

> For the law of Moses has been preached in every city from the
> earliest times and is read in the synagogues on every Sabbath.[22]

That doesn't seem like much of an explanation. But you're a
thoughtful Christian, so I'll let you connect the dots. Why would
James suggest they send that particular message to Gentile Christians
living three hundred miles away in Antioch? What does "Moses has
been preached in every city" have to do with these *four*, not *ten*, but *four*
Old Testament-ish instructions? If Gentile men weren't required to be
circumcised, if Gentile men and women weren't going to be required to
keep the law of Moses, why burden them with these four commands?
And why these four? Why not, "You shall not murder"?[23] Or, "You
shall not steal"?[24] While you're thinking, here's the text from the actual
letter they sent:

> Greetings.
>   We have heard that some went out from us without our
> authorization and disturbed you, troubling your minds by what
> they said. So we all agreed to choose some men and send them
> to you with our dear friends Barnabas and Paul—men who have
> risked their lives for the name of our Lord Jesus Christ.
>   Therefore we are sending Judas and Silas to confirm by
> word of mouth what we are writing. It seemed good to the
> Holy Spirit and to us not to *burden you with anything beyond the*
> *following requirements: You are to* abstain from food sacrificed
> to idols, from blood, from the meat of strangled animals, and
> from sexual immorality. You will do well to avoid these things.
>   Farewell.[25]

Pretty straightforward.

> So the men were sent off and went down to Antioch, where
> they gathered the church together and delivered the letter. The
> people read it and were glad for its encouraging message.[26]

Especially the men.

So, what do you think? What's the connection? Of all the command-ments, why those four? Why choose not to "burden" them with any other requirement beyond those four? And what does any of this have to do with Moses being preached in every city?

Raise your hand and I'll call on you.

BIG FOUR

To begin with, those four imperatives had nothing to do with Gentiles *keeping the law of Moses*. That was a settled issue. Jewish believers were free to keep doing things the way they had always done them, but Gentile believers would not be required to follow suit.

Those four imperatives had nothing to do with keeping the law and everything to do with *keeping the peace*. Specifically, peace *in the church*. Peace between Jewish and Gentile believers.

Regarding the food restrictions, James knew good and well that Jewish believers in Antioch were not about to mix and mingle freely with Gentile believers unless Gentiles made some concessions. As we saw with Peter, the dietary law was not an emotionally neutral subject. James was simply asking Gentile believers to be sensitive to Jewish sensitivities.

Several New Testament scholars see a parallel between these three dietary requirements and Moses' instructions to foreigners, i.e., Gentiles, who chose to live within the borders of ancient Israel.[27] Foreigners were not obligated to embrace Israel's religion, but they were required to make several concessions while living on Israel's soil. But there is one important difference between the old covenant dietary restrictions imposed on for-eigners in ancient Israel and the dietary instructions outlined by James. Under the old covenant, foreigners who violated the dietary restrictions would be held responsible. They would be "cut off."[28] There was a spe-cific penalty attached to the violation of these dietary prohibitions.

But James didn't include a penalty clause.

Why?

Because the point of the letter was not to obligate Gentiles to a slice of Jewish dietary law. The point of the letter was to obligate Gentile believers to maintaining unity in the church. Corporate unity would require personal sacrifice.

From both groups.

Which brings us to the fourth requirement included in the letter. In addition to curbing their appetite for certain kinds of food, Gentiles were required to curb their sexual appetites as well.

> You are to abstain from food sacrificed to idols, from blood, from the meat of strangled animals and from *sexual immorality*.

So what did the Council mean by "sexual immorality?"

This is where I part ways with some of the brightest New Testament scholars of our time. So, you'd probably be better off opting for their answer to this question. These fine folks believe "sexual immorality" is shorthand for the Levitical law regarding sexual conduct.

I don't think so.

Here's why.

If you've been a Christian for more than ten years, read your Bible on a somewhat regular basis, and attend church at least once a month, I would like for you to find something to write on and list the Levitical prohibitions regarding sexual conduct.

No peeking.

No guessing.

You either know or you don't.

I'll wait.

You own several copies of the Jewish Scriptures (Old Testament). You know how to read. You have discretionary time. You've attended church for years. But you cannot list from memory the Levitical laws pertaining to sexual conduct.

So . . .

How likely is it that Gentiles, three hundred miles from Jerusalem, who never owned a copy of the Jewish Scriptures, never read a copy of the Jewish Scriptures, and didn't grow up having Jewish Scriptures read to them would know the Levitical prohibitions pertaining to sexual conduct? Is it realistic to think these Gentiles knew the Levitical law so well that the mere mention of "sexual immorality" immediately brought to mind the entire list of prohibitions outlined in Leviticus?[29]

I don't think so. That assumes too much.

I'm convinced there's a much better explanation as to what James meant by "sexual immorality." He meant what Paul meant when Paul used the phrase. Actually, in Greek, it's a word, not a phrase. And Paul used the term quite frequently in his letters. So we can safely assume he used it quite frequently in his preaching and teaching as well. And where had Paul been preaching and teaching most recently?

Antioch.

And where did Paul go after things wrapped up in Jerusalem?

Antioch.[30]

And when Paul taught on the topic of sexual immorality, what did he point to as the basis of his instruction?

Antioch.

Kidding.

You'll have to wait till chapter sixteen for the answer to that question. But I'll go ahead and tell you what he did *not* leverage or point to as the basis for his teaching on appropriate and inappropriate sexual behavior.

The Levitical law.

As we will discover, Paul did not consider the law of Moses the go-to source for Christian behavior. I hope that makes you so nervous you actually finish this book.

The decision of the Jerusalem Council is mind-boggling. Against every Jewish fiber in their Jewish bodies they determined that Gentiles everywhere would have access to the God of *their* fathers without making a single trip to the temple and without sacrificing a single animal. All the benefits, none of the blood. But what's more mind-boggling than that, they decided *unity* in the church was more important than the *law* of Moses.

Did that send a chill down your spine?

No?

Peter, Paul, and James agreed that keeping the church together took precedence over keeping the law. To put it another way, unity in the church was more important than about half your English Bible.

Congregational unity trumped ceremonial purity.

Chills? No?

This was an extraordinary day in the history of the church. It was precisely what Jesus prayed for just before he was arrested.[31]

The same Jesus who warned his followers not to tamper with the law.[32]

The same Jesus who claimed to be the fulfillment of the law.[33]

The same Jesus who predicted the destruction of the temple that housed the law.[34]

BUT THERE'S MORE

In addition to laying the groundwork for unity between Jewish and Gentile believers, the Council's letter signaled a permanent break with the Jewish Scriptures as the foundation for orthopraxy.

Orthopraxy?

Orthopraxy is a compound term that simply means *correct practice*. In theological contexts, orthopraxy is what orthodoxy (right belief) looks like in the real world. It's the behavior, both ethical and moral, associated with a faith or belief system.

Up until this point in the history of the church, Jewish believers were taking their behavioral cues from both the teaching of Jesus and their first-century understanding of the law of Moses. Case in point, Peter's reluctance to visit a Gentile's home. Peter considered himself a follower of Jesus, but he wasn't about to run the risk of violating Jewish law. The decision of the Jerusalem Council was intended to change that, at least for Gentile believers. This is why the instructions in the letter weren't anchored to anything other than the authority of the Council.

The apostles' decision regarding Gentiles and the law left so much open to interpretation that Paul would spend a great deal of his spare time acting as referee between believing Jews and Gentiles. We can't fully appreciate the lengths the early church went to in order to blend two groups that had a long history of not blending. But blending those two groups required an uncompromising refusal to blend the two covenants.

Whereas Gentile believers abandoned their pagan beliefs, they did not abandon their pagan behaviors. They brought their Gentile customs, habits, and values right along with them, many of which were offensive to Jews.

It was messy.

It took twenty years, but the leaders of the Jesus movement were finally starting to understand the old had no place in the new. The decision of the Jerusalem Council should have been the final nail in the mix-and-match coffin. From that point forward, the law of Moses was no longer the point of reference for how Gentile believers were to conduct their lives. But old ways die hard. Paul's entire career as a church planter was encumbered by a run 'n' gun battle with the blended covenant model gang. They are identified in the New Testament as the Judaizers. As we will see in the next chapter, Paul reserved his harshest criticism for those who insisted on blending the old with the new. Harsh, as in . . . well . . . leg-crossing harsh.

Chapter 11

THE APOPLECTIC APOSTLE

If the previous couple of chapters left you wondering why I spent the previous couple of chapters making an argument for salvation apart from the law, you missed the broader implications of the previous couple of chapters. Worse, you missed the point of the previous couple of chapters.

Which is easy to miss.

It's easy to miss because we were taught to view the tension between the old and new covenants as a tension between two different approaches to salvation. And while that's true, there's more to it than that.

Paul thought so anyway.

CAPED CRUSADER

The decision of the Jerusalem Council was a watershed moment in the church's campaign for new covenant independence. But the struggle would continue. On the forefront of the struggle was none other than the former destroyer of all things Christian, Paul. Paul brought his passion, pedigree, and energy to the Jesus movement. He brought something else as well.

Clarity.

Extraordinary clarity.

Paul immediately saw the problems associated with blending the old with the new. As an educated Pharisee who spent his adult life studying, teaching, and defending the law, he instantly recognized the incompatibility of Moses and Jesus. From day one, he recognized Jesus was not an add-on or a continuation of the old ways. In Jesus, he recognized the introduction of something brand-new.

The *new* he recognized encompassed more than who was included in the kingdom of God and who wasn't.

No doubt it was Paul's clarity around the teaching of *The Way* that fueled his hatred of *The Way* to begin with. Prior to his conversion, Paul recognized the incongruence of Moses and Jesus. The two were incompatible and unblendable.

He didn't view the Jesus movement as a new version of Judaism. He viewed it as a perversion that must be eradicated.

Following his conversion, Paul channeled this same energy and determination into convincing his fellow Jews that God had, in fact, inaugurated something new. But as Paul saw it, embracing the new required complete disengagement from the old. In searching for a way to describe the relationship between old and new, Paul latched onto the term *mystery*—the mystery of the gospel—a mystery that, while heralded, illustrated, and foreshadowed by the Law and the Prophets, was not revealed until the arrival of Jesus.

The prophets knew something new was coming.

They knew somebody new was coming.

But no one grasped the fullness of God's ultimate ambition. That remained a mystery. A mystery alluded to in God's promise to Abraham. A mystery resolved in Christ. The mystery was Gentiles becoming heirs of God's promises together with Israel. Together, they would become members of one body, a new body, the *ekklesia* of Jesus. Together they would share in the fulfillment of God's promise to Abraham.[1]

But there was a hitch.

A big hitch.

Between God's promise to Abraham in Genesis and the arrival of Jesus, there were 1,500 years of covenant-keeping, law-observing, animal-slaughtering, temple-constructing, nation-building history. To law-abiding Jews, Paul's message seemed to discount all that. The notion of the Jewish nation paving the way and paying the price for something that would now be made available for free to cootie-ridden Gentiles didn't sit well with either the Jesus-following or non-Jesus-following Jews.

If Paul was correct, the Gentiles would get all the benefits with none of the costs. All the rewards with none of the surgery. Within the context of their centuries old "I will, if you will" arrangement with God, this was a bit hard to swallow. Paul understood that. He was an all-star law keeper. But Paul was convinced this was God's plan all along. His global plan. Everything between God's original promise to Abraham and the birth of Jesus was a means to a Gentile-including end. From the beginning, everything prescribed on Mount Sinai was designed to end.

For Paul, the law of Moses was a directional sign, not a final destination. The law was good, but the law was temporary. The law, and everything associated with it, was a means to an end. And the end had come. The law had a purpose. But it had served its purpose. So mixing, matching, blending, cherry-picking, and retrofitting were not options for Paul. He insisted they weren't options for any Jesus follower.

From day one, the day the scales fell (literally) from his eyes, Paul was at odds with the Jewish religious establishment, the very people he had spilled blood for the day before. Paul was commissioned by Jesus to get out of town and take the gospel to Gentiles, and it was an assignment he readily accepted. True to his word, he packed his bags and embarked on a tour de force of the major port cities of the Mediterranean. It is no exaggeration to say Paul's missionary journeys changed the world. But his message of inclusion apart from the law infuriated the blended-church Christians back home. Following the decision of the Jerusalem Council blended model, Jewish leaders continued to commission missionaries of their own to come behind Paul and "correct" his heretical, Jesus-first teaching. This didn't sit well with Paul, the former inquisitor-interrogator-imprisoner of Christians. While Paul was a man of great faith, he was not a man of great patience or tolerance for those who opposed the gospel.

But that was okay.

God didn't choose him for his manners.

LAYING DOWN THE LAW

In his letter to Christians living in Rome, Paul leaves us a somewhat academic summary of his thoughts regarding the relationship of the old and new covenants.

> So, my brothers and sisters, you also died to the law through the body of Christ, that you might belong to another, to him who was raised from the dead, in order that we might bear fruit for God.[2]

Paul leverages two points of contrast here. First, Jesus followers are dead to the law. The law, along with the covenant arrangement that served as the context for the law, has no say in the life of a believer. None. The second point of contrast centers on the term *belong*. Believers *belong* to Jesus.

You probably didn't underline that.

This is a big deal when understood within the context of the contrast Paul is making. Believers belong to Jesus, not the old covenant. Believers are accountable to Jesus, not the old covenant. Believers take their cues from Jesus, not the old covenant. Specifically, we don't not commit adultery because the Ten Commandments instruct us not to commit adultery.[3] According to Paul, Jesus followers are dead to the Ten Commandments. The Ten Commandments have no authority over you. None.

To be clear: Thou shalt not obey the Ten Commandments.

If that makes you uncomfortable, it's because you have unwittingly embraced the version of Christianity the Jerusalem Council declared unnecessary—the version Paul spent his ministry warning against. You are attempting to straddle two incompatible covenants.

You're not alone.

Hopefully, you won't run out and commit adultery. Jesus wouldn't like that. Remember, you belong to him now. You have been bought with a price. The Ten Commandments didn't even offer to rent you, much less buy you. The Ten Commandments never lifted a finger to help you. Worse, the Ten Commandments sat back and waited for you to screw up. And when you did, they finally spoke up, not to defend you but to condemn you! Once you were condemned, do you know what they did next? They demanded you go to a priest and make a sacrifice to purchase atonement for your sin.

That's a problem, now, isn't it?

You see, all the temple priests retired when the temple burnt down two thousand years ago. I suppose you could build an altar in your backyard. But my guess is animal sacrifice is illegal where you live. Not to mention, you really need an official, flesh-and-blood Levite for your sacrifice to be official. Good luck with that. So not only have you screwed up, you are . . . well, you are condemned. You are out of favor with God and there's absolutely nothing you can do about it!

Have a nice day.

"But wait!" you say. "God forgives sin. All I have to do is ask!"

Not under the old Ten Commandment's covenant, he doesn't. You've gotta kill something or burn something when you break a commandment. You're getting your covenants confused. Asking for forgiveness in Jesus' name is the new covenant, not the old.

Does it matter?

Oh yeah.

Back to Paul's letter to the Romans for a moment.

> But now, by dying to what once bound us, we have been released
> from the law . . .

Here's a bit of tragic irony. When Paul uses the term *we*, he's not talking about "you-and-me" we. We were never bound to the old covenant to begin with. Paul is trying to convince Jewish believers that they have been released from the law of Moses, including the Big Ten. Meanwhile, a gazillion modern-day Gentile believers have managed to wiggle themselves up under a covenant they were never included in to begin with. It's crazy. And if you were offended when I said you aren't accountable to the Ten Commandments, you're one of 'em.

Just sayin'.

What comes next helps explain how the two sections of your English Bible got their titles.

> But now, by dying to what once bound us, we have been released from the law so that we serve in the new way of the Spirit, and not in the old way of the written code.[4]

Once again, Paul leverages pairs of contrasts. Important ones. Under the old covenant, Jews were accountable to a "written" code, the law of Moses. But under the new covenant, we are accountable to the Holy Spirit. Big difference. The written code was housed in the temple, libraries, synagogues, and portions of it in the homes of wealthy Jews. The Spirit? Not so much. Under the new covenant, we don't visit the temple. We are the temple. Paul wasn't sure you knew that, so he wrote:

> Do you not know that your bodies are temples of the Holy Spirit, who is in you, whom you have received from God? You are not your own.[5]

As we saw earlier, this would have been considered scandalous in the first century. The temple was the epicenter of the Jewish world. God lived there . . . well . . . that was the rumor anyway. When Paul penned this statement, the temple was still operational. Operational, but according to Paul, no longer necessary. The mobile God had moved yet again—from tabernacle to temple to the hearts of those embracing God's final sacrifice for sin. The indwelling of the Holy Spirit in Jesus followers was yet another indication that the Sinai covenant, the old, was limited in scope, inferior, and temporary.

Before we leave Paul's letter to Roman Christians, I want to point out one other super important contrast: new vs. old.

> . . . in the *new* way of the Spirit, and not in the *old* way of the written code.[6]

You'll think I'm making this up. The Greek term translated *old* actually means obsolete or outdated.[7] Paul uses a derivative of this same term in his second letter to Corinthian Christians. Speaking of his Jewish brethren, he writes:

> But their minds were made dull, for to this day the same veil remains when the old covenant is read.[8]

This isn't old as in ancient. We don't refer to the U.S. Constitution as the old constitution. Why? Because it's still in force. If we ratified a new constitution, we would immediately, as in the next day, refer to the original constitution as the old constitution. Not because it suddenly got older, but because we were no longer using it.

Remember when you got your current cell phone? The moment you took possession of it, how did you begin referring to the one you walked into the store with? The one you kept by your bedside the night before? The one you showed off to friends when you first got it? As soon as you took possession of your new phone, the other phone immediately became your . . . old phone. Not because it suddenly got older. But because you were replacing it with something newer. Better. And I bet you didn't carry both phones around with you. Why? You're not the blended-phone type. Once you got your new one, you . . . well . . . what did you do with your old one?

Paul could not be any clearer. God's covenant with Israel was made obsolete the moment Jesus ratified the new covenant. This explains why the Jerusalem Council did not instruct Gentiles living in Antioch to obey the Jewish law. It was obsolete. They instructed the Antiochian Gentiles to be sensitive to believing Jews who were still in transition.

These next two sentences are so important.

Jews weren't expected to be accommodating to Gentiles moving in their direction, because Gentiles weren't moving in their direction. Gentiles were asked to be accommodating to Jews moving in their direction.

That's a lot of *theirs*. So you may need to read that again.

The Jews were exiting a covenant that had shaped their worldview for centuries, a worldview that had informed their consciences, their parents' consciences, and their parents' parents' consciences. It's no wonder it took 'em so long to make a clean break. A conscience is a difficult thing to shake. Just ask Peter.

Or my dad.

For us religious folks, our consciences define religious reality whether they reflect reality or not. My dad won't drink coffee. It's a conscience issue for him. He was raised in a religious environment that banned pretty much everything enjoyable. Including coffee. He laughs about it. But he still won't drink it. Oddly enough, bacon wasn't under the ban.

Bottom line, if Paul had been around in the fourth century when the bishops and theologians were brainstorming titles for the major divisions of what would eventually be called the Bible, I'm pretty sure he would have opted for the term *obsolete* over *old*. Imagine that? The Obsolete Testament and the New Testament. It's not pithy, but it's accurate. And it might have prevented a great deal of suffering along the way. The most shameful and embarrassing chapters in church history were not the result of anything Jesus or the apostle Paul taught. Our most embarrassing, indefensible moments resulted from Christians leveraging the old covenant concepts.

THE SMACKDOWN

I imagine Paul's comments ruffled a few feathers among the Jesus-following Jews in Rome. But these comments were mild in comparison to what he wrote to Christians living in the Roman province of Galatia. There's debate as to whether his letter was written before or after the Jerusalem Council. Either way, the New Testament book of Galatians reveals the depth of Paul's zeal to maintain the purity and exclusivity of the new covenant.

As referenced earlier, it wasn't uncommon for the church in Jerusalem to send missionaries to tidy up Paul's unorthodox theology. Apparently, that's what happened in Galatia. And when Paul heard about it, he fired off a letter.

After a very brief introduction, he jumps right in:

> I am astonished that you are so quickly deserting the one who called you to live in the grace of Christ and are turning to a different gospel—which is really no gospel at all. Evidently some people are throwing you into confusion and are trying to pervert the gospel of Christ.[9]

Paul calls the blended covenant model a "perversion."

> But even if we or an angel from heaven should preach a gospel other than the one we preached to you, let them be under God's curse![10]

Paul calls down a curse on the missionaries who preached mix-and-match. Then, just for good measure, he repeats himself.

> As we have already said, so now I say again: If anybody is preaching to you a gospel other than what you accepted, let them be under God's curse![11]

That's harsh. But we salvation-by-faith-alone types can't help but cheer him on. Right? After all, he's defending the gospel. Grace alone. Faith alone. Christ alone.

Actually, he's doing a lot more than that. But we miss the "a lot more than that" part because of how we've heard these passages taught. Here's what we hear:

> If anyone tries to convince you that salvation comes through the works of the law rather than grace, let them be under God's curse!

Not only is that not what he said, that's not what he meant. That's included in his point, but his point is much broader. The issue Paul was responding to in the Galatian church was not how one gains salvation. The issue was the relevance of the entire Mosaic covenant. The group that followed Paul to Galatia wasn't holding evangelism crusades. They were there to convince Jesus-following Gentiles to become Jewish in order to become "fully Christian." They were arguing for a blend of old and new.

So Paul, in his lawyer-like fashion, compares and contrasts God's unconditional promise to Abraham with God's conditional covenant with Israel. His point being, if you're gonna blend two things, blend Abraham and Jesus, because God's promise to Abraham was fulfilled through Jesus.

> Scripture foresaw that God would justify the Gentiles by faith and announced the gospel in advance to Abraham: "All nations will be blessed through you." So those who rely on faith are blessed along with Abraham, the man of faith.[12]

Hard to argue with that. But that approach leaves God's covenant with Israel spinning in the wind. Orphaned. Paul assumed someone reading his letter would wonder about that, so he addresses it.

> Why then was the law given at all?

Good question. If the law of Moses was destined to become obsolete, why establish it in the first place? Why did God establish a covenant that had a shelf life? Paul's answer:

> Why then was the law given at all? It was added because of transgressions until the Seed to whom the promise referred had come.[13]

There it is again. The law was intended as a temporary measure until God fulfilled his promise to Abraham. For good measure, Paul threw in a word picture.

> So the law was our guardian until Christ came that we might be justified by faith. Now that this faith has come, we are no longer under a guardian.[14]

The law was like a nanny. Guardians, or nannies, are responsible for watching over children until they're old enough to care for themselves. God's covenant with Israel served that same purpose. The law was in place for a limited time while God prepared the world for the introduction of the King who existed before time. Consequently, the law was in effect only "until Christ came." With the inauguration of the new covenant, the old covenant lost its authority. Following his word picture, Paul opts for an analogy the Jews in the audience would understand—and then he pretty much loses it.

> Mark my words! I, Paul, tell you that if you let yourselves be circumcised, Christ will be of no value to you at all. Again, I declare to every man who lets himself be circumcised that he is obligated to obey the whole law.[15]

It would be wise to pause here and allow the implications of that last statement to sink in.

No cherry-picking. If you pick and choose, you lose! The old covenant, like the new covenant, is an all-or-nothing proposition. As Peter learned from his encounter with Cornelius . . . as James affirmed at the Jerusalem Council . . . as Jesus announced in his mountain message . . . the old and new covenants are not compatible. They are not blendable. They are sequential. The old became old because it was fulfilled in Christ and replaced by the new. The moment anyone attempts to smuggle anything old into the new, the new becomes old. And the smuggler is obligated to embrace all of the old. The smuggler is obligated to slit animal throats and stone adulterers. The smuggler is obligated to marry his daughter off to the teenage idiot that steals her virginity.

Let that sink in.

Still not finished, he tosses out another analogy:

> A little yeast works through the whole batch of dough.[16]

Yeast is a single-cell fungus. Add a little single-cell fungus to a dense mass of dough and before you know it, you've got something completely different than what you started with. Which, of course, was Paul's point. A little thing can make a big difference.

It only takes a small dose of the wrong thing to corrupt the whole thing.

Even a pinch of the old covenant will corrupt the taste and texture of the new covenant. Then Paul goes Lorena Bobbitt on 'em. Remember Lorena? She's the woman who cut off her husband's . . .

Now you remember.

> As for those agitators, I wish they would go the whole way and emasculate themselves![17]

The Greek term for *emasculate* is . . .

Never mind.

You get the idea. If not, check the footnote.[18] And if you need to get up and walk around the room for minute, I understand.

FRESH EYES

So why the harsh language?

Why so worked up?

Paul saw what his contemporaries missed. He saw what we miss. Paul had allowed himself to go where few of his contemporary law keepers dared to go. Paul had taken the old covenant to its logical extreme. He had been to the dark side. When operating under the authority of the old covenant, Paul was free to track down, arrest, torture, and execute apostate Jews.

According to his understanding of the Jewish Scriptures, his unbridled cruelty was God's will. His violence was God's work. Paul, who prided himself on being the most law-abiding Pharisee in the Middle East, believed he was acting on God's behalf when he assumed the role of inquisitor and executioner. When we read or hear about the unimaginable atrocities carried out in the name of Christianity, we wonder how such things could be justified.

Paul knew.

Paul weaponized his religion.

With a clear conscience.

But Paul wasn't the only one who felt empowered to leverage violence against apostate Jews. Paul's old boss back in Jerusalem deputized him. Paul's old boss back in Jerusalem was none other than the high priest. Imagine that. The high priest, the man entrusted with and intimately acquainted with the sacred texts, had no qualms commissioning Saul of Tarsus to arrest, and if need be, exterminate followers of *The Way*.[19] In the minds of those closest to and most intimately acquainted with the old covenant, extreme violence was a justifiable means to an end.

Fun fact: When Paul became a Jesus follower, he could find nothing in the teaching of Jesus or Jesus' apostles to justify violent opposition against those who opposed *The Way*.

Don't rush by that.

When Paul became a Jesus follower, he could find nothing in the teaching of Jesus or of Jesus' apostles to justify violent opposition against those who violently opposed him. This is extraordinarily instructive as we consider how to handle the Old Testament.

Under the law, Paul could identify with King David's rants regarding the future of his enemies. We read the imprecatory Psalms and shudder, or worse, we spiritualize them to make David sound less barbaric and violent. But David was barbaric and violent. He raided and looted villages and murdered all the inhabitants to cover his tracks.[20] But he loved God's law. David saw no conflict between God's law and what we consider cold-blooded, racially motivated murder.

Neither did Saul of Tarsus—the fellow who wrote that lovely poem you had read at your wedding.

But when Paul unhitched his wagon from the old covenant and bolted it onto the new, his entire worldview changed. Not just his understanding of justification and salvation, his entire worldview. Paul had taken the old covenant to its logical extreme both in his personal devotion to it as well as his no-holds-barred defense of it. Which may explain why he was so happy to be done with it. He knew from personal experience the two covenants were incompatible. Yet Paul never, as in never ever, questioned the divine origin of the Jewish Scriptures. He never felt compelled to sanitize them either. They were what they were because of when they were written and for whom they were written. They were a divinely inspired means to a divinely ordained end, and in this way Jesus was both a beginning and an end.

With all that as a backdrop, I have a suggestion.

NOT HARMLESS

When we consider how to use and apply the Old Testament, let's take our cues from Paul. After all, he successfully navigated the transition from old to new while it was still fresh. Fortunately for us, he documented his transition. And from what we've read so far, if he catches us mixing and matching . . .

Well, just don't mix and match.

While Jewish Christians in Paul's day viewed a blend of ancient tradition with new revelation as harmless, Paul saw something different. He knew the legalism, hypocrisy, self-righteousness, and exclusivity that characterized ancient Judaism would eventually seep into and erode the beauty, simplicity, and appeal of the *ekklesia* of Jesus. Perhaps he knew that if the Jesus movement ever found favor in the empire, any trace of old covenant imperialistic thinking would tip the scale in the direction of the kingdoms of this world. Maybe he foresaw the day when mix-and-match husbands would leverage his words in attempts to force their wives into submission. No doubt he'd seen enough opportunistic evangelists to know they would not resist the temptation to claim for themselves God's covenant promises to prosper Israel. Perhaps he knew his words regarding slavery, when blended with old covenant narratives and assumptions, would be used to support the slave trade.

Whatever the case, Paul could not stand by while church leaders became self-righteous reflections of a priesthood that was disappearing. He refused to do nothing as the dual covenant model laid the groundwork for the very hypocrisy his encounter with Jesus liberated him from. He saw what others could not see, so yes . . . it would indeed be better if those corrupting the *ekklesia* of Jesus were to bleed out. Their pain would be a small price to pay to protect the church from the corruption that would ensue if old was blended with new.

KEEPING SCORE

If there were a ledger recounting the human rights violations committed in the name of Christianity, and we were privy to that information, there's no doubt we would join Paul in his visceral disdain for any attempt to borrow from the covenant Jesus fulfilled and replaced. But let's be honest. We don't need a list. Haven't we all seen enough to know he was right?

I have.

I bet if you stop to think about it, you have as well.

Years ago, I was asked by a gentleman I'd never met if I would meet with him and his daughter at my office to discuss her choice in boyfriends. It turned out her boyfriend was black and she was white. South-Georgia white. Dad brought his mom along. She never said a word. And she never smiled either. He also brought King James.

For two hours I listened to the dad explain why it was absolutely "against the Bible" for his daughter to marry a black man. It was amazing.

Ridiculous, but amazing. And no, he never quoted Jesus. He did remind her that Paul instructed children to obey their parents. Never mind she was nineteen. He told us all about Solomon's foreign wives. He'd underlined the verse in Ezra where Ezra instructs the men to separate themselves from foreign wives. But he saved the best for last. He concluded with his version of why God did not allow Moses to enter the promised land.

Any guesses?

Moses had married a dark-skinned Midianite woman.

When he finished and it was obvious his daughter was not inclined to change her mind, he stood up suddenly and reached into his interior suit pocket. I swear to you I thought he was going to pull out a gun and kill his daughter rather than see her date a black man.

Instead, he pulled out an envelope, opened it, and handed me the contents. It was an arrest warrant for his daughter. He'd had himself deputized by the sheriff back home, and then he'd somehow convinced a judge to declare his daughter mentally unstable, authorizing him to transport her, against her will if necessary, to the local hospital for evaluation. Grandma remained completely stoic while her granddaughter cried her eyes out.

Fortunately, there were a couple off-duty policemen in the building. I showed 'em the warrant, and they said the only option was for them to call a paddy wagon and have her locked up downtown.

She immediately agreed.

It was horrible.

Did I mention I was thirty years old? Newly married. No kids. No clue.

I asked daughter and grandma to step out so I could talk things over with Dad. I knew better than to get into a spittin' match with him over what the Bible says. I would have won. But she would've lost.

Instead, I asked him how important his relationship with his daughter was to him. He said it was extremely important. "In that case," I said, "you need to do something relational rather than legal." He just stared at me.

So I kept talking.

"You can make her go. But it will destroy your relationship. Or you can let her go and start working to win her heart." Then I looked him dead in the eye and said,

"But you can't do both."

Now, if I were you, I would be a bit skeptical at this point in the story. You're thinking, *How in the world do you remember what you said that long ago?* I'll tell you how in a bit.

I went out to the hall where both policemen and grandma were waiting with the most distraught nineteen-year-old you've ever seen. She was a mess. And who could blame her. I invited her to step back inside my office. She insisted the police officers join us, which they did. And I was glad. By this time I'd given the arrest warrant back to Dad, and after about thirty seconds of silence, he ripped the warrant in half and handed it to me. She started crying again. Heck, I started crying. Grandma wasn't crying. To this day I'm not sure she was even human.

Anyway.

Dad said, "Honey, I love you. Pastor Stanley says I need to win your heart. I'm not sure how to do that, but I'm going to try."

And that was it.

Grandma and Dad headed back down south. Daughter rendezvoused with her boyfriend, who'd been sitting in the parking lot the entire time. As for me, I sat down at my desk and wrote down the details of that last bit of the conversation. Why?

Let's face it.

I nailed it!

I handled that situation so deftly I knew I'd experienced a bit of divine intervention. I'm not that smart. And I didn't want to forget what I had so divinely said. So I wrote it all down.

LIFE AND DEATH

Extreme? Sure it is. But I bet you know someone who's experienced something equally as devastating at the hands of a blended covenant Christian. Again, when you blend old with new, you'll get the worst of both. But once we decide to dispense with the old and fully embrace the *new* Jesus unleashed in our world, the potential for amazing rises exponentially. The old and new covenants don't mix. They were never intended to mix. Again, sequential, not blendable.

In his second letter to the church in Corinth, Paul summarized it this way:

> He has made us competent as ministers of a new covenant—not of the letter but of the Spirit; for the letter kills, but the Spirit gives life.[21]

You can make her go.

Or you can let her go.

But you can't do both.

I have a hunch you pretty much know where Paul's story goes from here. He rescues the gospel from the blender and is lauded by many as a hero. The folks who had him arrested and shipped off to Rome for trial are the villains. Paul's letters make up half the New Testament. The letters written by his detractors . . . well . . . apparently nobody thought to make any copies.

Chapter 12

OBSOLETE-R THAN EVER

All this talk of unhitching the old from the new and calling portions of our English Bibles obsolete may be a bit unsettling. I get that. But if it's unsettling to you, imagine how first-century, Jesus-following Jews felt when it was suggested they bid farewell to texts that had shaped their culture and consciences. So before we move on, I want to invite another New Testament author into our discussion. Unfortunately, I don't know his name. In fact, I'm not even sure he's a he.

Reminds me of an Aerosmith song.

Nobody knows who authored the letter to the Hebrews. It was written around AD 64. It reads more like a sermon than a letter. The document is written to Jewish Christians pressured by the Jewish community to renounce Jesus and return to traditional Judaism. The author urges his audience to stay the new covenant course and resist the temptation to bend and blend. In a point-by-point comparison, the author explains how everything about Jesus is superior to everything about the old covenant. Here's a brief summary:

- Jesus is greater than Moses.

- Jesus is a better high priest than the current high priests.

- Jesus' covenant is superior to the covenant established at Mount Sinai.

- Jesus' once-for-all sacrifice is superior to the daily temple sacrifices.

Comparing Jesus' capacity as a priest to the priest down the street, he writes:

> But, in fact, the ministry Jesus has received is as *superior* to theirs as the *covenant* of which he is mediator is *superior* to the *old* one, since the *new covenant* is established on *better* promises.[1]

Note the compare-and-contrast terminology: "superior," "old," "new," "better." He's in complete agreement with the Jerusalem Council and the apostle Paul. The new covenant is a better, superior, preferable covenant. There's no mention of blending, mixing, or combining. According to our mystery author, the old covenant does not carry the weight or authority of the new one. He continues:

> For if there had been nothing *wrong* with that first covenant, no place would have been sought for another.[2]

This is an extraordinary and unsettling statement. Apparently there was something *wrong* with the old covenant. If he's correct, the Bible says there's something wrong with part of the Bible. If he's not correct, well, then, part of our Bible is not correct.

Oh well.

He goes on to quote the prophet Jeremiah who predicted the old covenant would eventually be replaced by a new one. But what the author of Hebrews says next is astonishing. It doesn't astonish most Christians because . . . well, most Christians don't read the Bible. But what he says doesn't astonish those who do read it because most Bible readers miss the fact that he's talking about their Bible. Here we go:

> By calling this covenant "new," he has made the first one . . .

Wait for it . . .

> *obsolete*

Farewell, author of Hebrews.

Come on, you can't label portions of the Bible *obsolete* and claim to be a Christian. Can you? The author of Hebrews says the new covenant rendered the old and everything associated with it *obsolete*. But that's not the most astonishing statement. What follows may be the reason our mystery author chose to remain a mystery.

> By calling this covenant "new," he has made the first one obsolete, and what is *obsolete* and *outdated* will soon *disappear*.[3]

"Obsolete" and "outdated"? Can you say that about something in the Bible?

Wait!

This is *in* the Bible. One author of the Bible is calling the work of another author of the Bible obsolete and outdated. Why didn't they tell us about this when they gave us our first B-I-B-L-E? Think about it. He just called three or more of the Old Testament books of your English Bible obsolete and outdated. And in case you didn't notice, he predicted the old covenant would disappear. Which, as we've discussed, it did. The fact that this was written before it disappeared adds to its credibility.

THE HOUDINI COVENANT

As we mentioned earlier, the old covenant *disappeared* on August 6, AD 70, the day the temple burned and the sacrificial system ended. That was the day ancient Judaism died. Orthodox Jews have been lamenting ever since. But the majority of Jews have moved on. The vast majority of modern Jews have no desire to see the temple rebuilt or the old covenant reinstituted. Most Jews consider the old covenant outdated and obsolete.

But not us Christians.

We just can't seem to let it go.

We insist on elevating it to the status of the new covenant. For insiders, that's Christianity. For outsiders, that's hypocrisy. We call the Bible the Word of God and ignore the inconvenient, offensive portions of the old covenant while freely resurrecting the portions that suit us in the moment. Paul had a suggestion for folks who do that.

REWIND, FAST-FORWARD, AND PLAY

To be clear, *obsolete* doesn't mean *bad*. Obsolete means something new and better has come along. Cassette tapes are obsolete, but they're not bad. Back in the day, cassette tapes were cutting-edge technology. Cassette tapes were the first technology to create the possibility for portable personalized music, until CDs came along, and now CDs are fast becoming obsolete. Not because they're bad. Because something better has come along. Each of those technologies played a critical role in the evolution of music storage and portability. They were necessary steps to get where we are today. The same is true of God's covenant with the nation of Israel. Sequential.

God's arrangement with Israel was a necessary step between God's promise to Abraham and the fulfillment of that promise. God's covenant with Israel served as the moral, ethical, cultural, spiritual, and civic road map for an ancient civilization that knew nothing but slavery. But from that nation of redeemed slaves, God brought forth the Redeemer of the world, the Redeemer whose own blood would free humankind from slavery to sin.

Now that he's here, we should put our cassette tapes away. We can appreciate them without playing them.

OUR FATHERS IN HEAVEN

Before we leave this ever-so-delicate topic, I want to tiptoe ever so delicately into the past to offer one additional bit of insight into why it's so difficult for us to adopt this perspective on God's covenant with ancient Israel.

Namely: We've never seen it done.

In fact, it's never been done. On a grand scale anyway.

The generation of church leaders that came along after the apostle Paul ignored his warning against mixing and matching covenants. The church fathers, as they are often referred to, immediately went to work harmonizing the old covenant with the new so as to make it play nice with the teachings of Jesus and the apostles. They reinterpreted, allegorized, and rebranded them to make them line up with developing Christian thought and theology. Instead of putting a bow on 'em, they baptized 'em.

In the fourth century, church leaders bound the Jewish Scriptures together with the Gospels and epistles for the first time and gave the collection a name: *ta biblia. The Bible.* Once the Hebrew Scriptures were bound together with Christian Scriptures, the texts of the Hebrew Scriptures were granted the same authority as the Gospels and epistles. The words of Moses became every bit as authoritative and binding upon Christians as the words of Jesus. The old covenant was granted new covenant credentials and new covenant status. It's been that way ever since. Consequently, much of what was sanctioned in the Old Testament would eventually be sanctioned by the church.

And that's unfortunate.

The church fathers' primary interest in the Jewish Scriptures was neither historical nor cultural. Their primary interest was Christological. They were convinced the Jews did not recognize and thus accept Jesus as Messiah because they didn't know how to interpret their own prophets. No surprise, the church fathers had little interest in Jewish interpretation of Jewish Scriptures. So they went looking for Jesus.

And they found him.

Everywhere.

For the church fathers, the Jewish Scriptures were a treasure trove of narratives, poetry, and prophecy to be mined and leveraged for the benefit of the church. Like modern Bible readers, they were looking for Jesus, not the Jews. They were looking for God the Father, not God the Founder. Gentile church leaders reduced the Jewish Scriptures to proof texts and illustrations to support the teaching of the church. In the course of a generation, Jewish history became Christian allegory. Preachers and teachers have been mixing, matching, allegorizing, and ignoring original context ever since.

Having their Scriptures hijacked by the church was deeply troubling to Jews. But it didn't concern the church fathers because the church fathers weren't all that concerned about the Jews. It's important to remember that the initial persecution of the church wasn't initiated by Rome. It was initiated by the temple. Rome didn't authorize Saul of Tarsus to track down and imprison followers of *The Way*. It was the Jewish high priest who deputized and commissioned him.[4] The earliest Christians weren't sent to Rome for trial. They were sent to Jerusalem.

Later, when the Roman Empire launched its own persecution of Christians, local Jews supported the empire and participated in the trials. When Polycarp, a second-century church father, was ushered into an arena in Smyrna[5] to be devoured by beasts, we're told Jews took part in gathering wood for the fire.

Needless to say, there was no love lost between devout Jews and Gentile Christians. Jewish persecution of Christians was not ancient history for the church fathers. It was current events. So while Gentile believers were enamored with the Jewish Scriptures, they were not all that enamored with the Jewish religion.

Consequently, traces of what would eventually blossom into full-blown anti-Semitism surfaced as early as the late first century—something both Jesus and the apostle Paul would have found abhorrent and utterly un-Christian.

Combined and shaken together, these events made it easy for the church to justify appropriating the Jewish Scriptures for their own purposes. Little did the brave church fathers know that by lifting the Jewish Scriptures out of their Jewish context and retrofitting them as Christian Scripture, they were laying the foundation for the reintroduction of old covenant style violence and bloodshed. It wouldn't be long before the violent God of the Old Testament became the violence-affirming God of the church. Combining the covenants paved the way for church support of slavery, anti-Semitism, inquisitions, forced conversions, and a host of other unJesus-like enterprises.

If only the early church had heeded Jesus' and Paul's instructions. If only they had heeded the decision of the Jerusalem Council. Instead, they rehitched ancient Judaism to the new covenant, thereby granting the old covenant equal authority with the new. This has haunted the church ever since.

By the time of the Reformation, the church was literally at war with itself. Tens of thousands of Christian men and women died at the hands of "Christian" soldiers warring over differing "Christian" theologies. The ferocity of the conflict between Catholics and Protestants was every bit as violent as the warfare described in the Old Testament.

THESE DAYS

Fortunately, the church no longer condones the violence and anti-Semitism that characterized the church following the era of Constantine and continuing right up through the Reformation. While modern Christians may struggle to reconcile the behavior of God in the two testaments, at least we've stopped using the Old Testament as an excuse to wage war on one another. But our refusal to fully embrace the fulfillment of the Mosaic covenant has left us with our own set of challenges.

When it comes to what's *in* the Bible, the Old Testament is one of the primary stumbling blocks for non- and post-Christians. The Old Testament is used far more than the New Testament to create doubt in the minds of undergrad and graduate students. You may not have noticed, but skeptics and opponents of our faith never say, "The Old Testament teaches." I wish they would. Instead, they cite "The Bible." "The Bible teaches . . ." "According to the Bible . . ." Why? Because the church has communicated for centuries that our faith rises and falls on the defensibility of a collection of documents that include the Hebrew Scriptures.

For the record, it doesn't.

But most non-believers are convinced it does. Most believers are as well.

Jesus treated the Hebrew Scriptures as authoritative. Paul insisted they were God-breathed. Peter believed Jewish writers were carried along by the Holy Spirit. But they never claimed their faith was based on the integrity of the documents themselves.

Christianity has a compelling, verifiable, historical story to tell. But the moment we anchor our story to an old covenant narrative and worldview, we lose our case in the marketplace. Not in a Bible college classroom. Not in a seminary classroom. Not in the apologetics class offered by your local church. In the real world. The world where science is gospel and folks are growing more and more skeptical of all things religious.

Besides . . .

Jesus, the apostle Paul, the author of Hebrews, and the Jerusalem Council have given us permission to unhitch our faith from God's covenant with Israel. Actually, they didn't just give us permission; they highly recommended it. Paul threatened to . . . well . . . you remember. They all knew what we will never know until we choose to let it go.

Mix and match and you don't get the best of either.

You get the worst of both.

You get the prosperity gospel, the crusades, anti-Semitism, legalism, exclusivism, judgmentalism, fourteenth-century Catholicism, don't touch God's anointedism, God will get 'emism, and other isms we will bump into in the next section. Pretty much everything that makes us resistible is tethered to some version of blended-model theology.

Chapter 13

OUR OLD FRIEND

If you've stayed with me to this point, you may be wondering what we twenty-first-century new covenanters should do with our old friend the Old Testament. How should we navigate, teach, and apply the narratives describing God's activity among a people bound to a covenant that is no longer in effect? What should we do with the prophets whose warnings leveraged old covenant assumptions and contexts? What do we do with bloody King David and his get-'em-God Psalms? What about Ecclesiastes? Should we really eat, drink, and be merry because life sucks and soon we're all headed down to Sheol anyway? If we aren't supposed to apply it, blend it, mix it, or edit it, what do we do with it?

Here are some suggestions.

AGREE WITH JAMES AND CO.

To begin with, we new covenant folks should embrace the decision of the Jerusalem Council regarding our relationship to the old covenant and everything associated with it. It's not our covenant. It wasn't given to us and it's not binding on us. That plane already landed. When it landed, everybody disembarked and the boarding gate was boarded up. Then the Romans came and destroyed the entire concourse. So, just accept the fact that everything in Exodus through Malachi, while fascinating, is not binding. It's not your covenant.

As uncomfortable as that sounds, consider this. The authors of the New Testament considered the old covenant *Scripture*, but they didn't consider it *binding*. The men who wrote the letter to Gentiles in Antioch held the Jewish Scriptures in high regard. These texts guided and comforted their ancestors. These were the narratives they had grown up with as children. These were the very texts that assured them of Messiah, that God would keep his promise to the nation and to the world. This was not an easy transition. It was hard to let go.

But they did.

And so should we. We twenty-first-century, new covenant folks should adopt the same view of the old covenant Scriptures as the men at the Jerusalem Council. Namely:

> God said it!
> That settles it!
> But Gentiles don't have to do it.

As inspired as the old covenant may be, it has no, nada, none authority over us, and any effort on our part to wiggle back up underneath its authority is tantamount to declaring the new covenant insufficient.[1] Once you accept the verdict of Peter, Paul, and James, along with the Jerusalem Council, the rest is easy.

Well, easier.

Suggestion number two.

WHAT IT IS

Accept the Old Testament for what it actually is rather than what you were taught as a child that it was.

And what is it?

First and foremost, the Old Testament is history. It is prima facie a history of ancient Israel. Last I Googled, there were 929 chapters in our English Old Testament. Abraham shows up in chapter eleven and the rest is history—Jewish history.

The Old Testament is not a comprehensive book about God. The Old Testament does not tell us everything God was doing everywhere in the world. It's not a biography of God's early years. The Jewish Scriptures describe God's activity in connection to one particular people group.

When you read American history, you learn a great deal about George Washington and Thomas Jefferson. But an American history book is not a book about George Washington and Thomas Jefferson. If you read a biography of George Washington, you will learn a great deal about American history. In either case, one would learn true things about both. But a history book is not the same as a biography. The Old Testament is not the biography of God. The Old Testament is a history of the ancient Jews from which we learn a great deal about God. But what we learn about God comes to us through the filter of Jewish history and a specific covenant.

The Old Testament makes no mention of Nebuchadnezzar's conquest of the Cimmerians and Scythians—only his conquest of Jerusalem. The poetry, songs, and wisdom literature were written primarily by two Jewish kings. There are no Chinese proverbs in the Old Testament. Only Jewish proverbs. The reason Psalms, Proverbs, and Ecclesiastes were copied and cared for was due to authorship, not content. Anything David or any of Israel's kings wrote or decreed would have been, and should have been, considered valuable and worth archiving.

The major and minor prophets address specific historical Jewish contexts, which even the above-average Gentile reader has a difficult time deciphering without the help of the handy introductions, outlines, and footnotes included in most modern English study Bibles. The Jewish law is so complex and linked to a specific historical context, we often skim it and thank God we didn't live back then.

Well, that's what I do.

Approaching the Old Testament as history in no way lessens its significance. The Old Testament is the backstory for the Christian faith. This carefully chronicled and meticulously copied history is the context for the introduction of the Savior of the world. And while they may not be our favorites, let's not forget that it was Jewish prophets who predicted his coming, hundreds of years in advance.

Third suggestion.

AVOID CONFLICT RESOLUTION

Resist the temptation to resolve theological, ideological, or ethical conflicts between the Old Testament and the teaching of Jesus and the apostles. Neither Jesus nor the apostle Paul felt the need to do so. We shouldn't either. Jesus warned his Jewish audience against tampering with the old covenant in one breath and then claimed to be the fulfillment of all things old covenant in the next. He made no attempt to harmonize the two. Again, neither should we. The apostle Paul pivoted from one covenant to the other within the course of an afternoon. Yet he did not attempt to harmonize God's behavior in the Hebrew Scriptures with the tone and teaching of Jesus. Why? That was then. This is now. What God did in the past was the necessary path to accomplish what he intended to do all along.

Once you accept the Old Testament for what it is, you'll feel less pressure to tidy it up, sand off the rough edges, or just ignore certain portions altogether. You'll spend less time trying to sanitize it and glamorize it in an effort to harmonize it with the New Testament. When you stop viewing the Old Testament as a spiritual guidebook or moral lessons to live by, the plotline and the lives behind the plot will leap off the pages in colors more vivid than you may be comfortable with. Mostly red.

The Old Testament is a saga of an ancient people struggling to survive in a world where food was scarce, enemies were real, and death was just a minor infection away. In spite of that, they clung to YHWH, and he in turn clung to his nation, careful not to override their freedom with his presence. It's gritty. Dirty. Powerful. It's ancient history with a divine purpose.

In our attempts to harmonize the values and ethics of the old and new covenants, we risk missing the real story. The energy we expend sanding off the rough edges of God's Old Testament behavior is energy we should apply to appreciating the mess God waded into in order to see the story of redemption played out to the bitter, bloody, "Crucify him, crucify him!" end. God did not spare his own Son. We shouldn't be surprised or offended by the fact that he didn't spare the sons and daughters of previous generations either. On the contrary, the saga of the Old Testament should cause us to drop to our knees in gratitude for what he has done on our behalf and on behalf of the world.

God does not need us to make excuses for him. He doesn't expect us to explain (or explain away) his old covenant behavior. To do so is insulting. Yes, his behavior was uncivilized by our modern standards. So what? While we think of God in terms of Father, in the Old Testament he was playing the role of founder, and founding a nation from dirt required a different set of tools.

Besides.

All the gods of the ancient world were human rights violators. Within the context of first-century violence, nobody batted an eye at the violence depicted in the Jewish Scriptures. This was standard fare. Standard warfare. That's just the way the world was. If the God of the Jews was going to establish a nation for himself, he would have to wade into the fray and play by the rules of the day.

Which is exactly what he did.

In the Old Testament, God played by the rules of the kingdoms of this world in order to usher in a kingdom not of this world through a covenant that stands as an invitation to everyone in the world. This is what makes the story of the exodus so epic. YHWH spoke in terms a Pharaoh could understand—the only terms an Egyptian pharaoh could understand—power and violence. We don't need to be embarrassed by that. We don't need to sanitize and spiritualize it. We certainly don't need to try to harmonize it with the Sermon on the Mount. It is what it is. Attempts to civilize the terms, conditions, and outcomes of the old covenant and its associated narratives undermine the credibility of the text and the credibility of the church. Even more, doing so diminishes the extent to which God went to redeem and rescue the world from sin.

The storyline of the Bible is both simple and compelling. Humankind screwed things up and God waded in to fix it. And then, when the time was right, when he had everything just the way he wanted it, he sent a baby, born of a woman, born under the old covenant with all its violent, bloody history. The Word became flesh and dwelt among us and he didn't cheat. He never played the God card. The power card. The kingdoms-of-this-world card. Paul said it best:

> Who, being in very nature God, did not consider equality with
> God something to be used to his own advantage;[2]

How very un-old covenant of him.

> . . . rather, he made himself nothing by taking the very nature
> of a servant, being made in human likeness. And being found
> in appearance as a man, he humbled himself by becoming
> obedient to death—

Surrender? Death? What happened to eye-for-an eye? You don't get any more un-old covenant than that.

You may have noticed in the Old Testament that people equated long life with God's blessing. You may have noticed how few of Jesus' followers lived long lives. Then again, you may have noticed how none of your friends named their sons Methuselah. But there are a lot of Petes, Jims, and Andys running around. Back to Paul:

> . . . he humbled himself by becoming obedient to death—even
> death on a cross![3]

Don't be confused. By old covenant standards, Jesus lost.

By new covenant standards, he won.

We do others and ourselves a great disservice when we retrofit the values, behaviors, and narratives of the Old Testament to make them compatible with the new. First-century Jewish Jesus followers felt no compulsion to tidy up and remove the sharp edges from God's behavior. It wasn't their problem. In fact, it *wasn't* a problem at all.

Fourth suggestion.

PRINCIPLES, NOT PROMISES

The promises found in most of the Old Testament are not your promises. Yours are better.[4] They may not be as promising, but they are better promises. Everything promised between Exodus and Malachi is promised within the context of a *bilateral suzerainty treaty* between God and a nation. It should all be interpreted within that context. Psalms, Proverbs, and Ecclesiastes were all written within the context of an *I will if you will* arrangement between God and a nation. An arrangement, by the way, that promised nothing in the afterlife.

That's right. No heaven. No hell. No nothing. Just Sheol.

You want to go to Sheol?

Didn't think so.

So don't go snooping around for promises in the old covenant. You may live long and prosper, but in the end, Sheol.

If you asked an ancient Jew how one could know for sure they were going to heaven, they may have responded by asking you what made you think *anybody* went to heaven. Most ancient Jews didn't believe in an afterlife. Why? Their Scriptures didn't assume one. In the Old Testament, when people died, it was assumed they went to Sheol. But Sheol wasn't an actual place. It was the term used to describe the realm of the dead.[5] Sheol became somewhat synonymous with hell after the Jewish Scriptures were combined with Christian writings.

Many a grieving parent has taken comfort in King David's response when he's told the baby he conceived with Bathsheba had died.

Can I bring him back again? I will go to him, but he will not return to me.[6]

This is a powerful, reassuring, hope-filled statement when read through the lenses of our new covenant-colored glasses. But there was nothing hopeful about it when David uttered it. His point was not that he would see his baby again one day in heaven. His point was that he would eventually join his baby in death.

Would I correct a grieving parent's misapplication of this text? Of course not. But I sure as Sheol wouldn't use it at the funeral service either. For lots of reasons. Most folks overlook the fact that God killed David's baby to punish him and Bathsheba. That's comforting. The reason we new covenanters believe mamas and babies will be reunited someday has nothing to do with anything in the old covenant. We believe the dead will be reunited because of an empty tomb.

Somebody say, "Amen."

Every promise you need today is found within the context of Jesus' new covenant. It's a better covenant. If you can't find it there, don't go looking elsewhere. You'll just get yourself in trouble. God's promises to Israel are not his promises to you. Again, yours are better.

Much better.

His promises to you are coupled to his original promise to Abraham. His promise to bless the world. To bless YOU!

On the other hand, there are principles, both stated and illustrated, throughout the Old Testament. Lots of sowing and reaping. Proverbs is full of common sense cause-and-effect relationships. Solomon's financial suggestions alone are worth the price of a genuine leather-bound study Bible. But for the record, don't do anything because Simon and Solomon say. They are not the bosses of you.

Which leads me to my fifth suggestion.

INSPIRATION, NOT APPLICATION

The Old Testament is great for inspiration, but not application. Don't do anything the Old Testament tells you to do because someone in the

Old Testament tells you to do it or because they did it themselves. Especially the *because they did it themselves* part. That could get you arrested. This is such a big idea I've devoted the entire next section to it. But life is uncertain and I wasn't sure you would make it to the next section. So there you go.

While the Old Testament is not our go-to source for application, it is a fabulous source of inspiration. Old Testament narratives are rich in courage, valor, and sacrifice. Everybody faces a Goliath or two. Most of us can relate to Moses' fear of rejection and Gideon's insecurity regarding his past. Who isn't inspired by Joseph's decision to forgive his wicked brothers or Daniel's decision to face Babylonian lions rather than violate his conscience. Besides, Old Testament stories of faith, fortitude, and grit are the dots that connect to create the storyline of our redemption. While it's not your covenant, it certainly connects to your story. Referencing the saga of ancient Israel, Paul places it in its proper new covenant context when he writes:

> These things happened to them as examples and were written down as *warnings for us*, on whom the culmination of the ages has come.[7]

He underscored this same point in his letter to believing Jews in Rome when he wrote:

> For everything that was written in the past was written to teach us, so that through the *endurance* taught in the Scriptures and the encouragement they provide we might have hope.

The Old Testament is filled with stories of endurance in the face of overwhelming obstacles. The Jews in Paul's audiences knew these stories well, as do most of us. He suggests they find encouragement in those accounts of God's faithfulness to their forefathers. But then he pivots:

> May the God who gives *endurance* and *encouragement* give you the same attitude of mind toward each other that Christ Jesus had.[8]

See what he did there? While the history of the ancient Jews serves as a reminder of God's power to sustain, Paul instructs his first-century new covenant audience to anchor their endurance in Christ, to take their behavioral cues from Jesus.

When teaching this content, I'm occasionally asked how Paul's words to Timothy regarding the usefulness of "all Scripture" fits this paradigm. Paul writes:

> All Scripture is God-breathed and is useful for teaching, rebuking, correcting and training in righteousness.[9]

And, of course, I wholeheartedly agree. All Scripture is useful for all those things. But here's something to keep in mind.

> If you want to know what someone means by what they say, listen to what else they say and watch what else they do.

If we want to know what Paul meant by "all Scripture is useful for teaching, rebuking, correcting and training," we should pay attention to how Paul used the Jewish Scriptures to teach, rebuke, correct, and train. Illustrations are scattered throughout his letters and his teaching as documented in the book of Acts. As we will discover in chapter sixteen, Paul never sets his application ball on an old covenant tee. When it came to how believers are to live, he was quick to point to Jesus as the standard. When Paul described the believer's relationship with God, he always spoke in new covenant terms.

FIRST DATE

If these five suggestions make you uncomfortable, I get it. I get it because I, too, was introduced to the Old Testament as part of a sacred book with no explanation as to how the different parts fit together. I, too, was taught from childhood that every word in the Bible is God's Word and, consequently, it's all *equally* important and applicable. Most of us accepted this as gospel before we ever got to the Gospels. As children we were given a set of lenses through which to view the Old Testament, and when we were able to read it for ourselves, we went looking for God.

And we usually see what we're looking for.

But if you were to pick up a copy of the Old Testament as an adult and you didn't know what it was, you would probably identify it for exactly what it is. A history of the ancient Jewish people.

If it sounds like I'm being harsh or critical of the Old Testament, I'm not. Jesus said if you diss the Jewish Scriptures, you'll be sent to the back of the line in the kingdom of heaven.[10]

And I hate lines.

ALL GOOD THINGS

God's covenant with Israel played an essential and important but temporary role in the story of our redemption. The letter from church officials in Jerusalem to the nervous men in Antioch represented the official break between the church and ancient Judaism. It signaled the official recognition that a new covenant had, in fact, fulfilled and replaced the old one. Faith alone in Christ alone became the official means of entry to *faith* and *fellowship*. But the Jerusalem Council's decision represented something else as well. Something deeper and wider. In addition to unhitching the church from the law of Moses, their decision unhitched the church from everything *associated* with the law of Moses. So the early church:

- Chose the first day of the week rather than the Sabbath as their holy day.

- Rebranded Passover.

- Abandoned animal sacrifice.

- Ditched circumcision.

- Dispensed with the priesthood.

- Served and prayed for rather than persecuting their enemies.

But even in the face of all the change and transition, we should always affirm the goodness and divine origin of the old covenant. After all, it is the cocoon that brought us life, light, and a kingdom that has no end. It's the backstory for the greatest story. It was the nanny whose purpose was to point God's people toward the One who was to come. It's the history of God's chosen people through whom he would eventually step foot personally onto planet earth. The old covenant is a perpetual reminder that God keeps his promises, that his love endures forever. Yes, it is obsolete. But it is an obsolete covenant for which Jesus followers should be forever grateful. N. T. Wright summarized it perfectly when he wrote:

> The Torah [law of Moses at Sinai] is given for a specific period
> of time, and is then set aside—not because it was a bad thing
> now happily abolished, but because it was a good thing whose
> purpose had now been accomplished.[11]

As followers of Jesus, we are people of the new covenant. And just as the old covenant was accompanied by a specific set of commandments that formed the guiding ethical framework for old covenant people, so too the new covenant of Christ has a *new* commandment that forms the *new* ethical framework for new covenant people. A framework that is far less complicated, but far more demanding. It is to that *new* unifying ethic that we now turn our attention.

SECTION 3

A New Ethic

INTRODUCTION

"So Andy, is _____ a sin?"

I get asked that question or some version of it quite often. Truth be told, I've asked it a few times myself. You've probably asked it as well. I was taught from childhood that sin offends God, so I should avoid sin in order to avoid offending God. Which is true, but I wasn't always sure where enjoyment ended and *sin* began. It's human nature to want to know exactly where the *okay* and the *not okay* lines are so we can snuggle up as close to *not okay* as possible without actually not being okay. I didn't want to be guilty of a sin. But I sure as heck didn't want to miss out on anything that wasn't off-limits. Thus the questions:

"What does the Bible say about _____?"

"Is it okay for a Christian to _____?"

"Is there anything wrong with _____?"

In the stream of Christianity I grew up in, sin avoidance was pretty much our guiding light. As I understood it, as long as I wasn't breaking a God rule, I was good with God and God was good with me. It was well with my soul. God was free to hear and, hopefully, answer my prayers. The whole thing was vertical. I was far more concerned about how my behavior affected my standing with God than I was about how my behavior affected anybody else. After all, the Bible says pleasing God is more important than pleasing people. Which led me to conclude that if I sinned against *you*, and asked God to forgive *me*, everything would be good between God and me even if things weren't good between you and me. I could have a clear conscience with God while continuing to avoid you in the grocery store.

Vertical morality, as I refer to it, assumes God's primary concern is how our behavior affects *him*. That's the *vertical* part. In this way of thinking, God is personally offended by certain behaviors because they are contrary to his nature, sensibilities, and holiness. While this is certainly true, it creates an eye-to-the-sky mentality. I was always wondering how my behavior sat with Holy God. And seeing as I couldn't see God's body language and facial expressions, I was often left wondering and guessing. Thus all the questions regarding what does and doesn't constitute sin.

Of course, there's a bit of hypocrisy woven into all this. My primary concern was not how my sin affected God. My primary concern was me! I was concerned that offending God might come back to haunt *me*. Not to mention, wondering how close we can get to sin without sinning is tantamount to asking how far away from God we can get without losing contact altogether.

It's a flawed approach to faith, to be sure.

But it's oh so common.

GO HIGH OR GO HOME

There's a second, perhaps less obvious, expression of vertical morality. Through the years I've run into lots of folks who aren't wondering *how low they can go*. They're wondering *how high they can get*.

Not that kind of high.

These folks are seeking a deeper experience with God. They ask a different set of questions. More virtuous questions, for sure. Questions like:

- How can I get closer to God?

- How can I know God more intimately?

- How can I receive all God has for me?

Strange as it may sound, these questions belie a vertical orientation as well. While seeking greater intimacy with God is a noble pursuit, we would be less than honest if we didn't admit that the intimacy sought is for the benefit of the seeker. People seeking a deeper experience are seeking something for themselves. Which is fine, except for the fact that folks looking for a way to get closer to God can be just as self-absorbed as those wondering how far they can go without going too far.

I know. That's harsh.

Maybe it will help you to know I've played on both playgrounds. The first one left me looking for loopholes and workarounds, ways to skirt the teaching of the New Testament in order to have my way while not wandering too far from the way. But the playground across the street sent me in another not-so-healthy direction as well.

Toward the end of college, I finally said goodbye to the *how low can I go* season of my life and began asking those more virtuous questions: How can I know God better? How do I ensure I'm experiencing all God has for me? I developed a rich prayer life, often praying an hour or more a day. I built a prayer closet under the stairs in my parents' basement. I attended just about every spiritual life conference that came to town. I endeavored to live a holy life. I went deep.

Well, I went a *version* of deep.

I went the version of deep modeled by the teachers and writers I was dialed into at the time. It was a version fueled by knowledge, insight, discipline, and personal experience. In the end, it was still pretty much about me. And as I'll explain in more detail later, the holier I got, the more intolerant and judgmental I became.

Whether one goes low and shallow or deep and high, both approaches are vertical in nature. Both are eye to the sky. And ... surprise, surprise ... both approaches are rooted in old covenant thinking. Both approaches are fueled by the tradition of mixing and matching old and new covenant texts and assumptions.

HOLY-ISH

A steady diet of personalizing and individualizing concepts from the Old Testament contributes to the creation of a vertically oriented faith. God's covenant with Israel was extraordinarily vertical. On purpose. He was creating a nation from scratch. He needed their undivided attention. The preamble to the Sinai covenant underscores that.

> I am the LORD your God, who brought you out of Egypt, out of the land of slavery. You shall have no other gods before me.

After a bit more elaboration on that theme, he concludes:

> ... for I, the LORD your God, am a jealous God, punishing the children for the sin of the parents to the third and fourth generation of those who hate me, but showing love to a thousand generations of those who love me and keep my commandments.[1]

In a nutshell, God's message to Israel was:

> *Keep your eyes on me and my commandments or else!*

Doesn't get more vertical than that. The *commandments* he references were all designed to keep the nation of Israel separate from all the other nations. They weren't to mix, marry, or mingle with anyone other than their own folks. They were to secure their borders and expel misbehaving foreigners. After Moses passed the leadership torch to Joshua, God reiterated this same idea to the nation's new commander in chief:

> Keep this Book of the Law always on your lips; meditate on it day and night, so that you may be careful to do everything written in it. Then you will be prosperous and successful.[2]

Implication: And if you don't? You won't!

Divine blessing was contingent upon the nation fixing their eyes on God and his law at all times. We're reminded again of the cause-and-effect nature of God's relationship with Israel. Obedience to the law would result in economic and military blessing. This is the tone and texture of everything associated with the old covenant. It's all very vertical.

On purpose.

Vertical morality will leave you wondering and vulnerable. It'll have you guessing at answers to questions the Bible doesn't directly answer. It leaves folks with sincere hearts longing for more and those with not-so-sincere hearts looking for ways to get by with less.

I would imagine somebody out there is thinking, *Andy, I'm not sure I buy it, but assuming vertical morality is even a thing . . . and assuming it's a thing to be avoided . . . what's the alternative? Horizontal morality?*

Good guess.

Where did I come up with all this nonsense?

Chapter 14

TRENDING HORIZONTAL

As we discovered earlier, Jesus said several things in his famous mountain message that served as a heads-up something new was on the horizon. He'd not come to "abolish" the law, though at times it certainly sounded that way. Then there were the six "you have heard . . . but I tell you" statements. Sandwiched between those two *who does this guy think he is* sections is something we brush right by but which undoubtedly raised a few first-century eyebrows.

> Therefore, if you are offering your gift at the altar and there remember that your brother or sister has something against you, leave your gift there in front of the altar. First go and be reconciled to them; then come and offer your gift.[1]

And the crowd went wild.

Actually, they probably shook their heads in disbelief. Most Jews visited the temple once or twice a year. The lines were long. The sun was hot. The kids were fussy. The animals unruly. The smell was . . . we can't imagine. Jesus and most of his crew were from Galilee. A three-day journey to the temple. While some of what Jesus taught was border-line blasphemous, this was just flat-out impractical. There was no way in hades anyone would give up their place in line at the temple to go searching for an unhappy camper back home. Especially if you were from Galilee. The offended party would have to wait. Besides, making things right with God was more important.

Right?

Right?

Bueller?

Did Jesus really mean to imply reconciliation with a brother or sister should come before reconciliation with God? That making things right with someone who *may* have something against us is more important than temple worship? Did he really believe horizontal should take precedence over vertical?

Surely not.

But that *is* what he said. Turns out, that *was* what he meant.

This was new.

HANG 'EM HIGH

Seventeen chapters later, we find the Pharisees, Herodians, and Sadducees taking bets on which group could humiliate Jesus in public.[2] The Pharisees went first. They sent a group of undercover assailants to ask Jesus an IRS question. Jesus did a coin trick and sent 'em scrambling back to their handlers.

The Sadducees were next. Their question was basically a riddle about a woman who married seven brothers, all of whom died, after which she died. All riddles end with a question. Theirs did as well: *Who then would she be married to in heaven?* It's important to note the Sadducees didn't even believe in heaven. The point of the riddle was to underscore the absurdity of an afterlife.

Jesus smiled and told them they needed to go home and read their Bibles; they didn't know the first thing about their Scriptures.[3] To prove it, he leveraged a verb tense from a passage in Genesis that left 'em speechless. They too disappeared into the crowd. The crowd who no doubt cheered every time Jesus publicly humiliated their hypocritical, graceless, merciless, overpaid religious leaders.[4]

By then, the Pharisees had regrouped and reloaded. This time they sent a lawyer. Matthew was taking notes:

Hearing that Jesus had silenced the Sadducees, the Pharisees got together. One of them, an expert in the law, tested him with this question:[5]

He wasn't there to learn anything. He was there to build his résumé. Since the theology questions hadn't put Jesus on the ropes, perhaps a legal question would.

"Teacher, which is the greatest commandment in the law?"[6]

This was not an unusual question. Every good Jew knew the textbook answer to this one. We aren't sure where the lawyer was going with this. In all likelihood, he assumed he knew how Jesus would answer this basic question. Perhaps his plan was to follow it up with a second question designed to stump this heretofore unstumpable rabbi.

Jesus replied: "'Love the Lord your God with all your heart and with all your soul and with all your mind.' This is the first and greatest commandment."[7]

Yes, it was.

Rabbis had been saying as much for some time.

The more difficult question, perhaps the lawyer's follow-up question, was *What exactly does it look like to love the Lord your God with one's heart, soul, and mind?* How does one actually go about doing that? Religious leaders had a textbook answer for that one as well. It was a vertical answer. After all, the question pertained to showing honor to an invisible God who dwelled in the heavens. Eye to the sky. The way ancient Jews demonstrated their love for God was by keeping his commandments. The law. The old covenant. The entire old covenant was an *I will if you will* arrangement. Keep God's laws and you keep God happy. If God's happy, everybody's happy. Even mama.

Perhaps the lawyer's intent was to demonstrate to the crowd that Jesus was guilty of breaking the most important command because he consistently disregarded the lesser commands. In the traditional Jewish way of thinking, obedience to the lesser was evidence of devotion to the greater. But alas, we'll never know where the lawyer's line of questioning was headed because Jesus went right ahead and gave *his* answer to that second question before the lawyer had an opportunity to ask it.

> And the second is like it . . .

The second?

The lawyer only asked for one. He asked about the greatest *commandment,* not the greatest *commandments.*

Perhaps Jesus held up his hand to indicate he wasn't quite finished.

> And the second is like it, "Love your neighbor as yourself."[8]

"Second" greatest? As in, almost as great as the first greatest? What did Jesus mean by "is like it"? How much like it is it like?

Before we go there, it's historically important to go here first.

FIRST TIME

This is the first time in recorded history that these two Old Testament statements were combined in this way. The first statement makes its debut in Deuteronomy. The other appears first in Leviticus.[9] But this unique formula is original with Jesus. This was new. This was yet another in a series of statements pointing to the change that was coming.

The majority of commentators are convinced Jesus' point was that there were actually *two* greatest commandments. The second commandment was not second in importance. It was second in sequence. The reason most commentators interpret Jesus' statement this way is the phrase "is like it." The command that comes second in the sequence of commands was equally as great or important as the first one. It was "like it" in magnitude and significance. The lawyer's question was front-loaded with an assumption. In this case, a false assumption.

Got kids?

Which one is greatest?

The question assumes something that's probably (hopefully) not true. The question assumes one of your children is greater than the other or others. Who am I to make that assumption? Similarly, what gave this lawyer the right to assume one commandment was greater than all the others? Perhaps *that* was the trap. Whatever the case, Jesus didn't allow himself to be boxed in by the assumption behind the question. There wasn't one greatest commandment. There were two. According to Jesus, these two commands summed up the Jewish Scriptures. Not just the law . . . the entire old covenant.

> All the Law and the Prophets hang on these two commandments.[10]

First-century Jews referred to their Scriptures as *the Law and the Prophets*. According to Jesus, their entire Bible, so to speak, could be summarized by those two commands. As one Greek lexicon puts it, "As a door hangs on its hinges, so the whole Old Testament hangs on these two commandments."[11] Another commentator writes,

> It is commonly recognized that this is fulfillment language, and that these two (commands) complete and bring into fulfillment all of Scripture . . .[12]

If you had asked first-century Jews what it looked like to love God, they would say, "Obey his commands." Jesus suggested a new answer. "Love your neighbor." His point was unmistakable. Love for God was best demonstrated and authenticated by loving one's neighbor.

That was a clue. A hint. A foreshadowing.

It was certainly horizontal.

These weren't just the greatest, as in the most important, commands. These two commands summarized every conceivable application of all the commands in the Jewish Scriptures. Anyone who obeyed these two commandments had, in effect, obeyed or fulfilled all the commandments. If they were to be taken seriously, anyone who mistreated a neighbor didn't love God. Vertical love for God was to be manifested through one's horizontal love for their neighbors. It was as if Jesus was saying,

> Don't claim adherence to commandment #1 if you're guilty of violating commandment #2.

This was disturbing.

Why?

It was disturbing because Jesus was constantly calling out religious leaders for their mistreatment of fellow Jews—their *neighbors*. Based on his twin commandments comments, the Pharisees and Sadducees were guilty of not loving the Lord their God with all their hearts, souls, minds, and strength. If Jesus was correct, they were guilty of violating what was widely accepted as the first and greatest commandment!

Which brings us to this.

Neighbor.

Love your "neighbor." I bet I know what comes to mind when you see the term *neighbor*. But it's important for where we're headed to understand what first-century Jews thought when they heard the term. Being an above average person, I bet you can figure it out for yourself. The following passage from Leviticus provides you with all the clues you need. This is where Jesus' second in sequence command originated. According to this verse, who did Jews regard as neighbors?

> Do not seek revenge or bear a grudge against anyone among your people, but love your neighbor as *yourself*.[13]

Maybe this will help.

> Do not seek revenge or bear a grudge against anyone among **your people**, but love **your neighbor** as *yourself*.

A Jew's neighbor was a Jew's people. Other Jews. For a Jew to love another Jew as they loved themselves made perfect sense, because in a sense, they were loving themselves. They were all Jews! They were family. They were all descendants of Abraham. *Loving neighbors* was code for *loving other Jews*. This explains the old covenant prohibitions and instructions regarding the treatment of foreigners (aliens). The civil law contained in the Sinai covenant was created first and foremost for kin.

Remember Peter's awkward introduction at Cornelius' home? Apparently, he'd never been expected to love anyone other than other Jews.

But Jesus' new movement would include more than his fellow Jews. His new movement would welcome the foreigner living among them as well as the foreigner living in foreign lands. So, as he had done on previous occasions, Jesus altered the rules and redefined terms. The era of defining *neighbor* ethnically was coming to an end. To prepare his followers for what was coming, Jesus once again veered outside the boundaries of the Levitical law and redefined *neighbor*.

Here's how it went down.

WHO'S YOUR NEIGHBOR?

Not too long after episode one of stump the rabbi, Jesus was approached by yet another lawyer with another trick question.

> "Teacher," he asked, "what must I do to inherit eternal life?"[14]

Good question. But Jesus knew there was a question behind his question, so he responded with a question of his own.

> "What is written in the law?" he replied. "How do you read it?"[15]

Translated: "You're a lawyer. You tell me and we'll both know." This is where things get interesting. This lawyer recites the answer they were both taught from childhood. But this fellow had been paying attention. He knew all about Jesus' greatest commandments formula. So in what may have been an attempt to throw Jesus off his game, he grinned and answered:

> "Love the Lord your God with all your heart and with all your soul and with all your strength and with all your mind"; and, "Love your neighbor as yourself."[16]

Nailed it!

> "You have answered correctly," Jesus replied. "Do this and you will live.[17]

Then he showed his cards. Luke writes:

> But he wanted to justify himself, so he asked Jesus, "And who is my neighbor?"[18]

This was the question behind the question. The unabridged version is as follows:

> If loving my neighbor is proof of my love for God, which is the key to eternal life, tell me *exactly* whom I'm expected to love so I can secure me some eternal life. What's the minimum requirement? What's the minimum amount of neighbor-loving I'm required to perform to ensure eternal life for myself?

Based on the Leviticus passage cited above, he assumed, as everyone in the crowd assumed, neighbor-love was restricted to descendants of Abraham. But which descendants? Which Jews? And how much love would be required? He was looking for a salvation formula. Not for God's sake. Certainly not for his neighbor's sake. For his sake. So very vertical.

But he may have had another trick up his sleeve as well.

His questions may have been designed to force Jesus into stating plainly what he had hinted at on other occasions. Jesus instructed his followers to love their enemies. That was code for non-Jews. If he could trick Jesus into equating Jews with non-Jews, the crowd was sure to turn on him. He, on the other hand, would go down in rabbinic history as the man who stumped the teacher from . . . where was it again?

So he asked:

"And who is my neighbor?"[19]

Jesus saw through all this. He also saw this as the perfect opportunity to deconstruct and then reconstruct his audience's concept of *neighbor*. He was months away from establishing his new covenant between God and the nations. If this good news, this gospel, was going to make it beyond the borders of Judea and Galilee, his followers would have to abandon their ancient racist ways. So he launched into his most disorienting, paradigm-shifting, mind-bending parable of all. We've reduced this parable to a figure of speech. In its original context it was so much more.

> A man was going down from Jerusalem to Jericho, when he was attacked by robbers. They stripped him of his clothes, beat him and went away, leaving him half dead.[20]

Weren't we just talking about neighbors?

You know this one. Two Jewish religious leaders pass by their bruised and bleeding Jewish neighbor and don't lift a finger. If Jesus' greatest hits formula was correct, these two were doomed. They did not love their Jewish neighbor. Therefore, they did not love the Lord their God. They could offer sacrifices for sin all day long, but if Jesus was correct, weren't nobody listening.

Everybody was leaning in.

He had 'em.

He always had 'em.

Wrinkling his brow as if he, too, were concerned with what followed:

> But a Samaritan . . .

Perhaps he paused to allow the murmuring to abate. It's safe to assume most of Jesus' audience assumed imaginary Samaritans were behind the imaginary robbery in Jesus' imaginary story.

> But a Samaritan as he traveled, came where the man was; and
> when he saw him, he took pity on him.[21]

Surely not, they thought. *Surely he's not going to make a Samaritan the hero?*

But he did.

Not only did he make the Samaritan the hero, he made him an extra-mile, are-you-kidding-me, who-would-do-that variety hero. This Samaritan didn't just pity the man:

> He went to him and bandaged his wounds, pouring on oil and
> wine. Then he put the man on his own donkey, brought him to
> an inn and took care of him.[22]

This was ridiculous. Few, if any, in Jesus' audience would do such a thing for a Samaritan. No Samaritan they'd met would show that level of concern for a Jew. These groups didn't speak to one another, much less touch one another. It wasn't how things were done in those parts.

But Jesus wasn't finished.

> The next day . . .

"The next day"? Did he really expect them to believe a Samaritan would spend an entire night caring for a Jew?

The next day he took out two denarii and gave them to the innkeeper. "Look after him," he said, "and when I return, I will reimburse you for any extra expense you may have."[23]

This was so over the top. No Jew should be expected to suspend that much imagination on a story designed to distract them from *the* question for which Jesus clearly had no answer. Something about a neighbor. Once folks settled down, Jesus did something his audience wouldn't live long enough to appreciate.

Jesus redefined *neighbor*.

For everybody.

Forever.

From this point forward, no one would have the latitude to limit the definition of *neighbor* to people like themselves. I love this insight from Scot McKnight:

> …the word "neighbor" is redefined by expansion and the temple cult itself suddenly becomes threatened. Subversive indeed.[24]

Jesus expanded *neighbor* beyond the boundaries of Judea and Galilee, beyond a single ethnicity. He broadened the definition beyond his first-century setting. And he did it with one perfectly timed and designed question. A question that continues to force even the most upright among us to examine our hearts and prejudices, our innate contempt for those who aren't like us. For more than two millennia, believers and skeptics alike have felt the weight of this parable and its inescapably disruptive closing question.

Every time I read it, teach it, or preach it, it challenges me. Like the Sermon on the Mount, the parable of the Good Samaritan was a signal. A sign. More breadcrumbs. Something new was on the horizon. Something better. Something simpler. Something for everyone. And thus everyone who hears the parable of the Good Samaritan knows the answer to Jesus' closing question. Jesus smiled and asked:

"Which of these three do you think was a neighbor to the man who fell into the hands of robbers?"[25]

The answer was obvious. The implications of the answer, not so much. Especially for us modern readers. As was the case with the lawyer, there was a question behind Jesus' closing question:

> Which of these three men loved the Lord their God with all their heart, soul, mind, and strength? Which laid claim to eternal life?

After perhaps the longest pause of the afternoon, the lawyer finally answered. Why do I read a pause into the story? Because this smart Jew knew the moment he answered that question out loud, he would be accountable for his words.

> The expert in the law replied, "The one who had mercy on him."

Apparently he couldn't bring himself to utter the ethnic identity of the hero. It was the Samaritan. It was the Samaritan who showed mercy. It was the Samaritan who laid claim to eternal life. Then, to add insult to injury, Jesus said:

> "Go and do likewise."[26]

Be the Samaritan.

No applause this time.

Stunned silence.

Something had changed.

Neighbor-love had no ethnic or geographical limits. Neighbor-love was evidence of God-love. It would be difficult to find a work-around or a loophole for this. If loving one's neighbor was the ultimate expression of one's love and devotion to God, the temple and everything associated with it suddenly became less important.

Perhaps unnecessary.

This was new indeed.

Public exchanges such as these combined with sermons and fireside chats were designed to prepare Jesus' followers for what was coming. Hours away from his arrest, he finally spelled it out, illustrated it, and then asked eleven of the Twelve to sign on. It turns out the signing table was the table used for their final Passover gathering. In conjunction with the inauguration of a new covenant, Jesus used the occasion to institute the new governing ethic for his new movement.

Chapter 15

A NEW COMMAND

Judas slipped out to run an errand.

Odd time for an errand.

There was still food on his plate.

When the door slammed, it signaled the first in a series of events that would culminate in a nightmare for everyone in the room. Whatever Jesus needed to say needed to be said now.

> My children, I will be with you only a little longer. You will look for me, and just as I told the Jews, so I tell you now: Where I am going, you cannot come.[1]

Several of the boys, Peter in particular, never heard anything after that. Why was Jesus *leaving*? Where was he going? Why couldn't they go along? Jesus was their security blanket. Wherever Jesus went, crowds gathered. Where crowds gathered, the temple henchmen weren't welcome. So if Jesus went missing, odds were good they would go missing as well.

Speaking of missing, where did Judas wander off to?

Jesus continued.

> A new command I give you . . .[2]

They needed a new command like they needed . . . well, they didn't need any new commands. The six hundred-plus they had kept 'em plenty busy. Besides, Jesus had already reduced their entire list to two: love God and love your neighbor.[3] So why add a third? And why now? Besides, what gave Jesus the right to add any at all? Grouping and prioritizing commandments was one thing. Adding to them? Only God had the authority to do that! Then again, only God had the authority to forgive sin.[4] Only God had the power to give sight to the blind. Only God had the power to raise the dead.

Oh well.

As it turned out, Jesus wasn't adding a command to an existing list of commands. He was doing something far more radical than that. He continued:

> A new command I give you, love one another . . .[5]

Jesus made *love* a verb and then used the imperative form of the verb. This was, in fact, a command. As in, go over there and love that guy. Imagine Jesus as a marriage counselor.

> Stop arguing, go home, and *love* each other.

Jesus wasn't commanding the guys to *feel* something. He was commanding them to *do* something. But loving one another wasn't really new.

As it turns out, Jesus wasn't really through.

He went a step further.

What came next was unthinkable. But what came next changed the world.

And perhaps if we would move what came next to the top of our agendas, it might change the world again. What came next made his message irresistible. What came next trumped the golden rule. I call it the platinum rule.

> As I have loved you, so you must love one another.[6]

That was new.

Jesus claimed to be the gold or platinum standard for love. Doing for others what one hoped others would do in return was so . . . so old covenant. Jesus instructed his followers to do unto one another as *he* had done unto them. He raised the bar. This was a whole 'nother kind of love.

This love was anchored in a person, which made it extraordinarily personal for the men seated around that table. When we read, "As I have loved you," we think of the cross. They didn't. They thought back over the previous three years. Perhaps each man in the room was transported back to a particular moment in time when Jesus had *loved* them particularly well. He could have called 'em out.

> Matthew, remember the first time we met? You were despised by your community and an embarrassment to your family. But I invited you to follow me anyway. Matthew, extend that same grace to everyone you meet for the rest of your life. As I have loved you . . .
>
> Nathanael, remember the day we met? Remember what you said about me? "Can anything good come from Nazareth?" You dissed my town, my family, my childhood friends. But I invited you anyway. Extend that same grace and forgiveness to everybody you meet. As I have loved you . . .
>
> Guys, you all remember the afternoon my blood-drinking, flesh-eating illustration offended and confused the crowd and we started losing 'em? Every single one of you yahoos was thinkin' about leaving me to fend for myself. I could have left you to fend for yourselves. You certainly deserved it. But I didn't. And I never brought it up again. Do unto others as I have done unto you.

For good measure he could have added:

> And gentlemen, if you think you've seen me love . . . tighten your sandals . . . you haven't seen anything yet.

FINAL SCORE

As the hinge between covenants, Jesus' mission was to lay the groundwork for the transition from old to new. Summarizing the entire Jewish law with two existing laws wasn't just genius, it was strategic. Just as the old covenant included laws for the nation to live by, so Jesus' new covenant would include instructions for his followers to live by as well. But his list wouldn't be engraved on stone tablets. It would be engraved in the hearts, minds, and consciences of his followers. The rules and regulations associated with Jesus' new covenant could easily be committed to memory. The reason being, they weren't a *they*. They were an it. There was just one.

The one commandment!

Doesn't sound very commanding, does it?

This should go without saying, but I don't hear many folks saying it, so I'll say it. The old covenant commands were part of the old covenant. The end of the old covenant signaled the end of the rules and regulations associated with it. Jesus didn't issue his *new command* as an additional commandment to the existing list of commands. Jesus issued his new commandment as a *replacement* for everything in the existing list. Including the Big Ten. Just as his new covenant fulfilled and replaced the old covenant, Jesus' new commandment fulfills and replaces the old commandments.

This is another one of those *don't rush by this too quickly* moments in our journey. So let me restate it a bit more offensively so as to make you curious enough to at least read to the end of this section:

> Participants in the new covenant are not required to obey most of the commandments found in the first half of their Bibles. Participants in the new covenant are expected to obey the single command Jesus issued as part of his new covenant. Namely: As I have loved you, so you must love one another.[7]

How's that?

THE MARK

The significance of what Jesus said next cannot be overstated. As circumcision was the distinguishing mark for a man included in the old covenant, so this new-command, one-another brand of love would be the mark of the man or woman who chose to participate in the new covenant. New-command-brand love was to serve as the unifying behavior for his *ekklesia*. This new command would be the governing ethic, the standard against which all behavior was to be measured for those who called him Lord.

> By *this* everyone will know that you are my disciples, if you love one another.[8]

The term *this* is a demonstrative pronoun. Remember those?

Demonstrative pronouns are used to point to something specific. In this particular case, it's a *singular* demonstrative pronoun. Jesus pointed to one specific thing that was to be *the* identifying characteristic of his followers—the way they loved.

His primary concern was not that they believe something. He insisted they *do* something. They were to love as he had loved. The men gathered that night had an inkling as to what that might look like. Three days later it became agonizingly clear.

And where the heck was Judas?

ANCHOR MAN

Jesus' new command involved another subtle, but striking shift in the world order. Jesus didn't tether his new command to the anchor all Jewish commands were traditionally tethered to: love for, fear of, dedication to God. Jesus tethered his new command to . . . this is big . . . to himself. Again, he inserted himself into an equation mere mortals have no business inserting themselves into.

Woven into all this subtlety was a not-so-subtle shift from vertical to horizontal. The eye-to-the-sky days were coming to an end. The litmus test for being a bona fide Jesus follower was not the ritualistic, day-of-the-week, festival-driven, don't-forget-your-goat worship of an invisible and somewhat distant God.

Following Jesus would not be about looking for ways to get closer to God who dwelled out there, up there, somewhere. Jesus followers would demonstrate their devotion to God by putting the person next to them in front of them. Jesus followers weren't expected to look up. They authenticated their devotion by looking around.

But the shift didn't stop there.

Conspicuously absent from Jesus' new-command instructions was an overt reference to his divine right to require such allegiance and obedience. In what is arguably his most future-defining set of instructions, Jesus refused to play the God card. Even in this final, if-you-forget-everything-else-I've-said-remember-this exchange, Jesus did not leverage his holiness, his personal righteousness, or even his divinely granted moral authority.

Jesus leveraged his example[9]—how he loved.

Jesus' love *for* the men in the room, rather than his authority *over* the men in the room, is what he leveraged to *instruct* and *inspire* the men in the room. On a personal note: Jesus' love *for* you, not his authority *over* you, is what he leverages to inspire you as well. The men in the room would not see him seated on a heavenly throne. They would see him hanging from a Roman cross. It was his gory and gritty sacrifice, not some old covenant, keep-your-hands-clean holiness that compelled his disciples to eventually take up their own crosses and follow him.

That should stop us in our tracks.

A few years later, it would stop Paul in his:

> In your relationships with *one another*, have the same mindset as Christ Jesus: Who, being in very nature God, did not consider equality with God something to be *used to his own advantage*;

Again, Jesus never played the God card.

> . . . rather, he made himself *nothing* by taking the very nature of a servant, being made in human likeness. And being found in appearance as a man, he humbled himself by becoming obedient to death—

But not just any death. A death no mere mortal would willingly subject themselves to.

> even death on a cross![10]

Jesus did not leverage his equality with God to stir us to action.

He leveraged his love.

This represented a total departure from the old covenant. Jesus didn't anchor his new command to his divine right as King. He anchored it to his sacrificial love. Why should his disciples obey his command to love? Because he loved them first. He loved them best. They were to do unto others as Jesus had already done . . . and was about to do . . . unto them. Hours later, Jesus staged a demonstration of love that took everybody's breath away.

Including his own.

It took the disciples' excuses away as well. Along with ours. Jesus leveraged his compelling love to compel his followers to love.

> By *this* everyone will know that you are my disciples, if you love one another.[11]

Toward the end of the evening, Peter couldn't contain himself any longer.

> "Lord, where are you going?"[12]

Aren't we glad John was taking notes?

COMMENTARY

Jesus' new covenant commandment established the governing ethic for his new movement. It was simple but all-encompassing. It was far less complicated than the current system but far more demanding. As we're about to discover, the imperatives we find scattered throughout the New Testament are simply applications of Jesus' new covenant command. New Testament imperatives are examples of how to love the "one-anothers" Jesus commanded us to love.

Again, far less complicated.

But far more demanding.

There are no loopholes in the love Jesus requires of us.

Chapter 16

PAUL AND THE IRRESISTIBLE ETHIC

I don't remember much about college.

The classroom part, anyway.

But one event I'll never forget took place in a requisite history of ancient civilization course. My professor, Dr. Davis, began his lecture on the influence of Christianity in the ancient world with the following statement:

> The apostle Paul had more influence on the development of Christian thought and theology than anyone who has ever lived. Including Jesus Christ.

I looked up from my doodling, certain I had misunderstood. But I hadn't. For the next fifty minutes, he made his case. Later I would discover pretty much every historian, along with most New Testament scholars, agree. When it comes to early church doctrine and theology, the consensus is that Paul's influence trumps everyone else's. Including Jesus. Whether that's true or not is beyond the scope of this book. I bring it up to highlight that Paul's church planting efforts and subsequent letter writing campaign had a massive influence on how ancients and moderns interpret the significance of Jesus' life, death, and resurrection.

But Paul did not limit his comments to matters of theology. His letters are packed with specific, as in exceedingly specific, instructions for how Christians were and are to conduct themselves both inside and outside the community of faith. At first glance, one might suspect our former Pharisee has relapsed and is attempting to resurrect some of the rules and regulations Jesus declared null and void. After all, few of Paul's specific applications are found in the teaching of Jesus.

If that's not disconcerting enough, in his letter to the church in Corinth, Paul admits that one of his applications is completely his idea. He goes out of his way to ensure nobody gives Jesus credit for what is his unique contribution.[1]

So, what's he up to?

DON'T LOOK BACK

If you read Paul's epistles carefully, you'll discover that while he considered the old covenant *Scripture,* he didn't consider it *binding.* Just the opposite. For Paul, the Old Testament narratives provide new covenant folks with encouragement, context, and hope—but not applications to live by. He's quick to point to the Old Testament passages that point us to Jesus. But then he's quick to point out that applying the Old Testament won't score us any points with God. But having closed the door on the moral and ethical imperatives found in the Old Testament, Paul turns right around and fills his letters with moral and ethical teaching and imperatives.

So what's up?

If he's not mining the old covenant for all his application gold, and if he's not quoting Jesus directly, what's the basis for all the do's and don'ts scattered throughout his letters?

Fortunately, he tells us.

And this may be new.

Most Christians miss this because they're still married to, or at least dating, the old covenant.

Here we go.

PLAIN SIGHT

Here's one of Paul's more famous lists of imperatives. These were directed to Christians living in the port city of Ephesus.

> Get rid of all bitterness, rage and anger, brawling and slander, along with every form of malice. Be kind and compassionate to one another, forgiving each other . . . [2]

That's good advice.

But why?

Why should we dispense with bitterness, rage, and anger? Why should we be kind to the unkind and compassionate to the undeserving? Why forgive? Forgiveness is a gift to the guilty. Paul, who are you to set such lofty behavioral standards for the rest of us? Besides, we know your story. You've got no moral authority!

Anticipating our question, he completes his statement by citing his source:

> . . . just as . . .

Just as the law commands? Just as Moses taught? Just as the Scripture teaches? Just as the Bible says?

> . . . just as in Christ God forgave you.

That should sound familiar. According to Paul, we are to do for others what God through Christ has done for us. Everything in Paul's short list is simply an application of "do unto others as Christ has already done unto you."

He continues:

> Follow God's example, therefore, as dearly loved children and walk in the way of love . . .

"The way of love." Sounds romantic. But there's another "just as" around the bend.

> ... and walk in the way of love *just as* Christ loved us and gave himself up for us as a fragrant offering and sacrifice to God.[3]

According to Paul, Christian behavior is to be patterned after Christ's sacrificial love for humankind. A way of life that Paul brands *the way of love*. It sounds a bit mushy until we consider *the way of love* culminated in a man hanging from a cross covered in his own sweat, blood, and feces. We don't like to think about that last part. After all, we're talking about Jesus. But there's nothing to gain, and perhaps much to lose, when we lay a filter over the gruesome nature of Jesus' death. If nothing else, embracing the full scope of crucifixion removes any modern misconceptions regarding *the way of love*. There is certainly nothing soft or mushy about it. Paul, who had seen his share of crucifixions, would be quick to remind us that *the way of love*, while simpler than *the way of Moses*, was far more demanding. He continues:

> But among you there must not be even a hint of sexual immorality, or of any kind of impurity, or of greed, because ...

Because why?

> ... because these are improper for God's holy people.[4]

Not surprisingly, Paul doesn't leverage the old covenant to establish the standard for Christian morality. He leverages the believer's inclusion in Jesus' new covenant. These Ephesian Gentiles were now considered "holy people" or "saints" based on their inclusion in the new covenant. In light of who they were by the gift of God's grace, Paul instructs them to walk in a manner worthy of their place. Everything that follows is simply more application of what it looks like to live as one forgiven by and, therefore, devoted to Christ. He closes and punctuates this section with this:

> For you were once darkness, but now you are light in the Lord. Live as children of light.[5]

When in doubt ask, *What would a forgiven child of the light do?* So simple. So beautiful. So clear. No instructions necessary. Live as children of the light. Embrace *the way of love*. Clearly, this was Paul's rendition of Jesus' final words to his disciples, to love as he had loved them. And this is not an isolated instance.

So, what is the basis of Christian behavior?

The Bible?

No.

Sit on that for a moment. This is distinction with a significant difference. The basis for Christian behavior is the sacrificial love of Jesus. We don't love because the Bible tells us to love. We love because God the Father through Christ the Son has loved us.

THE ONLY THING THAT COUNTS

Earlier we looked at a portion of Paul's letter to Galatian Christians. Remember? The one where he made it painfully clear that mixing and matching old covenant with new was off-limits? Maybe a quick review would help.

> As for those agitators, I wish they would go the whole way . . . [6]

Now you remember.

Immediately following this rather inelegant declaration of contempt for his detractors, Paul returns his attention to his primary audience:

> You, my brothers and sisters, were called to be free. But do not use your freedom to indulge the flesh; rather, serve one another humbly in love.[7]

There's that *way of love* thing again. And again he tips his hat as to where he got this all-encompassing idea.

For the entire law is fulfilled in keeping this one command:
"Love your neighbor as yourself."[8]

Where do you think he got that? Jesus, of course. Taking his cue from
Jesus, Paul ties everything back to loving God and loving others. For Paul, as
was the case with Jesus, everything else is commentary and application. If that
seems like a stretch, here are Paul's words from earlier in the same chapter.

This is extreme.

This is so extreme you may be tempted to pull out your personal copy
of the Scriptures to see if I'm putting words in Paul's mouth. Feel free.
This is so rich; I'll feed it to you line by line.

For in Christ Jesus . . .

That's Paul's shorthand for *new covenant*.

For in Christ Jesus neither circumcision nor uncircumcision has
any value.

Circumcision was shorthand for the *old covenant*. How much value
does the old covenant have? Not any. How much value does the old covenant have now that the new one is here? None. But it's his next statement
that's the show-stopper. This next statement would revolutionize the
church if we took it as seriously as Paul did:

The only thing that counts is faith expressing itself through love.[9]

Seriously? "The *only* thing that counts"?

The only thing that counts is faith expressing itself through love?
Really? That's it? Perhaps he meant, "*one* of the only things that counts."
Another translator stated it this way:

Neither circumcision nor uncircumcision means anything.
But faith working through love means everything.[10]

Everything? Really? Everything? The defining characteristic of the old covenant was circumcision. The defining characteristic of the new covenant is "faith expressing itself through love." What circumcision was to the old covenant, faith *expressing* itself through love is to the new covenant. For ancient Jews, circumcision was the defining characteristic of someone in covenant with God. For those embracing the new covenant, the defining characteristic is *faith expressing itself through love*.

Big difference.

Circumcision was invisible to the public. A once and done. All male. Decided by parents. The mark of the new covenant is visible and public. It involves daily decisions. It's not gender-specific. It's an all-skate. And while it doesn't require surgery, it's painful. Love requires sacrifice, and sacrifice is always a bit painful.

Notice Paul doesn't say that the only thing that matters is "faith." That's the version of Christianity I grew up with. The *faith without love* version fuels vertical morality. Faith that doesn't feel obligated to express itself through love expresses itself through manufactured religious routines. Faith disconnected from love leads to legalism, an eye-to-the-sky, vertical morality that doesn't concern itself with loving others.

Been there.

Stayed there way too long.

The mark of the new covenant is faith expressing itself, working itself out, through *love*. That's an important distinction. It's a distinction James, the half-brother of Jesus, would make as well. He would argue faith unaccompanied by works of love is "dead faith."[11] Useless faith.

REDUCTION

So Paul, taking his cue from Jesus, embraced the new, irresistible, unifying, all-encompassing ethic of love. This is amazing in light of Paul's personality and pedigree. As far as law keeping went, he was as good as they came. He claimed as much:

If someone else thinks they have reasons to put confidence in the flesh, I have more . . . as for righteousness based on the law, faultless.[12]

"Faultless." Not too shabby. Not too many first-century Jews would claim such a thing. But Paul could. And yet once this best-in-class law keeper encountered Jesus, he walked away from the entire circumcised enterprise.

But whatever were gains to me I now consider loss for the sake of Christ.[13]

You've heard or read that before. Perhaps you've taught or preached it. But have you ever stopped to consider what was included in Paul's *whatever* bucket? His *whatever* bucket wasn't full of sin. It wasn't full of secular accomplishments and pursuits. Paul wasn't talking about sales awards or Super Bowl rings. When Paul writes, "But whatever were gains to me," he's referring to old covenant accomplishments and pursuits. His *whatever* bucket was categorized and organized around the Jewish Scriptures. Our Old Testament. Paul dismisses the primary relevance of the Scriptures he grew up with. They were once the gold standard. Once upon a time, his Scriptures guaranteed him divine approval based on the blood that ran through his veins. But compared to the value of the new covenant . . . compared to what God had done through Christ . . . Well, again, it's better to let him tell you:

What's more, I consider everything as loss because of the surpassing worth of knowing Christ Jesus my Lord, for whose sake I have lost all things. I consider them garbage, that I may gain Christ.[14]

Compared to the value of knowing Christ, made possible through the new covenant, Paul considered the things that were once most valuable unworthy of the recycle bin. He equates the value of his past pursuits to *garbage*. Perhaps the best translation of the term is *filth*.

He wraps up with this:

> . . . that I may gain Christ and be found in him, not having
> a righteousness of my own that comes from the law, but that
> which is through faith in Christ—the righteousness that comes
> from God on the basis of faith.[15]

What was of great worth to Paul as he approached Damascus that fateful afternoon was, within the course of a few hours, reduced to ashes and dust.

What was once of great value held no value once he regained his physical sight and his spiritual bearings.

With all that as a backdrop, we shouldn't be surprised to discover Paul *never* leverages the old covenant as the basis for Christian behavior. He'd been there, done that, and was done with that. Perhaps we should be done with it as well. Earlier in this same letter, Paul draws upon the same formula we saw in Galatians.

> Do nothing out of selfish ambition or vain conceit. Rather, in
> humility value others above yourselves, not looking to your own
> interests but each of you to the interests of the others.[16]

Why? Based on what?

> In your relationships with one another, have the same mindset
> as Christ Jesus.[17]

Sorry I asked. That's a pretty high standard.

We are to look to the interests of others rather than our own because that's what Jesus did for us. If you were to ask Paul a relationship question, he wouldn't refer you to Genesis, Proverbs, or even Song of Solomon. He would look you square in the eye and say:

> In your relationships with one another, have the same mindset
> as Christ Jesus.[18]

This was Paul's contextualized version of Jesus' new command. Every application was connected to Jesus' new covenant command.

Less complicated.

More demanding.

No loopholes.

Chapter 17

IT'S MUTUAL

Paul applied this new covenant *way of love* command to everything imaginable—parenting, finances, conflict resolution, generosity, compassion, adversity.

He applied it to marriage as well.

Thanks to the church's habit of mixing and matching old with new, his instructions to married folks have been distorted to the point of being unrecognizable. As you know, Paul is the one responsible for telling wives to *submit* to their husbands. Most women cringe at the thought of such misogynistic notions. Men, on the other hand, shrug and praise God from whom all blessings flow.

As it turns out, Paul's instruction to married people is one of the best examples in the New Testament of how he leveraged Jesus' *new* new covenant command to shape Christian behavior. Let's begin with the dreaded *S* verse:

> Wives, submit yourselves to your own husbands as you do to
> the Lord.[1]

Fun fact: The term *submit* doesn't appear here in the oldest Greek texts. The Greek text reads: "The wife to her own husband as to the Lord." Which doesn't make sense because it's missing a verb. What's a wife supposed to do to her own husband as to the Lord?

That's uncomfortable.

The term *submit* shows up in our English text because it's inferred from the previous verse. And everybody who knows about these things agrees the term *submit* from the previous verse is, in fact, the proper verb to insert here. The point being: the verse before this verse provides the verb for the verses that follow. Without the verse that comes before the *wives submit* verse, nobody would know what wives were to do to their husbands as unto the Lord. So before we tell wives to submit to their husbands, we should probably take a look at the verse that introduces the S verb. Here it is:

> Submit to one another out of reverence for Christ.[2]

I know you're in a hurry to finish this book. You've got things to do. You've got other, better books to read. But would you pause for thirty seconds and think about the far-reaching implications of that one statement? Imagine growing up in a family that embraced that one guideline. How many rules would we need if everybody just did that? Can you think of a marriage conflict that couldn't be resolved if both parties decided to submit to one another, freely, out of reverence for Christ? This was Paul's way of saying: *Put others first just as Christ put you first.*

MUTUAL SUBMISSION

I call this *the principle of mutual submission*. I'm convinced this is the most powerful, transformational, relational dynamic on the planet. The term *submit* doesn't play well in our culture. Understandably so. The term *submit* literally means to subordinate or place oneself under the authority of another.

Can't wait.

What could be more enjoyable than handing over control of our lives to someone else? But Paul isn't calling for an unequivocal, unilateral abandonment of personal independence. This is a *one-another* thing:

> Submit to one another . . . .

In a relationship characterized by mutual submission, both parties choose to submit themselves to the other. Mutual submission doesn't work unless it's mutual. It only *works* when both parties work it. But like Jesus, Paul didn't stop there.

> Submit to one another out of reverence for Christ.

New covenant participants are to submit to one another in view of what Christ has done for them. Paul doesn't instruct believers to submit to one another out of reverence for one another. Let's face it, most "one-anothers" don't deserve to be submitted to. Paul takes us back to the dynamic Jesus introduced in the upper room. The phrase *out of reverence for Christ* suggests we are to submit to one another out of reverence for the fact that Christ submitted himself to each of us on the cross to pay our sin debt. His sacrifice is to serve as the inspiration and standard for our submission to one another. It's that *just as* thing again.

When you connect what follows to this simple admonition, Paul essentially reduces marriage to a *submission competition*—a race to the back of the line. Any man who leverages *submission* to convince, or worse, force, his wife to do something she doesn't want to do is not submitting to his wife out of reverence to Christ. A man who leverages Scripture to pressure his wife into anything is operating under old covenant thinking and assumptions. This is why I don't use the phrase *biblical marriage*. I say Christian marriage or New Testament marriage.

Besides . . .

Guys, when Paul instructed women to submit to their husbands, he wasn't talking to you. The statement is addressed to "wives." So if you aren't a "wife," that verse isn't for you. Not to worry, Paul didn't leave us out. Husbands have a specific application of mutual submission as well:

> Husbands, love your wives . . .

Wait for it . . .

just as . . .

There it is again.

> Husbands, love your wives just as Christ loved the church and
> gave himself up for her.[3]

Where should we husbands go for advice on how best to love our
wives? Song of Solomon? Hardly. Paul says we're to take our cues from
Jesus.

How should we Christian husbands love our wives?

As Christ loved the church.

And how did he love the church?

You may be sorry you asked. There aren't any loopholes, shortcuts,
or old covenant workarounds. Christ loved the church by laying down
his life. In a Christian marriage, husbands lay down their lives for their
wives. Not because of what the Bible *says*. Because of what Jesus *did*.
Real quick, go back and read through the Old Testament and count the
number of times husbands laid down their lives for their wives.

I'll wait.

Clearly, that wasn't the old covenant way. Under the old covenant,
husbands laid down the law, not their lives. Things had gotten so bad
that a group of Pharisees had no misgivings asking Jesus his opinion on
the proper guidelines and procedures for trading in a wife for a newer
model. Their specific question was:

> Is it lawful for a man to divorce his wife for any and every
> reason?[4]

We cringe.

They weren't the least bit conscience-stricken. Under the old covenant, women were essentially commodities. But with the inauguration

of the new covenant, that changed. Women were elevated to the status of joint heirs and partners in the kingdom of God. They were to be granted the same recognition and respect as men. This was scandalous. Peter said it best:

> Husbands, in the same way be considerate as you live with your wives, and treat them with respect as the weaker partner and as heirs with you of the gracious gift of life, so that nothing will hinder your prayers.[5]

We read that and think, *Well, of course!* First-century Jews and Gentiles read that and thought, *But they're women!* It's impossible to overstate the elevated status women enjoyed in the early church. The notion of mutual submission within marriage was unheard of until the birth of Christianity. It's a uniquely Christian idea. And for Paul it was an obvious and logical application of Jesus' new covenant command.

THE OTHER ONE-ANOTHERS

Submit to one another wasn't Paul's only *one-another*. He left the church with some other *one-anothers*. According to Paul, the primary duty of church folks is to one-another one another. Here's his list:

- Submit to one another.

- Forgive one another.

- Encourage one another.

- Restore one another.

- Accept one another.

- Care for one another.

- Bear with one another.

- Carry one another's burdens.

If we were to ask Paul what *faith expressing itself through love* looks like, he might rattle off this list. And if you asked him where he got the list, he might suggest you add the phrase *just as Christ* after each item. This is the short list of all God through Christ has done for each of us. When we decide to love as Christ loved us, it will look a lot like the items on Paul's list. He simply teased out specific applications of Jesus' new command. His single command designed to serve as the overarching ethic for his *ekklesia*.

Love one another, just as I have loved you.[6]

IMAGINE

Imagine a world where people were skeptical of what we believed but envious of how well we treated one another. Imagine a world where unbelievers were anxious to hire, work for, work with, live next door to Christians because of how well we "one-another" one another and how well we "one-another" them as well.

Once upon a time it was so. Once upon a time the *one-another* culture of the church stood in sharp contrast to the "bite and devour" one-another culture of the pagan world. Within that context, pagans found the church to be somewhat *irresistible*. This was especially true for women, children, and the economically disadvantaged.

What was true then should be true today. Paul's *one-another* list should epitomize the reputation of those who call themselves Christians. When people outside the church think about folks inside the church, the items on Paul's list should come to mind. We should be the best neighbors, employers, employees, friends, partners, and coaches in the community.

Everybody wants to be one-anothered. Everybody wants to feel included in a community characterized by one-another love. And while the gravitational pull of vertical morality is always toward individual spirituality, the driving force behind horizontal morality is *one another*. The *one-another* way, the way of Jesus, appeals to something that resides in the soul of every man, woman, and child. The *one-another* way appeals to our desire to be included, recognized, and loved.

So, what if we just did that?

What if we just *one-anothered* one another better?

Why not?

After all, Paul said, "The only thing that counts is faith expressing itself through love."[7]

Chapter 18

DON'T EVEN THINK ABOUT IT

You know who I hate?

Okay, "hate" may be too strong.

Do you know who I have a hard time not hating?

Anyone who mistreats one of my children.

Sandra and I have been lucky. "Mistreatment" has been limited to a couple of teachers who just didn't *get it*, a couple of coaches who thought their boys were better batters than mine, and one unfaithful girlfriend. If you're a teacher, you're thinking, *Andy,* you *are the one who doesn't get it*. You may be right. But that's the point. Even the perception that one of my children is being mistreated touches off something inside me. I had a hard time liking some of my kids' friends because of the way they treated my kids. My daughter had a friend in middle school I struggled to even be polite to because of how she manipulated my perfect angel of a daughter. I know. I should be more mature. But my papa bear instincts are age- and gender-neutral.

Juvenile?

Perhaps.

But if you've got kids, you get it. It doesn't take much for us parents to get pretty worked up when somebody messes with our children. It's instinct. Most of us would die for our kids. Some of us would kill for them. We can't help it. It's just in us. Mess with my kids and you'll find yourself messing with me.

If Sandra doesn't get to you first.

Pray to God she doesn't.

AIN'T NO USE

If you mistreat one of my kids, don't invite me to lunch. I'm not going. If you mistreat my kids, don't pretend everything is okay between us. It's not. You can buy me gifts, send me flowers, offer to loan me your beach house. It won't do any good. You can sing me songs on Sunday, praise my holy name, and tithe 10 percent of your income to my 401(k). That won't help either. Until you make things right with my son or my daughter, things won't be right between us.

The opposite is true as well.

Years ago, during a double elimination baseball tournament in which my son Andrew's team was on the verge of being double eliminated, I experienced something I'll never forget. The game was tied. Bases were loaded. Andrew was up to bat with a 3-2 count. He was twelve. I could hardly breathe and Sandra could hardly look. The pitcher threw a change-up that grazed Andrew's shoulder. He dropped his bat, trotted off to first base. The crowd (about two dozen of us) went wild. We were one run ahead.

Or so we thought.

The umpire stepped out in front of the plate, called the play dead, sent the scoring runner back to third base, and called Andrew back to home plate. He claimed Andrew leaned into the pitch in order to be hit intentionally. Andrew was still up to bat with a count of 3-2.

Sandra gave me that look.

The look that says, *Everybody here knows who you are and what you do. It's just a game.* It's a look I'd seen and ignored a thousand times. I was about to ignore it again when God saw fit to intervene on behalf of my reputation by sending an angel from heaven.

Actually, Allison from Milton.

But in the moment, she was an angel from heaven.

Before I could "ruin my witness" as we say in the South, Allison jumped up, grabbed the chain-link backstop, and started screaming at the umpire. He turned and gave her that look umpires give overly enthusiastic parents and then turned back around to call the next pitch. But she wasn't having it. She didn't back down and she didn't sit back down. She would be heard!

"Are you kidding me? Are you kidding me? You've got to be kidding me! He didn't lean into that pitch! This is ridiculous!"

It was awesome.

I turned to Sandra and said, "I love that woman." Then the umpire turned back around to Allison and threw her out of the park!

Seriously. He threw her out of the park.

We still love Allison. Always will. She took up for our son. You take up for my kid, and I'll take you to lunch. Heck, I'll take you just about anywhere you want to go. You don't have to give me a thing. You don't need to sing me any songs. If you're good to the folks I love most, we're good. We're better than good. You're one of my faves.

I wonder where I get that?

I wonder where you get that?

I wonder if our heavenly . . . Father . . . is anything like that?

Actually, I don't wonder. I have it on good authority he's *exactly* like that. My good authority is the apostle John.

HE SHOULD KNOW

In addition to his unique account of Jesus' life, the apostle John wrote three letters that survived antiquity. Of all the documents included in our New Testament, the letters from John were some of the last to be written. It's believed John was an old man when he penned, or more likely dictated, his letters to the church.

Unlike Paul, John knew Jesus personally. He had a front-row seat for all Jesus said and did. He was there when Jesus called Lazarus back from the dead. He was at Golgotha as Jesus' cross was hoisted up and dropped unceremoniously into the shallow hole prepared for the occasion. John was given charge over Jesus' mother. John was among the first to peer into Jesus' vacated tomb. John had seen it all and lived a long life to tell about it. He may have been the last surviving member of Jesus' original posse when he dictated the document titled 1 John in our English Bibles.

In all likelihood, John expected to see his friend return in the clouds during his lifetime. As it became apparent that may not be the case, he called for a scribe to take down a few thoughts for the church at large. He begins by reminding his readers that he was, in fact, an eyewitness of all they had been taught:

> That which was from the beginning, which we have *heard*, which we have *seen* with our eyes, which we have *looked* at and our *hands* have *touched*—this we proclaim concerning the Word of life.[1]

> The life appeared; we have *seen* it and testify to it, and we proclaim to you the eternal life, which was with the Father and has *appeared* to us.[2]

> We proclaim to you what we have *seen* and *heard*, so that you also may have fellowship with us. And our fellowship is with the Father and with his Son, Jesus Christ.[3]

It was John's firsthand experience with Jesus, combined with decades of reflection, that led him to pen one of the most remarkable declarations declared by anyone, anywhere, at any time. With three words, John redefined God for his readers and, ultimately, for the world. The fact that his declaration will not strike you as remarkable points to just how remarkable it is. What was outrageous and completely indefensible in the first century is assumed by tens of millions of believers and unbelievers all over the world today. But until John's first letter, this concept was neither assumed nor celebrated by Jews or pagans. He writes:

Whoever does not love does not know God, because *God is love.*[4]

Eight verses later he repeats this novel idea.

God is love. Whoever lives in love lives in God, and God in them.[5]

John equated God with love. This was novel. This was unique. This would change the world.

God is love is a uniquely Christian idea.

Uniquely.

No one credited the pagan gods with being *love* or *loving.* They were jealous, fickle, capricious, and entertained themselves by trifling in human affairs. For Jews, God was holy. Separate. Unapproachable. He lived behind a curtain. His love was reserved for his covenant people. For John to equate God with love was epic. Even more so considering the injustice and cruelty he'd witnessed in his lifetime.

Scholars believe John penned or dictated this document after the destruction of the temple in Jerusalem. The horror and loss of life associated with that event alone would cause even the most devout to doubt the love or even the existence of God. By this time in history, Peter and Paul had been executed in Nero's Rome along with hundreds of devout Jesus followers. If God was love, there was certainly no evidence of it in John's world. Yet he insisted it was so.

But how?

Many of us have a difficult time believing *God is love* in light of the suffering we read or hear about. John witnessed unspeakable horrors firsthand. Yet he concludes, God is love. What did he know that we miss?

PICTURE-PERFECT

On the night of his arrest, Jesus was asked by Philip, in the presence of the Twelve, to show them the Father. Jesus responded:

> Anyone who has seen me has seen the Father.[6]

Translated, *I'm as good as it gets.* Look past me and you'll miss him. Stop short of me, you'll miss him. In this life, I'm as close as you'll get to knowing and understanding the Father.

Blasphemous, to be sure.

But a few days after watching Jesus die, John would find himself face to face with his resurrected friend. His Lord. When someone predicts his own death and resurrection and pulls it off, you roll with pretty much whatever he says. If Jesus was, in fact, God in a bod, if he was as close as mere mortals would get to knowing or understanding God, it's no wonder John concluded *God is love.* After all . . .

Jesus was love.

If there is no greater demonstration of love than laying down one's life for a friend, Jesus was love personified. If Jesus was God personified, and if the Father was anything like the Son, John's declaration made perfect sense.

John had looked love in the eye. John watched love live. He watched love mistreated. He watched love die. John had clarity the rest of us can only dream of. He did not confuse the cruelty of *life* with the love that is *God.* Life is life. But God is love. Life is harsh. Cruel. Unjust. But God . . . God is love.

HOW WE KNOW WE KNOW

John's groundbreaking declaration would eventually become doctrine for Christians and an assumption for many non-Christians. Understandably so. A loving God was more attractive than the manipulative pagan gods or the seemingly ethnically exclusive God of the Jews. But John's intent in writing his letters wasn't to modify his audience's understanding of the nature of God. It was far more practical than that. John's exclusively Christian declaration came prepackaged with detailed instructions. According to John, God's love requires a response. But not a vertical response. Those days had come and gone. Earlier in this same letter, he says of Jesus:

> We know that we have come to know him if we keep his commands.[7]

Whose commands?

God's commands?

Nope. According to the preceding verses, John is referring to Jesus' commands. Which should lead us to ask, *What did Jesus command?*

> Whoever says, "I know him," but does not do what he commands is a liar and the truth is not in that person.[8]

That's harsh. Anyone who does not do what Jesus commands is a liar. Why a liar? Because he's addressing folks who claim to be followers of Jesus. If you claim to follow the teaching of a teacher but don't do what the teacher requires, you're not a follower and that makes you a liar.

> But if anyone obeys his word, love for God is truly made complete in them. This is how we know we are in him.[9]

This is significant. John claims love for God is made complete, or brought to maturity, by obedience to Jesus. In making this connection, John equates Jesus with God. But what about these commands he keeps referring to? What commands? He continues:

> Dear friends, I am not writing you a *new* command but an old one, which you have had since the beginning.[10]

John's reference to "the beginning" is not a reference to Genesis but the beginning of the Jesus movement. The beginning of the church. John is referring to a command they've had since the movement began some sixty years prior. This command was as old as the movement itself.

> This old command is the message you have heard.[11]

Then he gets a bit poetic.

> Yet I am writing you a new command; its truth is seen in him and in you, because the darkness is passing and the true light is already shining.[12]

Do what?

This command was not new to the church, but it was new to the world. This command, when observed in the life of Jesus and his followers, was like the sun slowly rising and dispelling the darkness in a bite-and-devour world. What was known to the church from the beginning was slowly becoming known to the world. For the world, this was, in fact, a *new* command.

But so far he hasn't told us what the command is. He assumes we know. Or at least he assumed his original audience knew, which makes sense. They'd had it from the beginning. So instead of stating it outright, John approaches it through the back door by stating the opposite.

> Anyone who claims to be in the light but *hates* a brother or sister is still in the darkness. . . . [13]

Anyone who claims to be living in the light of Jesus' command, whatever it is, but hates a brother or sister is *not* living in the light of Jesus' command. The term *hate* gives us all a pass because none of us actually *hates* anybody, do we?

I don't.

Well, there was that umpire a few years back.

The Greek verb translated *hate* can mean *disregard, disrespect, detest, dismiss as unimportant.* His point is that a Jesus follower who is dismissive or disrespectful of or hateful toward another believer is not fulfilling Jesus' command. Of all the things John could have chosen as the litmus test for living under the canopy of Jesus' command, why did he opt for how we treat other people?

How horizontal of him.

This certainly echoes what we discovered earlier in Paul's epistles. It syncs up with Jesus' directive to hit pause on temple activity when there's an issue with someone back home. Again, it's all so horizontal. In the verse that follows, John tips us off to this mysterious command he's hinted at throughout—the command he assumes his readers were familiar with since they'd had it from the "beginning."

> Anyone who *loves* their brother and sister lives in the light, and there is nothing in them to make them stumble.[14]

This is remarkable. According to John, who got it straight from Jesus, if we *love* well, all *is* well. Period. That's it. Love well, and you're in the light. Or to quote Paul, "The only thing that counts is faith expressing itself through love." Believers maintain fellowship with God by loving those God loves. That's it. John is simply explaining what it looks like to apply Jesus' all-encompassing new and very horizontal command. But the opposite is true as well.

> But anyone who hates a brother or sister is in the darkness and walks around in the darkness.[15]

According to John, Paul, and Jesus, our devotion to God is illustrated, demonstrated, and authenticated by how we treat people. The visible you beside you—not the invisible him above you. How can this be? Why can this be? Earlier in this same letter, John addresses this very tension.

> He is the atoning sacrifice for our sins . . .

That's the part we like. That's the part we sing about and celebrate on Sunday.

But implied in God's unconditional love for us is an obligation. God's love is free, but it's not duty-free. Unlike the old covenant, God's love does not oblige us to do something *for* God. He's fine. God's love obligates us to do something for those around us. Why? Because Jesus didn't die for your sins only. He didn't die for your family's sins only. He didn't die for the sins of the folks who are easy to get along with only.

> He is the atoning sacrifice for our sins and not *only* for ours but *also* for the sins of the whole world.[16]

God's love for us obligates us to love those God loves. And who does God, who *is* love, love? According to John, *the whole world*. Turns out God and I have at least this one thing in common. You can't be fine with either of us if you mistreat someone we love. John says God loves everybody on the planet.

Everybody is *somebody* for whom Jesus died.

Everybody is somebody God loves.

To celebrate God's love for me while withholding my love for the person next to me, whom he loves as much as me, is the epitome of hypocrisy. John's version:

> Dear friends, since God so loved us, we also ought to love one another.[17]

Again, this is a distinctly Christian idea. Next time you talk to a non-Christian who glibly states that God loves everybody, ask them if they know where that idea originally came from. It's not intuitive. There's little to no evidence for such a notion. The New Atheists have made that abundantly clear. But there was little to no evidence in John's generation either. John wasn't taking his cue from nature, the temple, or the empire. John had met the resurrection and the life. John spent three years with the "Word made flesh." John was one of the lucky ones included in the "us" he referenced when he wrote:

> The Word became flesh and made his dwelling among *us*.

Imagine that. John was part of the *we* when he stated:

> *We* have seen his glory, the glory of the one and only Son, who came from the Father, full of grace and truth.[18]

Full of grace and truth. John shared meals with and listened to the teaching of a man he described as full of grace and truth. Not the balance between grace and truth. That's what we attempt. That's old covenant. When we attempt to balance grace and truth, we get the worst of both, never the best of either. Jesus was not the balance of grace and truth. Jesus represented a full dose of both. He was full on grace and full on truth. He never dumbed down truth and he never turned down grace. He called sin "sin" and sinners "sinners," and then he laid down his life to pay for their sin. He was all grace and all truth and it made a lasting impression on John.

DOING MADE THE DIFFERENCE

John witnessed grace and truth in motion. It was powerful. It eclipsed the evil and violence that characterized the ancient world. It was John's three-year adventure with Jesus, not what he saw around him, that led him to conclude *God is love*. It was Jesus' closing comments in the upper room dialogue that led him to conclude those who claim to love God must love those God loves. For John's readers who wanted (or want) to add to, qualify, or "what about" his loophole-proof imperative for maintaining fellowship with God, he doubles down:

> For whoever does not love their brother and sister, whom they have seen, *cannot* love God, whom they have not seen.[19]

"Cannot love God"?

That's strong.

"Cannot" is a reference to opportunity, not ability. If I don't get on the bus, I cannot ride the bus. Not because I lack the ability to ride, but because I lost my opportunity by not getting on the bus to begin with. To refuse to love a brother or sister is to forgo the opportunity to love God.

John placed little value on feelings of love and appreciation for God. Understandably so. He watched Jesus bleed to death. He was not confused. Jesus didn't pay for sin via fond feelings and heartfelt compassion. John's sin cost Jesus his life. It was Jesus' sacrificial display of love that paved the way for John's sins to be erased. For John, *un*displayed love was no love at all. He says as much:

> This is how we know what love is: Jesus Christ laid down his life for us. And we ought to lay down our lives for our brothers and sisters . . .
> Dear children, let us not love with words or speech but with actions and in truth.[20]

For John, Paul, and Jesus, loving people *is* loving God. Not because people are God, but because they are loved by God. Refusing to actively love a brother or sister is paramount to refusing to love God. Under the new covenant, we do not love God *and* love our neighbors. Under the new covenant, we love God *by* loving our neighbors. So, once more, with feeling:

> For whoever does not love their brother and sister, whom they have seen, *cannot* love God, whom they have not seen.[21]

It's not the religious hoops we jump through, the prayers we pray, the sins we've confessed, or even the communion crackers we've consumed that demonstrate our love for the Father. It's far less complicated than that.

LIKE OUR FATHER IN HEAVEN

While preparing to share this content with our churches for the first time, I was struck by a thought that immediately brought tears to my eyes. Before including it in my message outline, I decided to run it by Sandra. With no context and no hint as to why I was asking, I walked into the kitchen and asked:

> Is there anything that brings you more satisfaction and joy in life than watching our children love each other?

Now, the correct answer would have been, "Next to spending time alone with you, Andy . . ." But I wasn't fishing for affirmation. I was genuinely curious. She paused for a moment and shook her head. "No," she said. "I can't think of anything that fills me up more than watching our kids talk, share, laugh together, and love each other."

I can't either.

I wonder where we get that?

If John is correct, we may very well have gotten it from our Father in heaven. It may be a reflection of the image of God embedded on our souls.

Did I mention that if you mistreat one of my kids, all the singing and offering-taking in the world won't make up for it? Did I mention that the best way to honor me is to honor my children?

Chapter 19

A BETTER QUESTION

At the beginning of this section, I highlighted the subtle hypocrisy behind asking, "Is _____ a sin?" And I confessed on your behalf that we're all tempted to snuggle up as close to sin as possible without actually sinning. In this chapter I want to suggest an alternative question.

A better question.

It's a question that introduces inescapable clarity to just about every moral, ethical, and relational decision we will bump up against. This question takes us to the heart of Jesus' new covenant command—the standard by which we are to evaluate our behavior, conversations, and attitudes. Here it is:

> What does love require of me?

This clarifying but terrifying question should stand guard over our consciences. It should serve as guide, signpost, and compass as we navigate the complexities of our cultural contexts. It should inform how we date, parent, boss, manage, and coach. It should form a perimeter around what I say and do in my role as husband, pastor, and neighbor.

This question gives voice to the new covenant on issues where our New Testament is silent. It fills the gaps with disquieting precision. It succeeds where concordances fail. It quashes the insipid justification, *But the Bible doesn't say there's anything wrong with* _____. It closes loopholes. It exposes our hypocrisy. It stands as judge and jury. It's so simple. But it's so inescapably demanding.

There are many things the New Testament doesn't specifically or directly address. That shouldn't surprise or concern us. Why? Jesus' overarching ethic of love intersects with every imaginable scenario. New covenant people don't begin or end with the question: *What does the Bible say about . . . ?* That's so old covenant. New covenant people begin with a better question: *What does God's love for me require of me?* Remember, for the first two hundred-plus years, the church had no *The Bible.* Sacred documents? Yes. Officially sanctioned Christian Scripture? Not yet. In the beginning, new covenant folks took their cues from Jesus' new command. The command they had "from the beginning."[1] Everything flowed from and reflected that one overarching idea. When teaching this content, I often ask the audience to commit the following to memory:

WHEN UNSURE OF WHAT TO SAY OR DO,

ASK WHAT LOVE REQUIRES OF YOU.

The commands scattered throughout our New Testament answer the question, *What does love require of me?* New Testament imperatives are examples of how to love others as God in Christ has loved us. New Testament imperatives are not there for your benefit, though you may benefit by complying. New Testament imperatives aren't there for God's benefit. As I've said, he's fine. New Testament imperatives are there for the benefit of the one-anothers around us. They illustrate what love for others looks like. They clarify what's required of those who have embraced the new covenant and the new covenant command. Again, Paul, Peter, James, and John did not add to Jesus' "new command." They applied it.

THE NEW WHY

Jesus' new command obligates us to wrestle with this new and better question. But it does something else as well. His new command provides us with a new and better answer to an old question. If you are a preacher, teacher, curriculum writer, or Christian author, I hope you will pay particular attention to what I'm about to suggest.

Jesus' new covenant command forces us to upgrade our answer to the question *Why?*

Why obey?

Why submit?

Why surrender?

Under the old covenant, *why* was answered with an eye to the sky. Israel obeyed to fulfill their part of their old covenant contract with God. They obeyed to be blessed. They obeyed to be protected and prospered. They obeyed to keep the nation foreigner-free. Old Testament prophets, writing in their old covenant context, reiterated the old covenant *why* throughout their instructions to the nation. Obedience brought blessing. Disobedience would result in punishment, perhaps banishment. Israel obeyed old covenant rules and restrictions for their own sake. With that paradigm in mind, consider this well-known old covenant command.

> Honor your father and your mother . . .

Why?

> so that you may live long in the land the LORD your God is giving you.[2]

Honoring Mom and Dad under the old arrangement wasn't really for the benefit of Mom and Dad. It was about the security and prosperity of the kids. This is the nature, force, and tone of the old covenant.

Unfortunately, that's the nature, force, and tone of a lot of modern preaching. One of the devastating consequences of our mix-and-match church culture is we invariably mix and match old covenant and new covenant *whys*. It's devastating because Jesus' new covenant came pre-packaged with a new answer to the question *why*.

With the inauguration of the new covenant, *why* would no longer be associated with appeasing God or purging property. Jesus followers aren't instructed to obey in order to gain something from God. We obey in light of what we've already been given. We new covenant types don't honor our fathers and mothers so we can "live long in the land" the Lord our God is giving us. He hasn't given us any land. I suppose one could contextualize this promise to mean kids would "live long" in their parents' basement. But that sounds more like a punishment than a reward. So, while we're on that subject, *why* should Jesus followers honor their fathers and mothers?

BETTER WHY

The New Testament, new covenant answer to *why* is always:

> That's what love requires of me because that's what's best for them.

New covenant obedience is always connected to a *who*. Often, the who beside you. The old covenant *why* centered on doing right by God. The new covenant *why* centers on doing right by your neighbor. Or your parents.

If you were doing a Q&A with a group of thirty high school students, how would you answer the following three questions?

- Why is lying a sin?

- What's the big deal about gossiping?

- Why do Christians think it's wrong to have sex before marriage?

Quick, what's your first response to those questions? What's your go-to *why*? If your go-to answer to the question *why* begins with "The Bible says" or "The Scripture teaches," I understand. But consider this: Christians don't "not lie" because the Bible says not to lie. Christians were not lying long before there was a *The Bible*. Christians were committed to truth-telling before there were universally recognized Christian Scriptures. Christians are not anti-lie because the Ten Commandments forbid it. The Ten Commandments are part of God's covenant with Israel. As we've seen, Paul warned us in the sternest language imaginable that if we adopt part of the law, we are obligated to all of it.

What's true for lying holds true for gossiping, adultery, stealing, and premarital sex as well. Christians have declared these things off-limits as far back as the first century, hundreds of years before the canon was established and our Bible was assembled. So how would you respond to a seventeen-year-old who wants to know why he shouldn't lie to a teacher or his parents? While you're pondering that, ponder this.

THE FIRST-CENTURY FOSTER MOVEMENT

First-century Christians developed a reputation for taking in and caring for abandoned babies. Infanticide was not only legal in the Roman Empire, in certain circumstances it was considered an obligation. Case in point, Emperor Claudius famously forced his wife Urgulanilla to abandon a baby daughter she conceived with a freed slave. *Exposure*, as it was sometimes referred to, was not considered murder since technically the child had some chance of survival. If the fates chose for a child to survive, so be it. The fates decided. Parents were guiltless. It was common practice for mothers to abandon their newborns on the banks of a river, on the edge of a forest, or outside the protective walls of a village. Babies were left to starve, freeze, or be eaten by wild animals.

Babies were abandoned for a variety of reasons, including birth defects, suspicion of infidelity, economics, and, as is the case in parts of the world today, gender. A letter dating from some time in the first century illustrates the detached indifference many in Rome had toward newborns. We don't know who wrote this letter. It appears to be sent by a husband to his wife while he was away on a work assignment:

> I am still in Alexandria . . . I beg and plead with you to take care of our little child, and as soon as we receive wages, I will send them to you. In the meantime, if (good fortune to you!) you give birth, if it is a boy, let it live; if it is a girl, expose it.

No discussion. No *wait till I get home and we'll decide*. If it's a girl, expose—not her—but "it."

Christians rejected and condemned infanticide from the beginning. The Didache, a first-century Christian handbook of sorts, states, *"You shall not kill that which is born."* This sentiment was echoed by church fathers and apologists. But early Christians took it a step further. They visited the sites where children were commonly abandoned and took exposed children home to raise as their own.

Why?

Rescuing abandoned babies isn't commanded or even commended in the New Testament. Food was scarce and expensive. Homes were small. Babies died all the time. Why would anyone put their own family in jeopardy on behalf of an abandoned child?

Christian Scripture didn't require it.

Jewish Scriptures didn't require it.

First-century Jesus followers were convinced *love* required it.

Long before there were chapters and verses, there existed an expression of sacrificial love that would eventually capture the attention of the empire. In the year AD 318, Emperor Constantine declared infanticide a crime. In AD 374, under Emperor Valentinian, exposure became a capital offense. A pitiless ritual practiced by pagan parents for hundreds of years in multiple cultures was eventually considered criminal through the influence of Christians who simply did what they were convinced love required.

Okay, back to you.

YOUR TURN

What are you going to tell those high school students who want to know *why* they shouldn't lie?

Here's the new covenant approach to the topic of truth-telling. There are at least three reasons Christians shouldn't lie. First, lying dishonors the one to whom the lie is told. Lying communicates *protecting me* is more important than *honoring you*. Secondly, lying devalues the recipient. Lying says, *You're not worth the truth*. Lastly, lying breaks the relationship. When my children were young, this was the reason I gave for why they should never tell a lie. If they heard it once, they heard it a thousand times, "The worst thing you can do is tell a lie. Lying will break our relationship." When Andrew was six, the two of us were driving somewhere and he was in the backseat thinking. I could always tell when Andrew was thinking. Sure enough, "Dad," he said, "I know something worse than telling a lie."

"Really? What's that?"

"Worshipping the devil."

Hard to argue with that. So from that point on lying was the *second* worst thing a person could do.

So, there are at least three good reasons *Christians* shouldn't lie. What do those three things have to do with being a Christian? Everything. Let's start with honor. Christians believe God honored us by sending his Son to die for our dishonoring sin. Including the lies we've told. If God honored me that much . . . if God honored you that much . . . if God honored my parents that much . . . who am I to dishonor those whom God has honored? Especially in light of the honor he has shown me.

Next up, value and worth. When God sent Jesus to pay for my sin, it was a declaration of my worth, my value. It was a declaration of your value as well. Who am I to treat as worthless those to whom God has bestowed the status of sons and daughters?

Last but not least, broken relationships. God sent Jesus to repair the broken relationship between himself and humankind. Who am I to break a relationship with someone for whom God paid so high a price to establish and restore one? The reason Christians should tell the truth is inexorably linked to the gospel, not a verse in the Bible. The issue isn't that it's written in a religious book. It's what God actually *did* about our lies, our sin, and our separation from him and one another. Under the old covenant, participants told the truth to gain and maintain God's covenant promises. Under the new covenant, we tell the truth to show honor to those God honored. In doing so, we honor God.

This same line of reasoning holds true for gossiping, stealing, cheating, defrauding, adultery, and all forms of immorality. I don't need a verse that references pornography directly to know media that dishonors Sandra or undermines the integrity of our relationship or has the potential to compete for mastery of my life is off-limits.

Why?

I know what love requires of me.

Do you know why a twenty-two-year-old college sophomore shouldn't pressure his girlfriend for sex or for anything she's uncomfortable with? Because pressuring anyone for anything that dings their conscience is dishonoring. Love says, "I'll respect your standards because they're your standards whether they're mine or not and regardless of whether they make sense to me or not." Love says, "I would never want you to violate your conscience for my satisfaction." Love says, "You first, me second."

But what if it's consensual and sexual? What if she suggests it and he's all for it? Is that a sin? If so, why?

What if instead of high school students you were talking to a group of thirty college students? The traditional answer to the consensual sex question is: *God designed sex to be enjoyed within the context of marriage.* The traditional response to the traditional answer is: *Good! I have every intention of enjoying sex within the context of marriage. And college!*

What do you say to that? The Bible says? The Scripture teaches?

When it comes to sexual purity, the Bible is a mixed bag with mixed messages. The New Testament isn't. But the entire Bible, especially the Old Testament, certainly is. But even New Testament authors don't address consensual premarital sex directly. Not because New Testament authors lacked an opinion on the topic. The highly misogynistic honor-and-shame culture that permeated the first century made premarital sex taboo and dangerous for women. For a woman, premarital sex was punishable by death or exile. A woman without the covering of a husband or family was destined for the slave market, prostitution, or starvation. Consequently, there's no verse that reads: *Thou shalt not have sex before marriage.* Nobody living in the first century needed that one. Paul commands Christian men in Corinth not to join themselves with prostitutes. Odds are, your hypothetical college gathering would agree. But their question isn't about hiring prostitutes. Their question is why consensual sex is off-limits.

And your answer is . . .

Here's mine.

First of all, consensual is irrelevant.

Consensual isn't an argument for or against anything. Bad judgment and consensual go hand in hand all the time. I know a girl who got in a car with her drunk boyfriend, knowing he was drunk. It was consensual. She gave her consent. She'll never walk again. Setting the bar at *consensual* is setting the bar low. As Christians, we've been called to set the bar high. Real high.

How high?

This high: If it's not good for him, it's a sin. If it's not good for her, defer.

Serial sexual experiences aren't *good* for anybody.

Doing anything that might diminish someone's potential for intimacy with a future spouse is not good for them or their future spouse. Intimacy is fueled by exclusivity, not experience. Sex before marriage robs the other person of their potential for exclusivity. It robs your future partner of the comfort that comes in knowing you are exclusively theirs sexually. Not only are you undermining the future of the person you have sex with along with their future spouse, you are undermining the joy and security of your own future spouse. Nobody wins. It's a lose, lose, lose, lose. It's not best for anybody.

It's sin.

It's sin because it harms people made in the image of God for whom Christ died.

Besides, what do people have to show for their sexual misadventures? Nothing. What do they gain? Nothing. What have they taken from the other person? Perhaps a great deal. What have they lost personally? The opportunity to honor a future spouse with a history of self-control for their sake. It's a terrible trade. Everybody involved loses. Under the new covenant, you are responsible for how your behavior impacts the you beside you. Consensual or not.

I always ask students: If you sleep with a variety of folks between now and graduation and then you meet someone you think might be the "one," will you be tempted to lie about your sexual past? The answer is always yes. Then I say, "Think about that. If your sexual behavior with people you hope you never see again sets you up to lie to the person you hope to see every day, what does that imply about sex before marriage?" Anything that makes us liars for life is a sin because lying dishonors the people to whom we lied. Beginning a relationship with a lie isn't good for either party. Two divine image-bearers are hurt in the process.

Okay, enough about sex.

The behavioral standard for new covenanters is straightforward: *If it's not good for* them, *it's sin*. We don't need chapter and verse. We have something better. Namely, Jesus' new, all-encompassing, inescapably simple command. We are to do unto others as our heavenly Father through Christ has done unto us. He did what was best for us when he sent his Son for us. We, in turn, are to do what's best for others. Even when less than what's best is embraced as acceptable by the others. Consensual is still sinful.

How do we know what's best?

How do we know what love requires?

According to the apostle Paul, God's Spirit will always nudge us in the direction of kindness, goodness, gentleness, faithfulness, and self-control.[3] When in doubt, max those out. That's what love requires. That's what following Jesus looks like. That's what's best. Again, it's less complicated. But more demanding.

NOTHING BUT NET

As we close this chapter, I want to leave you with some of the most familiar words in the New Testament. More than a decade before John declared, "God is love," Paul delivered a similar message to the church in Corinth. His words are so familiar I'm afraid they don't create so much as a ripple in the consciences of many Christians. We've relegated this passage to weddings and love songs. That's both unfortunate and inappropriate. His words are gritty. Earthy. Offensive. Extreme. Paul's language, like John's, signaled a break with the traditional approach to religion. A complete, as in *don't you dare mix and match* break with both the old covenant as well as the pagan approach to religious devotion. He writes:

> If I speak in the tongues of men or of angels, but do not have love, I am only a resounding gong or a clanging cymbal.[4]

Like John, Paul considered words cheap. Even the ones we sing standing in rows with a hand up and our eyes closed. Great oratory without love is noise. Great preaching, teaching, and singing without love is noise. Offensive noise. For the record, never judge the depth or quality of a person's faith while they have a microphone in their hand or draped over their ear. Speaking from personal experience, we public-speaker-preacher types are on our best behavior when we're on stage.

My behavior at home is a far better indicator of my devotion to God than my public speaking. This is why I bristle when Christians refer to their pastor as *anointed* based on their oratory skills. Paul would respond with, *Show me the love.* Jesus would caution us against evaluating anyone's *anointing* based on the dexterity with which they wield their gift. If there's no love, don't kid yourself. There's no special anointing. John, on the other hand, would be quick to remind us modern Bible readers that every believer is anointed.[5]

Paul continues:

> If I have the gift of prophecy and can fathom all mysteries and all knowledge, and if I have a faith that can move mountains, but do not have love, I am nothing.[6]

"I am nothing."

A better translation would be, "I'm a nobody." Love trumps insight, knowledge, giftedness, education, and IQ in God's economy. That's quite a list. But I left one out. Paul says great love trumps great faith. Never confuse giftedness or even great expressions of faith with spiritual maturity. Remember what Jesus told the disciples on their last night together: *You wanna be somebody? Wash more feet!* Christian leaders who elevate the *gifts* of the Spirit over the *fruit* of the Spirit don't understand the Spirit. A gift is a gift. It's not necessarily a manifestation of the Spirit of God. The fruits of the Spirit always are. And the list begins with . . . love.

> If I give all I possess to the poor and give over my body to hardship that I may boast, but do not have love, I gain nothing.[7]

This is a death sentence for all things prosperity gospel. But without a bit of commentary, it's difficult to grasp the depth, breadth, and power of this statement. It certainly doesn't belong in a wedding. It's perhaps Paul's clearest statement regarding the shift from vertical to horizontal morality.

His point?

God is not moved by generosity or personal sacrifice that is vertically rather than horizontally oriented or motivated. Giving to gain God's blessing doesn't gain God's blessing. To leverage Paul's inspired words, it gains you "nothing." There is nothing to be gained by giving in order to gain. Why? That genre of giving isn't an expression of love. It's an attempt to create leverage with God. And he don't play.

That's old covenant.

That's obsolete.

New Testament generosity is always, always as in 100 percent of the time, to be a compassionate response to the needs of other people. Christians give to people in need because they're in need. Christians are generous because of what their generosity does for others, not what it does for them. Giving out of genuine concern for others is new covenant giving. Why? Because that's what our Father in heaven did for us. God didn't give in order to gain. Christ didn't give in order to gain. Christians don't either. Not the mature ones anyway. And if Paul is correct, if we give to gain, we won't gain anything anyway.

THAT QUESTION

What would happen in the church, and ultimately the world, if we oriented our lives . . . our marriages, friendships, professional relationships, finances, and time . . . around this inescapably simple but all-encompassing question:

> What does love require of me?

Maybe we would stop cross-examining our Bibles looking for loopholes. Instead, we would search the pages of Scripture in pursuit of ways to love better. Youth groups and student ministries would be characterized by honor and mutual respect. Families would live on budgets so they could give more away. Marriages would become submission competitions. While folks outside our faith community may be critical of what we believe, they would be envious of how well we treat one another and stunned by how well we treat them.

People who were nothing like us would like us.

That kind of love moved the needle once. I'm convinced it can again.

But to love the way Jesus called us to love requires a complete break with the inspired but retired, beautiful but obsolete, old covenant. As long as we continue mixing old with new, we will never be free to love as we have been called to love. Until we dispense with the old and embrace the new, our love will be leverage. And love that is leverage is no love at all.

What does love require of you?

In the next chapter, I'll tell you what it required of me.

Chapter 20

WHAT LOVE REQUIRED OF ME

Under the old covenant, cleanliness was literally evidence of godliness. A form of godliness anyway. The Pharisees were constantly criticizing Jesus for violating some cleanliness regulation. But Jesus kept touching sick people and sinners anyway. And to the shock and awe of the crowds, Jesus didn't get sick. People got well!

Jesus was setting the table for the day when cleanliness would no longer symbolize holiness. With the establishment of the new covenant, God left the building and came to dwell among us. When he did, dirty became the new holy. Under the new covenant, the holiest people often have the dirtiest hands. After all, the holiest man in history died covered in his own blood and your sin. Our salvation took place on a hill where the smell alone would have driven us back into the city.

> We would have been most *horrified* by the moment God was most *glorified*.

I almost underlined that myself.

TEMPLES WITH PIMPLES

The old covenant was characterized by sacred places and spaces. With the inauguration of the new covenant, that changed as well. The new covenant commuted sacred. The you next to you is more sacred than the temple mount, Golgotha, and the garden tomb combined. There will always be special places, places that elicit a sense of nostalgia. But sacred? Not compared to the you next to you. Not compared to the lady in your office whose name you can't ever remember.

Paul put it in concrete terms. Actually, he put it in post-concrete terms.

> . . . do you not know that your body is a temple of the Holy Spirit who is in you, whom you have from God?[1]

That statement elicits no emotional response from most of us because we have no emotional connection to a temple. But for the Jews and pagans in Paul's audience, this was a show-stopper. Temples were holy. Sacred. Mysterious. For Jews, the temple was inhabited by the presence of God. Proximity to the temple corresponded to proximity to God. Under the old covenant, certain types of people were disqualified from even entering certain parts of the temple. The temple was a big deal. There's no equivalent in Western society. We don't think anything should be off-limits to anybody. But that was not the case in ancient times.

As we saw earlier, men and women were willing to die to protect the sanctity and integrity of the Jewish temple. The temple was considered more valuable than human life. More valuable than Jewish human life. So, for Paul, an educated Jew, to suggest Gentile believers were now on equal footing with the Jewish temple? That was unimaginable. The implications, staggering.

Like most believers, you probably internalize and personalize Paul's words. That was his intent. Paul wanted you to understand that you are a walking, talking, mobile device-toting temple. The Spirit of God, who once upon a time spent most of his time in Jerusalem, has taken up residence in you. His presence makes you sacred. His presence makes me sacred. After all, the value of a container is determined by what it contains. With the arrival of the Holy Spirit, your value skyrocketed.

It's a bit like Air Force One.

Most folks think Air Force One is a specific aircraft. It's not. Air Force One is whatever aircraft happens to be carrying the President of the United States at any particular time. Air Force One could be a single-engine Cessna. In fact, if the President of the United States boarded a single-engine Cessna, that aircraft would immediately become more valuable than the multi-million-dollar military grade Boeing 747 he normally travels in. Basically, you're a single-engine Cessna carrying a really important passenger.

But that's not my point.

My point is that you are often surrounded by, seated by, and served by, married to, and perhaps raising single-engine Cessnas carrying an important passenger. Consequently, you'll never be closer to the divine than you are when you are in the presence of other Spirit-indwelt people. That's as close to God as you'll get in this life. If what Jesus predicted and Paul confirmed is true, how could you possibly get any closer? God is Spirit. If the Spirit of God chooses to take up residence in the body of a believer, that's as close as you'll get.

God is not out there.

God is in there and over there.

Outside of the New Testament authors, perhaps C. S. Lewis said it best when he wrote:

> There are no ordinary people. You have never talked to a mere mortal. Nations, cultures, arts, civilizations—these are mortal, and their life is to ours as the life of a gnat. But it is immortals whom we joke with, work with, marry, snub, and exploit . . . Next to the blessed sacrament itself, your neighbor is the holiest object presented to your senses.[2]

Like the folks around us, we too bear his image. As image-bearers, we are to reflect the glory of the One whose image we bear. And his glory is most powerfully reflected through sacrificial love for others. Jesus thought so, anyway.

As convincing as all that sounds, I wasn't always convinced. For more years than I would like to admit, I thought God was most glorified through my high ethical standards and wait-until-marriage morality. While those are important things, they are not the entire thing. But you would have had a hard time convincing me of that.

The self-righteous are rarely self-aware.

I should know.

EASIER SAID

I would have made a good Pharisee. I grew up with a predilection toward self-righteousness. It wasn't really my fault. I'm the firstborn son of a firstborn son whose grandfather was a Holiness preacher. My dad's grandfather, George Washington Stanley ... I know, seriously. My dad's grandfather held to the doctrine of sinless perfection. Translated, it's possible to live a completely sinless life, and a sinning believer is no believer at all.

The doctrine of sinless perfection creates the ideal environment for vertical morality and religious hypocrisy of the worst kind. In the Holiness movement, holiness meant old covenant holiness. Clean hands. Don't smoke or chew or run around with folks who do.

As an adult, my dad broke with the more extreme expressions of the Holiness movement. But he carried much of those old covenant vestiges with him into both his personal life and preaching. Consequently, I grew up with a very vertical, internally focused, "come out from among them" view of faith. So, don't judge me for being so judgmental. The deck was stacked against me.

RULES AND RULERS

I was a good rule keeper. I was a good boy, a good teenager, a good college student. Not only was I good, I was good at being good. And when you're good at being good, you get good at judging all the not-so-good people. And as you may have noticed, judgmental people come across as dismissive and angry. Having spent too many years in that camp, I can tell you why. But this needs to stay in the room:

> Judgmental people are secretly jealous. It's such a well-kept secret, they don't even know.

Jealousy always manifests itself as disdain and anger. It's next to impossible to see jealousy in the mirror. Jealousy always wears a mask. Christians aren't supposed to be jealous or angry, so Christians are better-than-average cover-up artists. We sanitize and sanctify our jealousy-fueled anger by adding an adjective to it: righteous. We have righteous anger! The self-righteous justify their anger by claiming to serve as a reflection of God's attitude toward sin. After all, God hates sin. In fact, he got so angry with sinners that he . . .

Well.

Well, in the Old Testament he got so angry, he drowned 'em all. Under the old covenant arrangement with Israel, he got so mad he allowed his own temple to be torn down and then put everybody in time-out. Read the prophets, God's spokesmen. They were angry as Sheol. So, righteous anger is a thing, as long as we hover over the Old Testament anyway.

Here's something else we need to keep between us.

HELL, YEAH!

Judgmental Christians are glad there's a hell. They can't wait for Jesus to divide the sheep from the goats. They want sinners to get what they deserve so that . . . well . . . so they can finally get what *they* deserve. Except they don't use the word *deserve* because the proper thing to say is *we all deserve hell.* But I'm not convinced people who say that actually believe that.

Judgmental Christians use the term *reward,* meaning that in the end the faithful are rewarded for their faithfulness. But if you would have asked me what faithfulness looked like when I was in my Pharisee season,

I would have said that faithfulness meant not sinning. I grew up convinced that professional sin-avoiders like me would one day be rewarded for avoiding sin. I never gave much thought to the *one-anothers* scattered throughout the New Testament. It never crossed my mind that bearing someone's burden was grounds for a reward. But I was oh-so-aware of the moral and ethical purity passages, along with Jesus' parables concerning wealth. So I was generous in order to be rewarded later. I remained morally pure so I would have a better marriage later. I was honest so as not to get on God's bad side.

It was all about me. Thus the *self* in *self-righteous*.

JEALOUS OF

If judgmental people are jealous people in disguise . . . if their jealousy manifests itself as indignation and anger, which masquerades as righteous anger, the next best questions are: Jealous of what? Jealous of whom?

Judgmental people are usually jealous of the people they judge. The harsher the judgment, the more jealous they are. I judged most harshly the folks who were doing what I wished I could do and get by with doing. So, as you might expect, I was most judgmental of those who . . . well . . . it's complicated.

The behaviors I judged most harshly, the ones that sent me looking for my gavel, changed from season to season. Which makes sense. What I secretly wanted to get by with in high school and college was a bit different than what I secretly wished I could get away with in later seasons. That should have been my first clue. But Pharisees are like vampires. They can't see themselves in the mirror either.

If you had confronted me about my intolerance, I would have defended my indignation by extolling Christian values and virtues. I would have reminded you of how much God hates sin. Especially pride. If you'd asked me if I was jealous, I would have looked at you like you were crazy. But I was. I resented the freedom of my non-Christian friends and acquaintances. I envied their carefree pursuit of pleasure. I resented them because I wanted to do what they were doing and my Christianity prohibited me from doing so. So I judged them. I secretly looked forward to the day they would reap what they were sowing while wishing I could sow right along with them.

COUNSELING 101

A good counselor will tell you that when your emotional reaction to an event doesn't line up with the reality of the event, you have work to do.

I had work to do.

The proper new covenant response to sin is not jealousy. It's not anger. It's not even righteous anger. The proper response to sin is a broken heart. The new covenant response to sin is John 3:16. Or, as Paul put it:

> Brothers and sisters, if someone is caught in a sin, you who live
> by the Spirit should restore that person gently.[3]

The proper response to sin is to leave your gift at the altar and seek to repair the broken relationship. The proper response to sin is the Father in the parable of the prodigal son. Eyes on the road, praying for his sinning son's return. Jesus' point in telling that trilogy of parables was to illustrate our heavenly Father's attitude toward sinners. From God's vantage point, sinners are like lost things. If your phone is lost, you don't get angry at your phone. If you do, you have work to do. We don't get angry with things we lose. We get busy looking for them. If sin makes you mad but doesn't break your heart . . . you guessed it . . . you have work to do.

Judgmental people secretly revel in the calamity sin creates in the lives of sinners. It vindicates them. It makes their sacrifice, obedience, and faithfulness worth it.

If Jesus' parable of the prodigal son were an actual event, I can't help but think the older (firstborn) brother would've been thrilled at the cause-and-effect suffering of his irresponsible sibling. The younger brother's failure left the older brother looking better and more responsible

254   A New Ethic

than ever. But Jesus doesn't give the older brother a shout-out. The older brother's response reflected the perspective of the Pharisees and religious leaders in Jesus' audience. Jesus could not have been clearer. New covenant folks don't get angry at lost things.

They go looking for 'em.

Sin should break our hearts because sin breaks people. Every sin comes prepackaged with a "gotcha." My jealousy and indignation blinded me to that. I was genuinely concerned, but not for my sinning friends. I was genuinely concerned they were going to get by with something. That in the end, they would have their cake and eat it too. So their sin didn't break my heart.

It made me mad.

Then came Steve.

DEFINING MOMENTS

Steve was my dad's personal counselor. In my book *Deep and Wide*, I detail the events that ensued following my parents' widely publicized separation and divorce. For a time it looked as if my relationship with my dad would be a casualty of their divorce as well. In an effort to keep that from happening, he invited me to begin meeting with Steve and him. We met for two years, sometimes twice a week. From time to time, Steve and I would meet to share a meal and catch up. During one of those private chats, Steve asked me a question that I made the mistake of answering honestly and out loud.

Never let your guard down around a good counselor. Next thing you know you'll be learning stuff about yourself. Worse, you're instantly accountable for what comes out of your mouth. It's terrible.

Turns out my judgmental streak was not as camouflaged as I thought. Steve picked up on it early in our trilateral discussions. So one afternoon, while munching on a bowl of chips and salsa, I launched into the same script he'd heard me rehearse a dozen times before. I had been mistreated. I was misunderstood. Everybody else was wrong. I was right. I was a victim. How could they? How dare they? The Bible says. My dad has always said . . . on and on I went. Then, with no warning, no set-up, no transition, Steve said:

> "Andy, if you had been one of Jesus' disciples the night Peter denied him, how would you have responded to Peter?"

Before I could stop myself, I blurted out,

> "He would've been out."

Steve smiled and asked,

> "What did Jesus do?"

I was a bit slower to respond this time. This was my Luke 10:36 moment. Remember the self-righteous lawyer who found himself staring down the barrel of a question that the moment he answered would make him accountable to his own words?[4] This was that for me. I knew the answer. Anyone familiar with the book of Acts knows the answer. Steve's question was too straightforward and the answer too obvious to dodge indefinitely. How did Jesus respond after Peter denied him three times in public? I reached for another chip to avoid eye contact and said:

> "Jesus pretty much put him in charge of his entire enterprise."

Jesus forgave Peter and granted him extraordinary influence in the early church. Me, I would have kicked him out.

I had work to do.

FILL IN THE BLANK

In the parable of the prodigal son, when referring to the wayward younger brother, Jesus says:

> But while he was still a long way off, his father saw him and was
> filled with _____.

Remember what comes next? Don't look. How we fill in that blank says a great deal about how well we understand the *new* Jesus unleashed in the world. In the past, I've felt scorn, anger, and resentment toward sinners. Even repentant sinners. Who could blame me? These folks, in some cases friends, enjoyed the pleasure of sin and then turned around and leveraged God's forgiveness and forgetfulness. They were having it both ways. I didn't like it. I didn't like them. So, yeah, my word was different than the word Jesus put in the mouth of the prodigal's father.

What word would you choose?

What would you be "filled with" if you were a brother or sister to the prodigal? What word would your church or denomination put in that blank?

> But while he was still a long way off, his father saw him and was
> filled with *compassion*.

According to Jesus, the proper response to sin isn't jealousy, anger, or indifference. It's compassion. That's easy to say but difficult to do. Jesus knew that. In the end, he put his life where his mouth was. Again, Paul said it best:

> You see, at just the right time, when we were still powerless,
> Christ died for the ungodly.

Still powerless.

> Very rarely will anyone die for a righteous person, though for a
> good person someone might possibly dare to die.
>   But God demonstrates his own love for us in this: While we
> were still sinners . . .

Before we began our journey home.

> But God demonstrates his own love for us in this: While we
> were still sinners Christ died for us.[5]

Sin should break our hearts because sin breaks people and broken people break the Father's heart. That's the new covenant. That's the new way. That's the way of love. The way of Jesus. The way of his followers. The old covenant said, *Stone him.* The new covenant said, *Take him back, swine smell and all.*

It took me far too long to realize I can't be *for* people far from God until I feel what the Father feels toward people who are far from him. He's not angry. He's not jealous. He's certainly not indifferent. He's brokenhearted. He's got his eyes on the road.

So yeah, I had work to do.

I despised the Pharisee in me. The sin in me was far less excusable and of far greater consequence than the sin I was so quick to point out and call out in others. After my chips-and-salsa chat with Steve, the New Testament took on a different flavor. I saw what I had always seen, but more. Much more.

Moral and ethical purity was still important, but I discovered there was more to faithfulness than fidelity. There was more to following Jesus than staying out of trouble. And where had these *one-anothers* been all my life? Slowly, I laid down my old-covenant-mix-and-match approach to faith. I became less prone to sizing people up and writing them off. I began trading vertical for horizontal. Faith became more relational and less transactional. Not surprisingly, I found this new approach to be less complicated but . . . altogether more demanding. Engaging with an invisible God alone in my favorite quiet time spot is far less demanding than one-anothering people. But one-anothering was what love required of me. It was what Jesus required of me. Heck, it was what he had done for me!

BELIEVING AND BEHAVING

I'm not always sure what to believe.

My views on a variety of topics have morphed, evolved, or completely changed through the years. This includes my views on parenting, politics, marriage, pastoring, leadership, and money, just to name a few. One of the humbling things about being a preacher is that my views on just about everything are documented somewhere on a hard drive, CD, or a cassette tape. Every preacher I know wishes they could go back and re-preach, un-preach, or delete some old messages. We meant well. But then life happened. Kids happened. Tragedy struck. We grew. We matured. We saw the world differently. God didn't change. The world didn't necessarily change. *We* changed. But those old sermons live on forever somewhere.

I certainly hope my views and beliefs have matured. I hope they more accurately reflect the reality of our Father's world. I hope my views are in better sync with how God intends things to work. But regardless of my progress, there will always be a journey ahead. Even the apostle Paul, with all his mind-bending insight, wisdom, and experience, acknowledged this.

> For we know in part and we prophesy in part, but when completeness comes, what is in part disappears.[6]

Apparently, "completeness" hadn't come yet. Even for Paul.

> For now we see only a reflection as in a mirror; then we shall see face to face. Now I know in part; then I shall know fully, even as I am fully known.[7]

That's encouraging. Paul only knew "in part." Paul, who spent time with Peter, John, and James. Paul, who had the original Damascus Road experience. Paul, who provided us with half the New Testament. If Paul only knew in part, what do I know? What do you know? On our best days, we know "in part." But the part that makes these statements so fascinating is the context. These statements appear at the end of Paul's famous love chapter. They are sandwiched between the following:

Love never fails. But where there are prophecies, they will cease; where there are tongues, they will be stilled; where there is knowledge, it will pass away.[8]

And now these three remain: faith, hope and love. But the greatest of these is love.[9]

His meaning could not be clearer.

We know what we know, but we don't know everything.

We see what we see, but we can't see everything.

Once we've learned all we can learn, there will still be more to learn.

We believe what we believe, but our beliefs are limited by what we know, see, and experience. Yet while our knowledge and beliefs are in flux, one thing is not. There is one thing that transcends our limited knowledge, insight, and experience.

Love.

Love fills the gaps. Love reduces the friction created by our limited insight, knowledge, and judgment-inhibiting experiences. Love works in spite of the limitations imposed by the era in which we live. There is much I don't know. There are things I'll never understand. My ignorance limits my abilities and reduces my opportunities. But ignorance does not impede my capacity to put others first.

So while I'm not always sure what to believe, and while my views on a variety of things continue to mature and change, I almost always know what *love requires of me*.

So do you.

How remarkable that our first-century Savior reduced all of life to one trans-generationally relevant, unchangeable command that has the potential to change everything in spite of how things change. Once upon a time—an illiterate, geocentric, Acetominophen-free time—there was a group of Jesus followers who had little else to go on.

Their views about most things were wrong. But they knew what love required of them.

Apparently, that was enough.

Apparently, it's enough for us as well.

SECTION 4

A New Approach

INTRODUCTION

So here's something I probably should have told you up front but chose not to.

Everything we've discussed so far was written to prepare you for what lies ahead.

I'm convinced what follows is extraordinarily important for the church in the West, especially as it relates to reaching the next generation and *re*reaching the current one. You may find what follows curious or even unnecessary. If you attend a church designed for church people, you may very well be one among those many. If you can't remember the last time you prayed for someone far from God by name or if you can't remember the last time you invited an unchurched person to church . . . and it hasn't bothered you until I brought it up . . . you may find what follows strange at best and heretical at worst.

But . . .

But if you're part of a faith community that cares about the rest of your community . . . if your heart is broken over the faithlessness of a friend, coworker, or family member . . . if you're concerned about the faith of the next generation . . . and if you're open to reevaluating the approach to faith you were raised on . . . what follows may feel like a breath of fresh, life-giving air.

Why?

Every generation of Christians is required to engage their generation with the new covenant claims of Jesus. Peter said it best.

> But in your hearts revere Christ as Lord. Always be prepared to give an answer to everyone who asks you to give the reason for the hope that you have.[1]

The word *answer* in our English Bibles comes from the Greek term *apologia*, from which we get our English words *apology* and *apologetics*. So as not to miss the important connection between the two ideas in Peter's statement, I'll mix 'em up a bit.

> Always be prepared to provide an explanation to everyone who asks you to explain why you've chosen to put your hope in Christ and make him your Lord.

Every generation of believers must be prepared to defend their decision to follow Jesus. But Peter's exhortation implies something else. Something we dare not miss. Every generation of believers must be prepared to explain their decision to follow Jesus *in* their generation *to* their generation out of concern *for* their generation. Peter knew that. He wanted to make sure his original audience knew it as well. So he adds:

> But do this with gentleness and respect[2] keeping a clear conscience, so that those who speak maliciously against your good behavior in Christ may be ashamed of their slander.[3]

So there it is.

Our new covenant marching orders.

We're to be prepared with a verbal explanation for why we've chosen to follow Jesus. And while we make our reasons known, we're to live in such a way that our behavior underscores rather than undermines our message. There was a time when *the Bible says* was reason enough. And while it may still be reason enough for you, it's no reason at all for a significant percentage of the population.

RETRO

In this final leg of our journey, I lay out an approach for defending our hope in a culture where *the Bible says* may at best be considered a statement of fact but not an argument for or against anything in particular. Back in the day, churches taught folks to share their faith. The presentations assumed receptivity to and respect for the Bible. In a culture that was receptive and respectful, those systems bore fruit. This generation requires lower rungs on the ladder. Unfortunately, this generation requires something else as well.

Some unlearning.

Many, perhaps most, folks who've walked away from faith walked away for reasons that had virtually nothing to do with the *new* Jesus introduced. They walked away from a version of Christianity anchored to and supported by the old covenant. It's a version best described as a house of cards. If the earth wasn't created in six days, why should anyone believe Jesus rose after three? The correct answer is because two thousand years ago, God entered history. The Word became flesh and dwelt among us. And the "us" it dwelt among documented it for the rest of us.

While that's not the answer most of us were taught to give, it's the answer the next generation must be equipped to give.

Besides.

Once upon a time, that answer turned the world upside down.

Chapter 21

Dorothy Was Right

In 2015, I took seven staff members to Nashville to attend an ERLC conference. The ERLC, short for The Ethics & Religious Liberty Commission, is the public policy arm of the Southern Baptist Convention (SBC). The SBC is the largest Protestant denomination in the United States. It's made up of over 43,000 churches. I grew up in several of 'em.

In the opening session, Dr. Al Mohler, president of the Southern Baptist Theological Seminary, made a comment that took my breath away. Nobody else in the room seemed the least bit bothered. I wrote it down and then went back and listened to the session again online to make sure I heard correctly. Speaking specifically about Southern Baptist churches, he stated:

> The vast majority of people who've ever been baptized by our people are our own offspring. We've never been very evangelistic in terms of people who weren't those to whom we gave birth.

What?

The SBC has never been evangelistic beyond people to whom they gave birth? If that's the case, and he should know, it seems to me my friends in the SBC, along with conservative churches everywhere, need to hit pause and rethink things.

Perhaps everything.

It's no secret the religious landscape in America has shifted. Fewer and fewer Americans are self-identifying as Christians, while more and more are identifying as religiously unaffiliated. As you've heard by now, this group has been nicknamed the "nones" because they check "None of the Above" on religious affiliation surveys. According to Pew Research Center's *2014 Religious Landscape Study*, nearly a quarter of Americans claim no religious affiliation, representing a seven-point jump in just seven years. Nones represent nearly 23 percent of Americans. Think about that…23 percent. That's just under fifty-six million people. Young Americans are more likely to be religiously unaffiliated than older Americans, with millennials comprising 44 percent of the nones. Translated:

> Millennials are walking away from the faith they grew up with
> in record numbers.[1]

Chances are you're related to a none or two. You certainly know a few. You probably drove a few future nones to church camp. You gave some current nones their first Bibles. You know their parents—their heartbroken, disappointed, frightened parents. You may be one of those parents.

Surveys, podcasts, and blogs leave one with the distinct impression that the version of faith this generation of nones grew up with left them unprepared for the rigors and questions of academia and adulthood. This is especially true for those who pursue education beyond high school. The de-churched exited church because they found the version of Christianity they grew up with unconvincing, uninspiring, and, ultimately, *un*—as in not believable.

It's important to note, however, de-churched folks don't perceive their version of Christianity a *version* of anything. For them, the version of Christianity they were raised on and later abandoned *is* Christianity. They've concluded Christianity is ill-suited for the undeniable realities, both scientific and sociological, of the world in which they find themselves.

And this ain't new.

It's been going on for a long time. So long, in fact, we're past the tipping point. We are officially *post*, as in *after*, Christian. We live in a *post-Christian* culture.

TRENDING POSTAL

Former *National Review* editor John O'Sullivan provides the following definition of post-Christianity:

> A post-Christian society is not merely a society in which agnosticism or atheism is the prevailing fundamental belief. It is a society rooted in the history, culture, and practices of Christianity but in which the religious beliefs of Christianity have been either rejected or, worse, forgotten.[2]

In a non-Christian society, the majority may have never heard the gospel and, therefore, have few to no preconceived notions about Christianity or the Bible. A post-Christian society is the opposite. In a post-Christian society, the majority have been exposed to Christianity (in our case, for generations) but are opting out for a different worldview—a different narrative through which to make sense of the world. In post-Christian society, people know the stories. They just don't believe 'em. Or they don't believe 'em *anymore*.

According to the Barna Group, 48 percent of Americans qualify as "post-Christian."[3] Forty-eight percent. Bottom line: many, perhaps most, of the nones in America have had some connection to Christianity in their pasts but have rejected it. They're not *non-Christians* in the way the church is accustomed to thinking about non-Christians. They're post-Christians. That's a whole 'nother thing. This group has been there, done that, and has a closetful of camp T-shirts to show for it.

For post-Christians, science, philosophy, and reason are the go-tos for worldviews and decision making. Post-Christians, especially post-Christian millennials, have low to no tolerance for faith-based answers to fact-based questions. At the same time, like most of us, they aren't exactly on a truth quest either. They're on a happiness quest. Many walked away from faith because faith didn't make them happy. That's never a presenting reason. Nobody wants to appear that shallow. But scratch beneath the surface and you'll find the quest for happiness plays a big role. When faith becomes an impediment to happiness, good-bye faith.

The seemingly irrational, anti-science version of faith many were brought up on makes the departure that much easier. The reason our evangelistic endeavors result in more recycling than conversion is our methods and approaches assume non-Christian rather than post-Christian.

That must change.

If we're going to reach unchurched, under-churched, de-churched, and post-churched folks with the new covenant, new command message of Jesus in a culture that's trending post-Christian, we must rethink our *approach*. The right message with the wrong approach yields the wrong results. This is why parents obsess over how to *approach* their kids on certain topics. They know what needs to be communicated. But the wrong approach has the potential to send an important conversation in the wrong direction.

But there's another reason parents obsess over their approach.

They care.

When you care about someone, you're never content to simply make your point. When you care about someone, your goal is to make a difference. So you think long and hard about your approach.

The approach I'll unpack and recommend in the remainder of this book is neither new nor original. It's modeled on the approach of the earliest Christian evangelists—the ones who turned the world upside down and who against all odds fueled a movement that captured the attention and, ultimately, the participation of the pagan world both inside and outside the Roman Empire.

So yeah, I feel pretty good about it.

But before that, there's this.

POST-CHRISTIANS AND THE BIBLE

When asked about their view of Scripture, 72 percent of nones said it was *not* the Word of God.

More people have more questions about the origins, relevance, and authority of the Scriptures . . . the steady rise of skepticism is creating a cultural atmosphere that is becoming unfriendly—sometimes even hostile—to claims of faith. In a society that venerates science and rationalism, it is an increasingly hard pill to swallow that an eclectic assortment of ancient stories, poems, sermons, prophecies, and letters, written and compiled over the course of 3,000 years, is somehow the sacred "Word of God."[4]

That's the bad news.

Here's the good news.

And now you'll understand why I spent so much of your valuable reading time trying to pry you away from all things old covenant. Again, here's the good news.

The foundation of our faith isn't "an eclectic assortment of ancient stories, poems, sermons, prophecies, and letters, written and compiled over the course of 3,000 years." The foundation of our faith isn't even an *inspired* assortment of ancient stories, poems, sermons, prophecies, and letters, written and compiled over the course of 3,000 years.

The foundation of our faith isn't an assortment of anything.

But the majority of Christians *believe* it is.

And the majority of post-Christians *thought* it was.

So they left.

ODDS ARE

In 2011, 10 percent of Americans qualified as skeptics when it came to the Bible. In 2016, just five years later, that number had more than doubled. Currently, 22 percent of Americans do not believe the Bible has any divine underpinnings.[5] But the current *percentage* is not the real story. The real story is the current *rate* at which culture is dismissing the Bible as uninspired, untrue, and irrelevant.

But it doesn't stop there.

Twenty-seven percent of millennial non-Christians believe "the Bible is a dangerous book of religious dogma used for centuries to oppress people."[6]

Journalists, scientists, and scholars the likes of Sam Harris, Richard Dawkins, and the late Christopher Hitchens have provided plenty of one-sided commentary to support that narrative. When our culture held the Bible in high regard, leveraging the authority of the Bible was somewhat effective. Those days are over. They've been over for a long time.

How has the church responded?

Skinny jeans and moving lights.

We preach, teach, write, and communicate as if nothing has changed, as if "The Bible says it," still settles it. As if our target audience is *non,* not *post.*

That must change as well.

#ILMC

The modern church movement has made church more interesting, but fewer folks are actually interested. The modern church movement has made church more attractive, but fewer people are actually attracted. For years, conservative church leaders viewed the decline in mainline churches as corroborating evidence for their assumption that God blesses churches who remain faithful to his Word. But the defection infection has spread. No one is immune. Not even those who faithfully *preach the Word.*

And no wonder.

Appealing to post-Christian people on the basis of the authority of Scripture has essentially the same effect as a Muslim imam appealing to you on the basis of the authority of the Quran. You may or may not already know what the Quran says. But it doesn't matter. You don't view it as authoritative.

Close to half our population doesn't view the Bible as authoritative either. If we're trying to reach people with undergraduate degrees or greater, over half our target audience will not be moved by *the Bible says, the Bible teaches, God's Word is clear,* or anything along those lines. Reaching post-Christian people will require a different approach. The church has changed its approach to music. Churches have transitioned architecturally. Preaching styles have changed as well. But when it comes to reengaging post-Christians, none of those changes matter.

Here's why.

Nobody in our family rides horses.

REACHING THE UN-EQUESTRIANS

Out where I live, there are dozens of stables and riding rings. Covered. Uncovered. High end. Low end. There are signs everywhere advertising riding lessons, claiming to have the most qualified, experienced trainers and the finest facilities. But I've never once turned down one of those gravel driveways to check out a riding ring or interview a trainer.

Why?

We're un-horsed.

Nobody in our family rides horses.

We're not non-horse riders because we can't find a clean stable or a qualified trainer. We aren't un-equestrianed because we can't afford to rent or purchase a horse. We don't lack interest because we don't know what a horse is. Just the opposite. We know enough about horses to know we aren't horse people. It's not what we do. If the finest stable with the most qualified trainers in America moved into our area, we still wouldn't go.

Post-churched and de-churched folks find even the best churches perfectly resistible. Why? They aren't church people. It's not what they do. In many cases, it's not what they do *anymore*. It's not that they don't know what a church is. Just the opposite. They know just enough about church to know it's not for them. Creating better churches won't change that. And I'm all for better churches. I sit in two or three meetings just about every week to talk about how to make more churches and how to make the ones we have better.

But I'm not confused.

In our post-Christian culture, making better churches isn't the answer. The answer is a return to the resurrection-centered, new covenant, love-one-another version of our faith we've unpacked in the previous chapters. The version of faith that got this thing kicked off to begin with. Unchurched people may not be interested in church, but they certainly want to be *one-anothered*. Especially when things aren't going well. Post-Christians couldn't care less about my new sermon series. But they're still interested in matters of faith and spirituality. And . . .

And this is big . . .

Most post-Christians still have a crush on Jesus.

More on that later.

SO WHAT'S A GIRL TO DO?

As bleak as the stats and research sound, I'm not discouraged. I'm not discouraged because the majority of folks who left the church left unnecessarily. They left over things that have absolutely nothing to do with Jesus or his new covenant, new command gospel. Once we start resisting the things that make us so unnecessarily resistible, they're liable to return. In fact . . . don't tell anyone . . . some of them want to return.

They miss church.

Seriously, they do. Sometimes they show up and sit in the back by themselves just for old times' sake. They long to find a way to reconnect without having to check their brains, their interest in science, or their justice instinct at the door. If we're willing to migrate from our *The Bible says*-based faith and sink our roots into the fertile, blood-soaked soil of new covenant morality, much of what makes us so resistible will eventually evaporate. Against all odds, a small band of Jesus followers defied both empire and temple. Their message and their way of life were inviting and demanding. And two thousand years later, the *ekklesia* of Jesus is still thriving.

All over the world.

So I'm not worried. But I'm not sitting around praying for revival either. I grew up in the *pray for revival* culture. It's often a cover for an unwillingness to put the low rungs back on the ladder. Instead of doing what needs to be done, the revival crowd prays for God to do what he's already done. First-century Christians prayed for *boldness*, not *revival*.[7] Perhaps we should pray for a revival of boldness.

There's a thought.

Nine years ago, I did something bold.

Well, it was bold for me.

WITHOUT WARNING

Nine years ago, I changed the way I talk about the Bible, repentance, discipleship, sin, and even salvation. I didn't change *what* I believed. I changed *the way I talked about what I believed*. I didn't announce the change. I just made it. The results have been remarkable.

It's remarkable what happens when people don't feel like they have to choose between science and Christianity. It's remarkable what happens when Jewish folks are given the option to follow Jesus' teaching without feeling pressured to embrace him as Messiah. It's remarkable what happens when a high school student realizes the creation story is not the make or break for her faith. It's remarkable what happens when you give skeptics the benefit of the doubt.

After all, we all have doubts.

It's remarkable what happens when you allow people to discover they are sinners rather than accusing them of it. It's remarkable what happens when thoughtful Christians, who for years harbored secret doubts and questions discover that the foundation of their faith is not an inerrant text or non-contradicting Gospels. It's remarkable what happens when college freshmen discover that the violence and unsubstantiated historical references in the Old Testament don't undermine the message of Jesus. It's remarkable what happens when a biology major discovers his Christian faith doesn't teeter on the brink of irrelevance based on how long it took the universe to form.

It's remarkable what happens when thoughtful, educated, skeptical men and women are invited to embrace the message of Jesus without having to believe a man put two of every kind of animal on a boat after which God flooded the world and killed everybody but that man and his family.

Then again, it's remarkable how fascinated new Christians become with the Old Testament *after* they become Jesus followers.

The gospel is powerful.

Especially the unencumbered gospel.

In the chapters that follow, I'm going to invite you, encourage you, and if I could, I'd bribe you, to unencumber your gospel.

Chapter 22

NAME CALLERS

I'm obsessed with de-conversion stories.

Books, blog posts, podcasts, interviews, feature-length articles, editorials, Twitter rants, letters, email. I'll read or listen to just about anything on the topic. Like a lot of folks in my profession, I devour Pew and Barna research studies about who's leaving the faith and why. The reasons are all over the map, but for the majority of people, it comes down to belief. Half of currently identified "nones" raised in a religion acknowledge lack of belief as the reason they walked away from religion.[1] Science, logic, and lack of evidence were offered as explanations for the evaporation of faith. But in the end, it comes down to one thing: they just don't believe anymore.

But that raises an extraordinarily important question:

> What *did* they believe that they don't believe anymore that left them believing they are no longer believers?

To tease that out a bit, what exactly did post-believers find impossible to keep believing? What did the de-converted believe was necessary, or essential, to believe in the first place to be a believer, a.k.a. Christ follower? In my conversations with de-converted people, I've never heard a de-conversion story involving disbelief in something essential to following Jesus. I've talked to plenty of folks who found it impossible to continue believing things they were taught at home or church and assumed were essential to the Christian faith. They're often shocked and sometimes relieved when I assure them I don't believe what they don't believe either or that a person can follow Jesus without believing whatever it is they were sure put them outside the faith fold.

De-conversion stories I've encountered in blogs and books almost always involve an experience that created doubt that eventually blossomed into full-blown unbelief. But there's no necessary correlation between these experiences and unbelief. The same is true for those who lost faith because of something they read or heard in a classroom. After all, there are respected scientists, mathematicians, and historians whose faith remains unwavering in the face of the same facts, figures, and findings that cause others to walk away.

OLD VS. NEW

What de-converts find impossible to continue believing eventually intersects with something *in* the Bible or something *about* the Bible. And when it's something *in* the Bible, the Old Testament is usually the culprit. But folks walking away from religion aren't the only ones who struggle with the Old Testament. Right? Some of us diehards struggle to harmonize the front and back halves of our Bibles. But truth be told, most of our challenges with the Old Testament flow directly from our unwillingness to follow Jesus' and Paul's instructions regarding the old covenant. And that brings us to some really good news most Christians don't know.

Christianity can stand on its own two new covenant, first-century feet.

The Christian faith doesn't need to be propped up by the Jewish Scriptures.

In a post-Christian context, our faith actually does better without old covenant support. This was not the case in the first century. And therein lies part of the confusion. The apostles appropriately leveraged the Old Testament to make their case to their Jewish brothers and sisters. But they typically did not leverage the Jewish Scriptures to make their case to the Gentile world. When preaching to Gentiles, they leveraged a more recent development.

The resurrection.

We should follow their example.

When you've watched a man crucified and then share a meal with him afterward, your faith in that man doesn't need ancient props. Current events and eyewitness testimony will suffice. The apostle Paul would certainly "Amen" that. In his letter to non-Jewish believers in Corinth, he lists everything that should be considered an obstacle to faith in Jesus. It's a very short list.

> Jews demand signs and Greeks look for wisdom, but we preach Christ crucified: a stumbling block to Jews and foolishness to Gentiles.[2]

Later in the same letter he writes:

> For I resolved to know nothing while I was with you except Jesus Christ and him crucified.[3]

Why?

Because the *ekklesia* of Jesus can stand on its own two first-century, empty-tomb, Damascus-road feet. Unlike Peter and Paul, we have an additional advantage. Many, perhaps most, post-Christians and non-Christians tend to have a favorable view of Jesus. This is something first-century believers didn't have going for them. They faced the almost insurmountable obstacle of having to explain why their God would allow his Son to die in such a shameful and painful way. By both Jewish and pagan standards, the method of Jesus' execution was evidence he had been cursed by the gods. All the gods. Including his own Jewish God. While modern folks may be hesitant to recognize Jesus as divine, they're not in the least bit hesitant to laud him as someone whose life is worth imitating. People don't generally leave the church or faith because of Jesus.

He's not the stumbling block.

We've put other things in their way.

280 A New Approach

Things that have made our message unnecessarily resistible.

When it comes to stumbling blocks to faith, the Old Testament is right up there at the top of the list. It's usually a contender for second place right behind pain and suffering. That's both unfortunate and unnecessary. So what should we new covenant folks do with our old friend, the Old Testament?

To begin with, let's start by calling the Old Testament something else. I think we should call it something that more accurately reflects what it actually is. While the Old Testament includes the old covenant, it includes more than the old covenant. A lot more. The two most accurate and least offensive options are *the Jewish Scriptures* or *the Hebrew Bible*. Our Jewish friends will certainly applaud the change. Modern Jews refer to their sacred texts as the Tanakh or the Hebrew Bible. Using either of these designations will certainly remove an unnecessary obstacle for Jewish folks in your circle of influence.

Why?

For Jews, there's no such thing as the Old Testament. Technically, there's no such thing as an Old Testament for non-believers either. The phrase "Old Testament" is a declaration of belief. Technically, it's a doctrinal statement. To refer to the Jewish Scriptures as "old" *assumes* something newer or better has taken its place. Jews don't believe that. Neither do non-Christians. So let's take a step back and refer to the Hebrew Bible as, well, the Hebrew Bible. The content of the official Hebrew Bible is almost identical to our Old Testament. The primary difference is the arrangement and titling of the content.

Am I suggesting publishers recall our English Bibles and rebrand the two primary divisions?

Not gonna happen.

But if it came up for a vote, I would be tempted to vote *yes*.

What if, instead of Old and New Testaments, our texts were labeled *the Hebrew Bible* and *the Christian Bible*. That's clearer and more accurate.

Whereas our New Testament (new covenant) contains a description of the new covenant initiated by Jesus, it too contains more than that. And whereas our Old Testament (old covenant) contains the contents of God's covenant with Israel, it contains more as well. The term *bible* simply means "books." The Bible is a book of books. Why not be consistent and make it a book divided into two parts, the Hebrew books and the Christian books. Such a division would be clearer and more accurate. Combining the Hebrew Bible with the Christian Bible for convenience sake is a great idea. But why not call each by its actual name?

A BRIDGE TOO FAR

If renaming half your Bible strikes you as being a bit sacrilegious, have no fear. God didn't name *the Old Testament*. Neither did Jesus. As we discussed earlier, Jesus referred to the Jewish Scriptures as the Law and the Prophets.[4] So did Paul.[5] The designation Law and Prophets included the writings not technically considered law or prophecy. In the first century, this designation included the history and poetic literature as well.[6] So, if you really want to follow Jesus' example, drop *the Old Testament* and start referring to the first half of your Bible as the Law and the Prophets. If that seems a bit over the top, just go with *the Hebrew Bible*.

Nobody in the Bible used the term *Old Testament* to refer to the entire corpus of Jewish Scriptures. As we saw earlier, Paul, along with the author of Hebrews, uses the term *old* when referring to God's covenant with Israel.[7] But neither author used the term as a designation for the entire collection of Jewish texts.

Which raises an interesting question.

Interesting to me, anyway.

How did the Old Testament get to be so old? Who took it upon themselves to rename the Jewish Scriptures? It certainly wasn't the Jews. Then who?

Glad you asked.

Allow me to introduce you to a brave second-century church father who was executed for his faith during the reign of Marcus Aurelius. His name is Melito. Melito of Sardis.

MY FRIEND MELITO

Melito was a Christian bishop who lived, wrote, and bishoped in Asia Minor. While most of his works didn't survive, what we do have provides us with a great deal of insight into second-century Christianity. He is the first person we know of to refer to the Jewish law, prophets, history, and poetry as "old."

Because Melito couldn't get a consistent answer regarding the official contents of the Jewish Scriptures from the Jews in his part of the world, he felt compelled to make a trip to Palestine and compile his own list. Which he did around AD 170. In fact, Melito created the earliest list of Old Testament books compiled by a Christian. Once he found what he was looking for, he did us all a favor and documented his findings in a letter to his brother, or perhaps a friend he refers to as brother, Onesimus.

> Melito to his brother Onesimus, greeting! Since you have often, in your zeal for the Word, expressed a wish to have extracts made from the Law and the Prophets concerning the Savior, and concerning our entire Faith, and have also desired to have *an accurate statement of the ancient books*, as regards their number and their order . . .

Onesimus, like many second-century Christians, was fascinated by the Jewish Scriptures as they pertained to Jesus.

> . . . I have endeavored to perform the task, knowing your zeal for the Faith, and your desire to gain information in regard to the Word, and knowing that you, in your yearning after God,

esteem these things above all else, struggling to attain eternal salvation.

Here's the line that provided Melito with his claim to fame.

Accordingly when I went to the East and reached the place where these things were preached and done, I learned accurately the books of the *old covenant*.[8]

There you have it.

The earliest known usage of the phrase *old covenant* to refer to the Jewish Scriptures. Again, this is about 140 years after the resurrection. About 140 years after Melito, with the creation of the Latin Bible, the term *covenant* became *testament* and the Latin term *testament* smuggled its way into our English text.

Melito was as fearless as he was intelligent. He was given an opportunity to present a case for the veracity of Christianity before Emperor Marcus Aurelius. Just for fun, here's my favorite section from Melito's presentation to the Roman emperor:

We are not those who pay homage to stones, that are without sensation; but of the only God, who is before all and over all, and, moreover, we are worshippers of His Christ, who is veritably God the Word *existing* before all time.[9]

That's strong.

The emperor wasn't convinced. Following Melito's rather direct address, the emperor had our friend Melito executed.[10] But not before he'd made his mark in history as the person who labeled the Jewish Scriptures *old*. The point of all this being, if you start referring to the Old Testament as something other than *old*, it isn't going to hurt God's feelings. It wasn't his idea. And referring to it as something other than *old* may reduce the number of Jewish feelings we hurt along the way.

For my next bad idea . . .

REORDERING

For the sake of clarity, perhaps the Christian Bible should precede the Hebrew Bible in our published texts. Why does the Christian Bible begin with the story of ancient Israel? Consider this. Unless you are Jewish, if it were not for the New Testament, you would know virtually nothing about the Old Testament. Actually, if it weren't for the New Testament, there wouldn't be an Old Testament. There would be *the Hebrew Bible*. Your knowledge of the Hebrew Bible would be limited to what you remember from a college class or seminar on comparative religions. If there were no New Testament, there would be no church. Virtually everything you know about the Jewish Scriptures you learned in church. So while the church didn't put the Hebrew Bible on the map, it has certainly kept it there.

Granted, the events recorded in the Jewish Bible precede the events recorded in the Gospels and Acts. But the narratives surrounding the life of Jesus are more important to the church than the narratives associated with ancient Israel. Christianity begins with Jesus, not Genesis.

I can't help wondering if folks in the fourth century made a mistake front-loading *the Holy Bible* with the Law and the Prophets. As we discussed earlier, when we give a new or non-Christian a Bible, we usually suggest they start in the middle rather than at the beginning. Well, not the actual middle. That's usually Psalms. We suggest they begin with the . . . New Testament. Why? Because if they start at the beginning, they may never make it to the part that makes all the difference. Besides, the current arrangement assumes God. "In the beginning, God . . ." Once upon a time that was a safe assumption. Not so much anymore.

Perhaps our Bibles should begin with Luke. Imagine how powerful it would be if the first thing folks read when they opened the Christian Scriptures was an introduction to eyewitness accounts complete with a reference to a verifiable historical figure:

> Inasmuch as many have undertaken to compile a narrative of
> the things that have been *accomplished among us*, just as those

who from the beginning were *eyewitnesses* and ministers of the word have delivered them to us, it seemed good to me also, having *followed all things closely* for some time past, to write an *orderly account* for you, most excellent Theophilus, that you may have certainty concerning the things you have been taught.

In the days of *Herod*, king of Judea, there was a priest named Zechariah . . .[11]

And the rest is history.

Christian history.

Complete with verifiable names, dates, and events. And twenty-one verses later, it's Christmas! Everybody loves Christmas.

Why not?

Since the Hebrew Bible provides the background for the Christian Scriptures, why not put it in the back?

OUR HOPE

Peter's instructions are helpful here.

Quick review:

Always be prepared to give an answer to everyone who asks you to give the reason for the hope that you have.[12]

We are to be prepared to explain our reason for choosing to follow Jesus. Nowhere are we instructed to be prepared to defend a text or convince people to accept an authoritative book before considering the message of Jesus. Nowhere are we instructed to defend the morality of every event chronicled in the Old Testament. Just the reason for our hope.

And what is the reason for our hope?

On that question we should take our cue from Jesus' original hope-filled followers. Why did Peter choose to "revere Christ as Lord"? After all, there toward the end he swore he didn't even know the fellow. What changed? What happened? What caused Peter's hope in Christ to flare back to life?

The Gospel writers tell us exactly what reignited Peter's hope.

An empty tomb and breakfast on the beach.

A generation or two ago, a different answer sufficed. In a bygone era, it wasn't necessary for Christians to go directly to resurrection. If the Bible said it, that settled it.

Not anymore.

Peter, Andrew, James, and John did not decide to follow Jesus because of something they read in the Jewish Scriptures. They didn't abandon Jesus the night he was arrested because of something in the Jewish Scriptures. Their view of their Scriptures was essentially the same from the day they met Jesus, chose to follow Jesus, chose to un-follow Jesus, and then chose to re-follow Jesus. The reason Jewish folks in the first century decided to follow Jesus was . . . Jesus.

DEBATE OF THE CENTURIES

Perhaps it would help to imagine a debate with atheists Richard Dawkins and Sam Harris on one side and apostles Peter and Paul on the other. Dawkins and Harris would deliver their typical blistering critique of all things Old Testament. They would argue persuasively for a 13.8 billion-year-old universe and a 4-billion-year-old earth. They would highlight God's genocidal directives to the ancient Jews and then turn right around and point out the lack of evidence for a Jewish exodus from Egypt to begin with. They would rail persuasively about the dangers of religion and cite in excruciatingly clear detail the atrocities carried out in the name of God. Here are a few actual quotes that would fit well in their closing arguments.

> The God of the Old Testament is arguably the most unpleasant character in all fiction: jealous and proud of it; a petty, unjust,

unforgiving control-freak; a vindictive, bloodthirsty ethnic cleanser; a misogynistic, homophobic, racist, infanticidal, genocidal, filicidal, pestilential, megalomaniacal, sadomasochistic, capriciously malevolent bully.[13]

It is time that we admitted that faith is nothing more than the license religious people give one another to keep believing when reasons fail.[14]

To be fair, much of the Bible is not systematically evil but just plain weird, as you would expect of a chaotically cobbled-together anthology of disjointed documents, composed, revised, translated, distorted and "improved" by hundreds of anonymous authors, editors, and copyists, unknown to us and mostly unknown to one another, spanning nine centuries.[15]

The fact that my continuous and public rejection of Christianity does not worry me in the least should suggest to you just how inadequate I think your reasons for being a Christian are.[16]

How would Peter respond? How would Paul respond? I think Peter, who had no formal education,[17] might respond something like this:

Fellas, I've never given much thought to the age of the earth. So I can't really comment on any of that. Perhaps Paul can. I'm certainly familiar with the God of the . . . what did you call it again . . . the Old Testament? I know my people's history, including God's instructions to Moses and Joshua. I'm sure the reason I've never questioned those stories is because of how and when I was raised. But gentlemen, none of that . . . in fact none of what you've said . . . has anything to do with my decision to follow Jesus.

Sam, you referenced the inadequacy of my reasoning. Allow me to explain my reasoning. I only have one. One reason, that is. When my teacher was arrested, I ran. When asked if I knew him, I lied. When the Romans crucified him, he died. In that moment, I was like you. I had no faith. I had no reason to believe. I didn't know what to believe.

When the women burst into the room early that morning to tell us the tomb was empty, I didn't assume a miracle. I'm no fool. You ever seen a crucifixion? Of course not. Let me tell you, nobody survives crucifixion. I assumed someone had stolen the body or perhaps the women had gotten confused and went to the wrong place.

But I was curious.

So I went to see for myself.

Before I knew it, I was running. And yes, hoping. But as John and I stared into that empty cave, we didn't know what to think. Later that day, Mary Magdalene found us and insisted she'd seen the master, alive. But I wouldn't allow myself to believe it. I'd just spent three years chasing a confused rabbi. I wasn't going to spend another season chasing ghosts. Besides, I had a price on my head. If I wasn't careful, I would end up a ghost myself.

So that night, as was our habit, the boys and me, we found a safe house just outside of town. The doors were locked and we were huddled together whispering about everything that had happened.

And that's when he came.

Nobody saw him walk in. I swear to you the door was locked. But we looked up and there he was. Very much alive.

Fellas, I can't argue with anything you've said. But I would like to clarify one thing. My reason for believing isn't something I've heard or read or had read to me. I believe what I believe because of what I saw. I watched him die. And I know for a fact, Nic and Joe buried him. But God raised him. And fellas . . . I saw him. That's the reason . . . that's the only reason . . . for my hope.

Perhaps Paul's response would go something like this:

Gentlemen, you believe religion is dangerous. I wholeheartedly agree. I weaponized Judaism. I arrested, jailed, tortured, and oversaw executions in the name of God. Sam, you aren't fond of Christians. I wasn't either. But while you and your friends are content to attack with your pens, I used a sword and a noose. I wasn't content to write about it. I got deputized and did something about it. My intent was to stamp out *The Way*, as we called it back then. And yes, I was absolutely convinced I was doing God's work. Religion can indeed be a dangerous thing.

But then something happened.

You've heard about it.

I was on my way to Damascus to do more violence in the name of religion when I went blind. But it was while I was blind that I began to see. Richard, you mentioned weird stories. Well, this is a weird one for sure. But I'm just telling you what happened. I heard a voice. The voice asked, "Saul, why do you persecute me?"

Well, I had a hunch, but I asked anyway, "Who are you, Lord?" And gentlemen, I don't expect you to believe me, but the voice said: "I am Jesus, whom you are persecuting." Jesus, as in crucified and buried Jesus.

Long story short, I was commissioned by the God I thought I had been serving all along to take the message of Jesus to the Gentile world. Which is exactly what I did. And from what I understand, nobody in your modern world disputes that that's exactly what I did. The only thing you can dispute is why I did it. So, Sam, Richard, why in the world would a diehard Pharisee like me do an about-face and serve the very person whose memory I set out to destroy?

What's your theory?

If you're going to dismiss the Christian faith, it's not enough to discount the credibility of my Jewish ancestors. You've got to discount me!

Oh, and one last thing. Richard, for the record, there's really only one weird story that matters. The one Peter told you. The one Matthew and Luke documented. And if you think about it, it's not much weirder than something the two of you believe. You believe all of life arose from a single organism. Peter and I believe a full-grown man arose from a single tomb.

THE SHRUG

When scientific claims and archaeological discoveries threaten to undermine the credibility of the Old Testament, Christians often feel compelled to either rise up and defend the Bible or look the other way lest they see something that undermines their faith. Both responses are unnecessary and harmful. Both responses feed a false narrative regarding our faith.

Our faith doesn't teeter on the brink of extinction based on the archaeology or the history or the Old Testament. Anyone who lost faith in Jesus because they lost faith in the historical and archeological credibility of the Old Testament lost faith unnecessarily.

The faith of Jesus' earliest followers did not rest on a historically, archaeologically, scientifically accurate book. Yours shouldn't either. Neither should your kid's. Neither should the kids' in your church. If the Old Testament had been written as a scientific textbook or following modern notions of historical accuracy, chances are no one would have understood it until the modern era. Our faith does not teeter on the brink of collapse based on the historicity, credibility, or even the believability of the Old Testament.

When skeptics point out the violence, the misogyny, the scientific and historically unverifiable claims of the Hebrew Bible, instead of trying to defend those things, we can shrug, give 'em our best confused look, and say, "I'm not sure why you're bringing this up. My Christian faith isn't based on any of that."

And by the way, it isn't.

Or it shouldn't be.

Peter's wasn't. Paul's wasn't. Katherine's isn't.

At the time of this writing, Katherine is an above-average tenth grader who recently transitioned from a small Christian school to a large public high school in our area. I asked Katherine's mom to read and critique this manuscript. Katherine asked her mom what she was reading. When she found out, she asked if she could read it as well.

She did.

Fast-forward several months and Katherine found herself in an honors biology class where she was confronted for the first time with the theory of evolution through natural selection. During her private Christian school years, Katherine was taught creationism and was armed with a few basic, but somewhat simplistic, arguments against Darwinism. Katherine's public school biology teacher knew she'd transferred from a Christian school. He assumed what he was teaching was new for Katherine and, in all likelihood, contradicted what she'd been taught all her life.

To his credit, on two occasions, he asked Katherine in private how she was faring. On both occasions, she smiled and responded, "Fine." Her grades were certainly fine. Which may have been what piqued his curiosity. Toward the end of the semester, he asked a third time. "Katherine, I know all of this is new for you. How are you handling it, you know, personally?"

Instead of launching into a defense of creationism, Katherine said, "I find it all fascinating. Besides, this doesn't have anything to do with the foundation of my faith."

She was right.

Smart girl.

Chapter 23

FIRST THINGS FIRST

Question: What would happen to you if your birth certificate along with every copy of and record of your birth were to vanish from the earth?

Answer: Nothing.

Your birth certificate documents you. It didn't create you and it doesn't sustain you.

Question: What would happen to you if you discovered an error on your birth certificate?

Answer: Nothing.

For the same reason.

How would you respond to someone who claimed you were never born because of an error on your birth certificate? How would you respond to someone who refused to believe you existed until you produced a birth certificate? Crazy, I know. But this convoluted thinking mirrors the way most people think about our faith. And by "most people," I don't mean most non-believers. Most Christians are confused on this point as well. Consequently, as the Bible goes, so goes their faith.

One more.

WHICH CAME FIRST

Which came first, the resurrection or the written accounts that document the resurrection? Obviously, the resurrection. Documents that document an event can't preexist the event they document.

Neither do they create the event.

The New Testament documents are like a birth certificate of sorts. They document the birth of the church. They document why the church was birthed. Most importantly, they document the resurrection of Jesus. The first converts to Christianity did not believe Jesus rose from the dead because they read about it. There was nothing to read. They believed he rose from the dead because eyewitnesses told them about it.

When your mama's friends came to visit her after you were born, they didn't ask to see your birth certificate. They asked to see you!

The foundation of our faith is not an inspired book. While the texts included in our New Testament play an important role in helping us understand what it means to follow Jesus, they are not the reason we follow. We don't believe because of a book; we believe because of the *event* that inspired the book. The event, not the record of the event, is what birthed the "church." To say it a different way, the Bible did not create Christianity. Christianity created the Bible. The Christian faith existed for decades before there was a *The Bible*. Faith in Jesus existed for decades before the Bible as well.

But not before the resurrection.

Here's something our Sunday school teachers forgot to tell us.

MIDDLE EARTH

When Joseph of Arimathea and Nicodemus showed up to take Jesus' body off the cross, there were no Christians. No Jesus followers. Sympathizers for sure, but at that moment in time nobody believed Jesus was the Son of God. When Jesus uttered his last word and breathed his last breath, everybody who had believed stopped believing. There's no evidence any of his former followers were planning to keep the dream alive or the movement moving. If Jesus couldn't keep himself alive, what hope did they have of keeping his *ekklesia* alive.

Besides, why bother?

The fact that Nic and Joe were taking a lifeless body down from a Roman cross was all the evidence anyone needed to know Jesus wasn't who he claimed to be. Or at least he wasn't who they thought he was claiming to be.

Maybe that was it.

Maybe they misunderstood.

What's often overlooked is that the reason Jesus' crucifixion brought his *ekklesia* to an abrupt halt was not what Jesus taught. The Gospels leave us with the impression most folks had no idea what Jesus was talking about most of the time. Two thousand years later, we're still trying to figure some of it out. Jesus' teaching wasn't the driving force of his movement. The claims Jesus made about himself were the driving force. It was his outrageous claims that kept the band together and the movement moving.

Case in point.

After that disturbing and confusing message where Jesus referenced eating his body and drinking his blood, many of his followers decided to unfollow.[1] When he asked the Twelve if they were planning to unfollow as well, Peter spoke up. What he didn't say was as instructive as what he did say. What he didn't say was:

> Lord, to whom shall we go? Nobody teaches as well as you do. We've learned so much. Your content is compelling and your storytelling skills are without equal. Granted, today wasn't one of your better outings. But one mediocre message is no reason for us to abandon you.

Peter and the boys didn't choose to stay with Jesus because of what he taught. They chose to stay *in spite of* what he taught. They hung around because of who he claimed to be. Peter's actual response:

> Lord, to whom shall we go? You have the words of eternal life. We have come to believe and to know that you are the Holy One of God.[2]

Hope died when Jesus died. But it didn't die when he died because of what he taught. It died when he died because of what he claimed about himself. His death undermined his claims. Keeping his movement alive was contingent upon keeping Jesus alive. And, of course, he would stay alive. He claimed to be the resurrection and the life. The resurrection and the life can't die. Surely the Savior of the world would have the power to save himself.

Wouldn't he?

Especially from Rome. A foreign power exercising authority over God's people was a sign of God's displeasure. So when Jesus died, hope died. The movement died. There was no dream to keep alive. Consequently, there were no believers after the crucifixion. There were devoted Jews. There were imperial-cult following Romans. But no Christians.

Not convinced?

How 'bout this. Everybody ... as in even his most devout followers ... expected Jesus to do what all dead people do.

Stay dead.

Nic and Joe took a big risk asking Pilate for Jesus' body. No doubt they had to cough up a few silver coins in the process. They did their best to prepare his body for burial before the Sabbath officially got underway. Clearly they expected Jesus to stay dead. On Easter morning, there are no reports of anyone standing outside the tomb counting down backward from ten anticipating a miracle. On the contrary, a group of women left home just before dawn to re-prepare Jesus' body for burial. Why redo it? Perhaps the women assumed the men didn't do it right. After all, they were rushed.

After all, they were men.

Either way, these brokenhearted women, who loved Jesus and believed everything he claimed about himself, expected him to remain in that tomb until his body decomposed, at which time his bones would be collected and placed in an ossuary. Nobody was planning to keep the movement moving. But then again ...

Nobody expected *no* body.

Even when they found no body, nobody believed. They believed somebody took the body, which would explain *no* body to everybody.

PAUSE

In light of where we're headed, we need to sit in this space for a moment or two. Remember, at this particular moment in history, there was no church. There were no Christians. Just brokenhearted, disillusioned, discouraged ex-Jesus followers. Passover had just wrapped up. Jerusalem was filled to the brim with devout Jews. Copies of the Jewish Scriptures were tucked away safely behind the temple walls. Saul of Tarsus was somewhere up north preparing another brilliant post-Passover message. Back in Rome, Tiberius Caesar continued to make a name for himself. Rome remained the Eternal City. Everything was as it had always been. As it always would be. That is, until a handful of ex-Jesus followers encountered their risen Savior and decided to *re*-follow.

> Our Savior displayed on a criminal's cross
> Darkness rejoiced as though heaven had lost
> But then Jesus arose with our freedom in hand
> That's when death was arrested and my life began ... [3]

Something else began as well.

Something new. Something stand-alone. Something birthed in a nation for all nations. Something forecasted, foreshadowed, and foreseen. A new movement fueled by a new covenant and guided by a new governing ethic. The resurrection signaled the inauguration of the *ekklesia* of Jesus. The church. Jesus was right when he predicted that the gates of Hades—death—would not be able to stop it. Not even his death. As it turned out, his followers were right after all.

The resurrection and the life could not be conquered by death. The Savior of the World did, in fact, have the power to save himself. What they missed ... what everyone missed ... was that God would indeed allow his Messiah to be arrested, tried, and executed by pagan Rome. But not as evidence of his divine displeasure.

As evidence of his love for the world.

And so it began.

JESUS FIRST, BIBLE SECOND

This should . . . actually, this must serve as the reason we give for the hope that is in us. And here's the divine beauty of this divinely inspired sequence of events. This approach to faith in no way diminishes the importance of Scripture. Just the opposite. The resurrection serves as our apologetic or argument for the reliability of Christian Scripture.

Let me explain.

The Christian faith began with the resurrection of Jesus.

It was birthed by an event, not a document. A birth, not a birth certificate. Our faith began when a handful of Jesus followers saw him alive from the dead. Just as the resurrection of Jesus served as the reason they would later give for the hope that was alive in them, so his resurrection must serve as the reason for our hope as well. To state it more directly, we don't believe because the Bible says. We believe because Jesus rose!

Why do we believe Jesus rose?

We believe he rose from the dead because Matthew tells us so. Mark tells us so. Luke tells us so. John tells us so. Peter tells us so. James, the brother of Jesus, believed it to be so. And last but not least, the apostle Paul came to believe it was so. Eventually, church leaders collected these individual declarations of faith, including the four accounts of Jesus' life and teaching, bound them together, and titled it the New Testament.

And then there's this.

Once someone accepts the historicity of the resurrection, you don't generally have to convince them to lean in to what Jesus said and did. But it gets even better. When someone becomes fascinated with Jesus, they usually become fascinated with the backstory as well—the Jewish Scriptures.

Case in point.

Before the spread of Christianity, Gentiles as a whole showed little interest in the Jewish Scriptures. Jews were peculiar people with peculiar habits. But as increasing numbers of Gentiles embraced Jesus as Lord, their fascination with Jewish religious texts escalated. Remember, it was his curiosity about the Jewish texts that inspired Melito of Sardis to travel to Palestine. To say it a different way, Gentile fascination with Jewish Scriptures was not fueled by a conviction that Jewish texts were inspired. The Gentile world became fascinated with Jewish Scriptures once convinced that Jesus was divine. They became enamored with Jewish Scriptures after they became enamored with a particular Jew.

The moral of this particular episode in our journey should actually be quite encouraging. Your unbelieving friends and family members don't have to accept the Old Testament as reliable or the New Testament as inspired as a precursor to embracing Jesus as Savior. Your skeptical, unbelieving friends don't have to accept the authority of a book before accepting the historicity of the resurrection. To state it in rather indelicate terms:

> Resurrection is the horse.
> The Bible is the cart.

Most of us grew up with that particular cart sitting in front of the horse. We were taught to believe that everything in the Bible was true *because* it was in the Bible. We inherited a text-based faith. So we grew up believing Jesus rose from the dead because, well, because the Bible says he rose from the dead. This particular cart has been sitting out in front of that particular horse for hundreds of years. But it wasn't sitting there in the beginning.

Once upon a time, our faith was event-based. Perhaps we should start showing off the baby from Nazareth instead of trying to convince folks his birth certificate is accurate.

WHY SO DIFFICULT?

If you're having a hard time wrapping your mind around all this, I understand. Like me, you may have grown up on Bible-first, Jesus-second preaching and teaching. If so, like me, you *believed* the Bible was true before you read it. But let's be honest. What do you call someone who believes a book is true before they read it? What do you call someone who would take someone's word for something as epic as, "This book is the infallible Word of God"? What kind of person would go for that?

A child.

When did you come to believe the Bible was God's Word? After you read it? Probably not. Chances are you arrived at that conclusion about the same time I did. When your mama told you. Or your pastor told you. You accepted the authority of the Bible long before you read it. In my case, before I was *able* to read it! Only a child would accept the Bible as God's infallible Word before knowing what was inside the Bible.

Anything wrong with that?

I hope not. I did the same thing for (Richard Dawkins would say *to*) my children. And I'm glad I did. But it explains why we have a difficult time doing effective ministry outside the circle of the already indoctrinated and convinced. My hunch is very few people reading this book embraced the Bible as God's Word as adults. The few who did were probably predisposed to hold the Bible in high regard as the result of some childhood experience.

My point?

If the church is going to regain the first-century status of irresistible, we must change the way we *talk* about the Bible. Most educated people have an educated opinion about what the Bible is and isn't. They don't walk into our churches with blank slates. They walk in with full slates. Consequently, we must shift our approach. And as we've seen, there is a first-century precedent for doing so.

With that in mind, here's one last thing I'd like you to consider.

Chapter 24

THE BIBLE SAYS

Here's something you've probably paid little to no attention to.

Preachers, teachers, and evangelists are far . . . as in far, far . . . more likely to assert "The Bible teaches!" "The Word of God tells us," "The Scripture says," rather than "The apostle Paul wrote," or "Jesus said." Christians are generally quick to leverage the authority of the Bible. We are not as quick to leverage the authority of the authors of the New Testament or, strangely enough, Jesus himself. This is unfortunate. This approach has undermined and continues to undermine the credibility of our faith. Why? Because supporting our faith with "The Bible says" communicates the foundation of our faith is the Bible. As we've discovered, it's not. Not unless there weren't any Christians until after the Bible was assembled in the fourth century.

"The Bible says" insinuates that the roots of our faith go no deeper than the fourth-century decision to combine first-century documents with the Jewish Scriptures.[1] We would do our generation a great service if we would leverage the actual source of our authority rather than the fourth-century title someone gave to our collection of sacred manuscripts. I know that sounds strange and unnecessary, but consider this.

Which came first, the Gospel of John or the collection of writings we now call the Bible? The book of Acts or the Bible? Paul's letter to the Ephesians or the Bible? Clearly, the documents that make up our New Testament preceded the New Testament just as the creation of the short stories in a short story collection preceded the creation of the short story collection. Consider this.

When did John's Gospel become *inspired*?

When he wrote it, or when it was recognized as inspired by a later generation? Was John's Gospel inspired when he wrote it or did it suddenly become inspired two hundred-plus years later when it was bound up with the rest of the New Testament documents and labeled *The Bible*? If you believe John's Gospel is Scripture and that all Scripture is God-breathed,[2] then you believe John's Gospel was inspired when it was written, not when it was copied, collected, and included. This is true of all our New Testament documents.

My point?

Inspired Scripture predated what we refer to as *The Bible* by two hundred-plus years.

Is that important?

Before the internet, maybe not.

Now?

Now it's incredibly important. What I'm about to tell you may be new to you. I hope not. If it's confusing, that may stem from how you've heard the Bible referenced throughout your life. Here goes:

> The documents included in our Bible are not inspired because they are in the Bible. They were included in the collection of documents we call *The Bible* because of who wrote them, what they contain, and when they were written.

Hopefully you knew that. If you didn't, you do now.

So while we are accustomed to saying *The Bible is inspired*, it is more accurate and helpful to say, *The authors of Scripture were inspired*. That's what Peter and Paul thought anyway. Here's Peter's famous take on the topic:

> For prophecy never had its origin in the human will, but prophets, though human, spoke from God as they were carried along by the Holy Spirit.[3]

Here's Paul's:

All Scripture is God-breathed . . . [4]

Clearly, the individually inspired documents—Matthew, Luke, Romans, for example—predated the collection and publication of these individually inspired documents. Eventually, church leaders recognized these particular documents as authoritative and included them in our New Testament along with a version of the Jewish Scriptures. It was a fourth-century church leader, Athanasius of Alexandria, who was first to compile the list of documents that would eventually be recognized and sanctioned by the church as the official New Testament.[5] The list first appears in a letter dated . . . don't rush by the date . . . AD 336. Leading up to the drafting of this important letter, and for decades following this letter, church leaders debated, as Bob Seger famously said, "What to leave in and what to leave out."[6]

The documents that made Athanasius' list, and eventually our list, were considered valuable, credible, and reliable the moment they were written. First-, second-, and third-century believers took their cues from, oriented their faith around, and meticulously copied these documents long before they were listed, compiled, and bound in gold. During the reign of Emperor Diocletian in the late third and early fourth centuries, men and women were arrested, and in some cases executed, for possessing portions of what would later become part of our New Testament. Clearly, these documents were considered sacred long before they were collected and published.

And this is important, why?

In light of the post-Christian context in which we live, it's time to stop appealing to the authority of a sacred book to make our case for Jesus. In the information age, that habit unnecessarily undermines the credibility of our faith. It makes our message unnecessarily resistible. We know for a fact this one bad habit has paved the off-ramp for a generation of millennials who felt they had no choice but to exit the version of faith they were raised on. The all-or-nothing version. The *non-contradicting book* version—a version of faith that didn't exist and could not have existed in the first century.

As twenty-first century new covenant Jesus followers, we must break the habit of saying "The Bible says" as the basis of our appeal. Instead, it's much better, and more accurate to say "Jesus taught" or "Paul wrote" or "Peter declares" or "According to the apostle John, who knew Jesus, peered into an empty tomb, and had breakfast with him on the beach." I can tell you from years of personal experience, this approach immediately reduces resistance among post-Christians, non-Christians, and Christians who are struggling to maintain faith.

Especially for those whose faith took a hit because of something someone said about some portion of the Bible.

Besides.

Let's be honest.

The problem with "The Bible says" isn't what the Bible says. It's what else the Bible says.

WHAT ELSE

The Bible *says* there was a worldwide flood. Archaeology claims there wasn't. The Bible *says* Israel migrated from Egypt to ancient Canaan. Historians claim they didn't. If there was, in fact, no global flood and no migration to Egypt, the Bible isn't true. If the Bible isn't true, our faith, like the walls of Jericho, comes tumbling down. Except, archaeologists say the walls of Jericho didn't come tumbling down. At least not as described in the Old Testament book of Joshua. If we can't trust what the Bible says about those things, can we trust what it says about *any*thing?

Yes.

We can, and we should.

But most Christians don't know that and most post-Christians didn't know that.

As it turns out, there is, in fact, evidence to support the flood narrative, Israel's exodus from Egypt, and the Hebrew Bible's account of what happened at Jericho. But even if there wasn't, that would in no way undermine the reliability of the accounts of Jesus' life found in the documents that comprise the New Testament. But for too many Christians, their faith hangs by the thread of an all-or-nothing proposition.

Why?

Because of the way the Bible was first explained to them and the way pastors and teachers consistently refer to it. And if you are a bit perplexed that I'm convinced the entire Bible doesn't have to be true for part of it to be true, you are probably guilty of laying that oh-so-fragile foundation for the folks who look to you for leadership.

So, don't go anywhere.

The Bible says husbands are not to divorce their wives, but gives men instructions on how to proceed with a divorce.[7] The Bible says Jesus died for our sins, but that parents must die for their own sins and their children must die for theirs as well.[8] These conflicting *biblical* notions may not pose a threat to your faith. Perhaps your old and new covenant filters are screwed on tight. But my concern here is not *your* faith. My concern is the faith of the next generation. A generation with an all-access pass to all things skeptical, critical, and contemptible. I'm concerned about folks who've lost faith and those struggling to maintain faith. And many . . . perhaps most . . . of the *lost faith* crowd lost faith when they lost faith in the Bible. For them, Christianity was a house of cards.

Sixty-six cards.

Discredit one, and the entire edifice comes tumbling down.

Unnecessarily.

The way most of us talk about the Bible leaves folks with the impression that if it's not all verifiably true, then none of it can or should be trusted. You may be convinced the worldwide flood or exodus from Egypt is historically and archaeologically verifiable. But you won't be sitting beside the college freshmen from your church when a professor with more education than you shows them evidence to the contrary. The good news is even if none of those things actually happened, it does nothing to undermine the credibility of our new covenant faith.

Why?

As I've said over and over during our journey together, the credibility of our faith has never hung by the thread of the credibility of a collection of ancient texts. Even inspired ancient texts. Especially Old Testament texts. Once upon a time, a group of *textless* Jesus followers, sandwiched between empire and temple, defied both. The credibility of our faith is not contingent upon the credibility of the events recorded in the Jewish Scriptures. The credibility of our faith is not contingent upon our text being infallible or inerrant. It rests securely on an event.

And then there's this.

The Bible doesn't actually *say* anything.

SAY WHAT

Jesus said some things. As did Moses, Isaiah, Paul, James, and a host of others. But the Bible has never uttered a word and we would do well to stop putting words in its mouth. The world would be a less confusing place if thoughtful Christians would refrain from quoting the Bible and would reference instead the extraordinary people God chose as his spokesfolks.

Semantics?

Nope.

Got a highlighter?

The next sentence may be worth highlighting.

> Anyone who lost faith in Jesus because they lost faith in the Bible lost faith unnecessarily.

When pastors, teachers, writers, and parents say *The Bible says,* they set the next generation up for an unnecessary crisis of faith. When we say *something* or *somebody says* something and, therefore, we ought to *do* something, we establish that person or thing as an authority. The Constitution says! The principal says! The company handbook says! The Bible says!

"The Bible says" establishes the Bible, as in everything in the Bible, as equally authoritative. It's not. If it is, we have a schizophrenic faith because, as we've noted, the Bible contains two covenants[9] with two different groups for whom God had two different agendas.

Case in point: biblical marriage.

What is a biblical marriage?

A marriage we find in the Bible? Solomon had a lot of biblical marriages. Heck, Solomon broadened the definition of biblical marriage to include concubines. As did David, a man after God's own heart. Abraham lied about Sarah's identity to save his skin. Adam and Eve? Maybe we should focus on what the Bible says about how to conduct a marriage. Like, if either party commits adultery, they should be put to death.[10] Or, if a man discovers his new wife is not a virgin, he can take her back to her father's house where she is to be put to death.[11]

I know. I'm being ridiculous. But it's ridiculous to you because when it comes to these commands, you don't feel obligated to do what *the Bible says*. In fact, when it comes to most of the Old Testament, you would argue against doing what *the Bible says*.

So, for the sake of clarity, let's stop saying that.

If we have to qualify it, why say it? Surely there's a better way. Again, the problem with *the Bible says* is what else the Bible says. If you preach, teach, write curriculum, lead a small group, or talk about your faith in public, drop the phrases *the Bible says* and *the Bible teaches*.

There's nothing to be gained.

There's much to be lost.

As in our credibility and the next generation.

WINSOME TO WIN SOME.

The apostle Paul makes the clearest argument for adjusting our approach based on our audience. He writes:

> Though I am free and belong to no one, I have made myself a slave to everyone . . .

Why?

> . . . to *win* as many as possible.[12]

And how do you plan to do that?

> To the Jews I became like a Jew, to *win* the Jews. To those under the law, I became like one under the law (though I myself am not under the law), so as to *win* those under the law. To those not having the law, I became like one not having the law (though I am not free from God's law but am under Christ's law), so as to *win* those not having the law. To the weak I became weak, to *win* the weak.

Hang on, Paul . . . you keep switching approaches. Why all the back and forth?

> I have become all things to all people so that *by all possible means*, I might *save* some. I do all this for the sake of the gospel, that I may share in its blessings.[13]

"All possible means"? Really? Is that really necessary? Doesn't the Spirit do the work?

> All possible means.

But isn't it enough to preach the Word?

All possible means.

And why do you go to such lengths?

. . . for the sake of the gospel.

What if we just did that for a year? What if we opted for "all possible means"?

Clearly Paul was not married to an approach. He was married to his mission. He was willing to do whatever it took to "win" some and "save" some.

OVERQUALIFIED

If there was ever a first-century preacher who had the goods to leverage *the Bible says* and *the Scripture teaches*, it was Paul. As a Pharisee, he was trained in the law. He studied under Gamaliel. His intellect and reasoning abilities were second to none. This is best evidenced in his message recorded by Luke in Acts 13. It's mind-blowing. Standing in the synagogue of Pisidian Antioch, surrounded by somewhat hostile Jews, Paul begins his message by recounting Israel's migration from Egypt. Common ground, for sure. From there he walks his audience through their own history right up to the era of King Saul and King David. But when he gets to David, he pivots:

> From this man's descendants God has brought to Israel the Savior Jesus, as he promised.[14]

From there he dives right into the details of Jesus' arrest, crucifixion, burial, and, of course, the main event:

> But God raised him from the dead, and for many days he was seen by those who had traveled with him from Galilee to Jerusalem. They are now his witnesses to *our* people.[15]

Then he connects the dots:

> We tell you the good news: What God promised our *ancestors*,
> he has fulfilled for us, their children, by raising up Jesus.[16]

But he's not finished. Diving back into the Jewish Scriptures, Paul quotes from the second psalm. He makes application to Jesus and then wraps it all up with a warning from the prophet Habakkuk.

No notes.

No net.

It's dizzying.

But his point is unmistakably clear and no doubt offensive to many in the room.

> Therefore, my friends, I want you to know that through Jesus
> the forgiveness of sins is proclaimed to you. Through him
> everyone who believes is set free from every sin, a justification
> you were not able to obtain under the law of Moses.[17]

Translated: Jesus did what Moses couldn't. Jesus is greater than Moses.

But later, in the same document, Luke recounts another of Paul's evangelistic messages. This time to a non-Jewish audience with which he leverages a completely different . . . here's our word . . . approach.

SOMETHING ELSE

While Paul's pedigree made him a formidable opponent for Jews intent on discrediting the Jesus movement, Jews were not his primary audience. Paul was called to take the gospel to Gentiles. The majority of Acts is dedicated to Paul's missionary endeavors throughout the Mediterranean Basin. During one of these trips, he took the opportunity to preach to a gathering of educated, upper-class Greeks. In Athens. Fortunately, his traveling companion, Luke, documented the event.

In Acts 17, we find Paul waiting in Athens for the arrival of Timothy and Silas. While wandering through town, he couldn't help but notice the place was full of idols. This eventually led to a heated debate with a group of Epicurean and Stoic philosophers who were confounded by Paul's insistence that . . . ready for this . . . someone had risen from the dead.[18]

They brought Paul to the Areopagus and gave him an opportunity to make his case, which, of course, he was more than happy to do. But his message in Athens is nothing like his message to the Jews in Antioch. He doesn't begin with the story of the Jewish exodus. He begins by complimenting his audience on their interest in the gods.

> People of Athens! I see that in every way you are very religious.[19]

Not only does he choose not to mention the Jewish exodus, he chooses not to quote from the book of Exodus. And this was the perfect opportunity for him to have done so.

> You shall not make for yourself an image in the form of anything in heaven above or on the earth beneath or in the waters below.[20]

How could he resist? The place was full of idols!

But resist he did.

Why?

His mission in life wasn't to make a point. His mission was to make a difference. He was there to "win" some and "save" some. So he chose not to quote from his Scriptures. He quoted one of their poets instead. He referenced something his audience may view as evidence.

Sneaky.

Or to quote Jesus, "shrewd."[21]

Rather than telling the Athenians their gods didn't exist, he chose to talk about the God they missed. He referenced an altar dedicated to an unknown god. This was the ancient Athenian way of playing it safe.

You know, just in case they missed one. My grandmother always set a spare place at the dinner table in case someone dropped by. Same idea.

At this point in his message, Paul employs an unusual preaching technique. He summarizes the Genesis account of creation, including a reference to Adam, without referencing Genesis or Adam. He teaches Scripture without referencing Scripture.

But why?

Why not do what he did in Antioch? Why not give 'em chapter and verse? Why so outsider, seeker sensitive all of a sudden? Was he afraid of what people might think of him?

Paul? Hardly.

If Paul had referenced his Jewish source, his non-Jewish audience may have checked out. When your mission is to win some and save some, you *never* give up influence unnecessarily. When your mission in life is to be *right*, maintaining influence isn't important. I bet you know parents who wish they could go back and parent with the goal of maintaining influence rather than simply being right all the time.

You can *right* kids *right* out the door.

You can *right* kids *right* out the door of the church as well.

Paul does two more unusual things in this message. He tells the Athenians they need to repent of their idolatry. But that's it. He doesn't reference all the other things they needed to repent of. The list was long. But the most unusual facet of his message to this elite group in Athens is that he *never mentions Jesus*.

One more time for effect.

Paul chose not to name the name of Jesus in his evangelistic sermon to Greeks in Athens. This is as close as he gets:

> For he has set a day when he will judge the world with justice by the man he has appointed. He has given proof of this to everyone by raising him from the dead.[22]

According to inspired Luke, that's how the message concluded.

He left his audience hanging.

Was that a good idea?

> When they heard about the resurrection of the dead, some of
> them sneered, but others said, "We want to hear you again on
> this subject."

Ah! A two-part series.

Nice.

> At that, Paul left the Council. Some of the people became fol-
> lowers of Paul and believed.[23]

Paul's approach to the Gentiles in Athens differed significantly
from his approach to the Jews in Antioch. But his central message
was the same. God has done something in the world on behalf of
humanity. He has punctuated and authenticated this great work by
raising someone from the dead! Come back for part two and I'll tell
you his name!

When preaching to non-Jewish audiences, audiences who did not
view the Jewish Scriptures as authoritative, both Peter and Paul leveraged
the life, death, and resurrection of Jesus. They put the spotlight where
the spotlight needed to be—on Jesus and the resurrection.

WRAPPING UP

The approach to preaching, teaching, writing, and evangelism most of
us saw modeled and, consequently, unwittingly inherited, is perfectly
designed for a culture that no longer exists. "The Bible says" doesn't carry
the weight it once did. Fortunately, first-century church leaders showed
us the way forward. They put all their eggs in one basket.

The Easter basket.

They leveraged the event of the resurrection. The time has come for us to do the same. The time has come for us to acknowledge the new normal and adjust. If we genuinely care about the unchurched and post-churched, we will. If we genuinely care about the faith of our kids and grandkids, we will. If our passion is in sync with Paul's, we will adopt his mantra: So that by all possible means I might save some.

If this entire discussion strikes you as unnecessary, unorthodox, or just plain weird, hang on to your birth certificate.

You know where it is, right?

If not, you need to go look for it right now.

You may not exist without it.

SURPRISE

It may help to know I've used this approach throughout this book. I have purposely avoided phrases along the lines of *The Bible says* or *The Word of God states*. Yet this book is filled with references to what Jesus said and what New Testament authors wrote. As I mentioned earlier, I've been avoiding these phrases for years in my preaching as well. I made this change because of the relative ease with which the New Atheists and others undermine faith by attacking *The Bible*. The trustworthiness of the Bible is defensible in a controlled environment. It's not defensible in culture where seconds count and emotions run high. So I changed my approach along with some of my terminology.

As part of my shift, I stopped leveraging the authority of Scripture and began leveraging the authority and stories of the people behind the Scripture. Shifting the conversation away from the authority of Scripture to the authority, courage, and faithfulness of the men and women behind our Scriptures has not only enabled me to better connect with post-Christians, it's done wonders for the faith of the faithful.

The stories of the men and women behind the Scriptures are rich, inspiring, and, unfortunately, not as well-known as you might think.

This approach underscores the historical roots of our Scriptures and our faith. Many, perhaps most, Christians view the Bible as a *spiritual* book that says *true* things to live by as opposed to a collection of documents documenting *events* that actually took place. Again, the foundation of our faith is not an inspired book but the events that inspired the book.

So...

Here's my ask.

THE INVITATION

In light of what's at stake and who is at stake, would you consider unhitching your teaching of what it means to follow Jesus from all things old covenant? Would you be willing to transfer your faith from a book to the events behind the book? Will you embrace this more endurable, defensible, liberating, culture-transforming version of our faith? That's a lot to ask. But while you're considering that, ask yourself this.

What is the faith of the next generation worth?

What is the faith of your children and grandchildren worth?

I say, everything.

I say it's worth any change necessary to ensure the version of faith passed on to the next generation is the enduring version—the faith of our first-century fathers. The version that was harder than Roman steel and tougher than Roman nails. So will you consider retooling how you communicate in order to win some and save some? Will you adjust your language to avoid making it unnecessarily difficult for those who are turning toward God or turning back to God? Are you willing to embrace the realities of the world we live in and let go of cultural assumptions that characterized the world you grew up in?

Granted, these will be hard habits to break.

But break them we must.

The faith of the next generation may depend on it.

Conclusion
History Worth Repeating

If you get a chance to go to Rome, go.

Sandra and I visited for the first time in 2007. I could have stayed for a month. There is so much to see. So much history, so much beauty, and so much traffic. Did I mention we drove to Rome from Venice? Everybody warned us against driving in Italy and especially in Rome. And everybody was correct. So, if you get a chance to visit Rome, go.

But don't drive.

I drove.

Don't drive.

I've been to the Holy Land several times. As a Christian, it's impossible to walk where Jesus walked and not be moved. Just driving into the city of Jerusalem is always emotional for me. But I saw something in Rome that stirred and inspired me more than anything I've seen or experienced in the Holy Land. I spotted something just inside the gate to the Roman Coliseum that I'll never forget and most visitors miss.

CELEBRATION OF DEATH

The Roman Coliseum[1] was originally known as the Flavian Amphitheater. Construction began in AD 72 during the reign of Emperor Vespasian and was completed in AD 80 by his son Titus. After Titus died, his brother Domitian became emperor and continued to add to the already enormous structure.

The Coliseum has four levels. It could seat or stand over 50,000 spectators. The floor was constructed of wood and was covered with sand. Fresh sand was continually brought in to cover the gore created by the games. The floor rotted away centuries ago. Modern visitors to the Coliseum have a bird's-eye view of the stone walls that supported the expansive floor. These walls create a maze of passageways and windowless rooms. It was here, in the dark, damp underworld of the Coliseum, that wild animals, slaves, hunters, and criminals gathered to await what might be their final moments in the sun on the sand above.

Spectators entered the Coliseum through eighty arched entrances. All but four were numbered. The four unnumbered entrances were the emperor's gate, reserved for the emperor and his family, two VIP gates, and the gladiator gate. The gladiator gate is directly across the arena from the emperor's gate. When we visited, guests were being ushered into the Coliseum through the emperor's gate. And it was there, just outside the emperor's gate, that I saw something from which I hope I never fully recover.

MY EYES ONLY

As we waited outside for our tour guide to purchase our tickets, I couldn't help but reflect on what took place centuries ago just a few yards from where we were standing. For almost four centuries, the Roman Coliseum was a place where death, strength, and brutality were celebrated. The Coliseum stands as a memorial to ancient Rome's lust for conquest and disregard for life. Specifically, the life of the weak and the conquered. Mercy was weakness. Good was what was good for Rome. Jupiter reigned. Rome was eternal.

It is impossible for us to fathom the gore that covered the floor of this ancient arena. Titus celebrated the opening of the Coliseum with a hundred days of games. As the final day came to a close, over five thousand animals[2] were killed by "hunters" to the cheers of the bloodthirsty mob.

Each afternoon, gladiatorial matches entertained spectators, all ending with blood. Some with death.

The Coliseum was not the first Roman arena designed for the glorification of gore. Within walking distance of the Coliseum is the site where Nero's Circus[3] once stood. It was here, just a few years before the construction of the Coliseum, that the first state-sponsored persecution of Christians took place. It was in Nero's Circus that Christians were first fed to lions and forced to fight wild beasts. According to tradition, it was in Nero's Circus that the apostle Peter was crucified. Tacitus, a second-century Roman senator turned historian, documented Nero's habit of having Christians wrapped in the skins of animals and thrown to wild dogs where they were torn apart. It was Tacitus who accused Nero of illuminating his gardens at night by burning the crosses of Christians who had been crucified during the daylight hours.[4]

So with visions of gladiators, ravenous animals, and the roar of the bloodthirsty mob, I followed our guide through the turnstile and into the shadow of the Coliseum. As we approached the emperor's gate, surrounded by hundreds of Canon- and Nikon-laden tourists, I looked up and saw the last thing I would have expected to see. Hanging in the archway of the emperor's gate is an enormous wooden cross.

No one warned me. Worse, no one else seemed to notice. In fact, as I've shared this story with friends who've visited the Coliseum, none of them recall seeing that cross. But every single person who enters the Coliseum walks directly beneath it. When I caught up with our Italian guide, I interrupted her lecture and asked where the cross came from. She looked back and I could tell by her expression she'd never noticed it before. And sure enough, she hadn't. In fairness, I should let you know that the only thing there are more of in Rome than cars and cameras are crosses. They're everywhere. So for the average tourist, the cross hanging over the emperor's gate in the Roman Coliseum was just one more cross. But that was not the case for this tourist. It was, and still is, the most significant cross I've ever seen.

When I got back to our hotel, I went online and discovered that Pope Benedict XIV had the cross placed there in the eighteenth century.

By that time, the Coliseum had fallen into terrible disrepair. Anything of value had been stolen. All the copper and brass ornaments had long since been stripped away and used for other purposes. Vagrants lived in the abandoned lower level. As a safety measure, town planners decided to demolish the entire structure. To keep that from happening, Pope Benedict declared the Coliseum a sacred monument dedicated to the suffering of Christ. As part of his declaration, he commissioned the construction of a cross to be hung over the emperor's gate to commemorate Christian martyrs.

STRANGER THAN FICTION

When I saw the cross in the Coliseum, I was overwhelmed with the realization that the gospel *is* the power of God. The contrast was staggering. Here were two symbols representing two kingdoms. The kingdom of this world and the kingdom of God. And in the end, the kingdom of God in Christ prevailed.

The Roman Empire is no more.

The Coliseum is a tourist attraction.

A symbol that once represented the most horrible kind of death represents eternal life.

Everywhere.

When I hear Christians and church leaders in the United States complain about the obstacles the church faces today, I don't know whether to laugh or cry. Obstacles? Seriously? What kind of obstacles? When compared to the insurmountable challenges faced by first- and second-century believers, our obstacles are laughable. The secularization of America? Moral decline? Loss of religious liberty? Hollywood's mischaracterization of Christians?

That's it?

Imagine voicing those complaints to a handful of first-century Roman Christians huddled in the back room of a second-floor apartment reading a portion of Matthew's Gospel by candlelight, the only scrap of Scripture they possessed. Imagine transporting the folks who've abandoned faith for all the wrong modern reasons back in time to that harrowing era of church history. Imagine how hollow, shallow, or completely nonsensical their arguments would sound to Jesus followers who had never owned any portion of Scripture but who sat under the teaching of the apostle Peter himself.

Imagine transporting this same group of time travelers to a house church in Corinth or Ephesus. Picture the confused looks they would receive when these modern skeptics began complaining about the violence depicted in the Jewish Scriptures. First-century followers of *The Way* weren't put off by violence. They were surrounded by it. Besides, the message of Jesus stood in stark contrast to the bloody violent methods of empire and temple.

How would our time travelers respond to a version of faith that had nothing to do with the creation account or the history of the Jews? Imagine their surprise once they discovered that these extraordinary people chose to follow Jesus because he offered eternal life and rose from the dead to authenticate his right to make such an outrageous offer. And they believed this, not because a book told them so, but because the apostle Paul himself told them so.

But enough of imagining.

How would we respond?

How would you respond?

This is no fiction. This is the actual, verifiable history of your faith. How would your version of faith hold up under the scrutiny of that mostly illiterate but oh-so-brave generation of Christians? A generation of Jesus followers whose tried-and-tested faith fueled their conviction that the documents that documented the words and works of Jesus were to be protected at all costs because his was a message for all generations.

So yes, there once existed a version of our faith that rested securely on a single unprecedented event—the resurrection. That's the version I'm inviting you to embrace. The original version. The endurable, defensible, new covenant, new command version.

So why doesn't everybody in America go to church?

Perhaps it's because our modern version of faith is easy to resist and thus easy to dismiss.

Perhaps it's because we're too caught up in what's in it for us rather than what love requires of us.

Perhaps we should change that.

Why not?

We know it's possible.

After all . . .

There's a cross hanging over the emperor's gate in the Roman Coliseum.

> Now to him who is able to do far more abundantly beyond all that we ask or think, according to the power that works within us, to him *be* the glory in the church and in Christ Jesus to all generations forever and ever.
> Amen.[5]

Appendix

Q&A with Andy Stanley and Reggie Joiner

For the launch of Irresistible, *I spoke to thousands of people in multiple cities around the United States. At each tour stop, people were invited to text questions, which were collected and answered during a podcast with my friend Reggie Joiner in Indianapolis, Indiana. This is an edited transcript of our conversation.*

* * *

ANDY: Before we get started, I'd like to set the context for this Q&A. One of the things that creates tension with this book is that I'm not standing in the same place that many pastors or academics are standing. What I'm trying to do with *Irresistible* is bridge the gap between the person who grew up in church and has walked away and the person who has maintained their faith but is thinking about walking away. I want to create a different kind of conversation, not around theology, but about the process or sequence of how we arrived where we are today. I want people to understand *sequentially* what happened, beginning with the resurrection. I want readers to re-engage, or perhaps engage for the first time, with the narrative connected to Jesus' death, burial, and physical resurrection in the hopes that they would embrace him as Savior and Lord.

At that point, I'm happy to hand them off to just about any theological persuasion they choose—be that covenant, dispensational, Reformed, Anabaptist, or Pentecostal. I'm far less concerned about the theological framework they embrace or re-embrace. I'm convinced the *nones* (and those who grew up in our evangelical churches and walked away) have walked away for all the wrong reasons. I want to create an on-ramp for them to re-engage with faith. Or more to the point, re-engage with Jesus.

Every single twenty-five-year-old who has walked away from faith didn't simply walk away from the Christian faith. They walked away from a *version* of the Christian faith. Every de-conversion story I read about or listen to, the belief they no longer believe, the "it" they no longer believe, all stem from the Christian *tradition* they grew up in. And often the tradition or the framework gets confused with the essence of Christianity. I'm trying to stand at an empty tomb and say, "This is it. If Jesus rose from the dead, game on. Choose your religious tradition; choose your framework. I don't really care. But if he didn't rise from the dead, to paraphrase the apostle Paul, it doesn't really matter what we believe. It all rises and falls on the resurrection."

I'm attempting to shift the spotlight away from theological frameworks, off the sixty-six books of the Bible, and onto the moment in time that changed and clarified everything. I'm asking readers to engage the question of whether or not Jesus rose from the dead. That is the question I want the *nones* and potential *nones* to wrestle to the ground. The resurrection is where our faith begins. The resurrection is why we have a Bible to begin with.

Is my approach the best approach? I don't know. I just know the current approach is no longer adequate. And, as I argue throughout *Irresistible*, the current approach is certainly not the original approach.

REGGIE: Some of the questions we're getting from leaders are very smart questions, great questions. And as people are reading the book and readjusting their approaches, we want to unpack those and talk about what this looks like. One of the questions is about the role of Scripture in general. Second Timothy 3:16 is a passage that speaks about Scripture, saying that all Scripture is given by God and is profitable for various purposes. Can you talk about that?

ANDY: For the record, I'm all for everything the apostle Paul said— including this. For us to be informed by what Paul meant by that verse, we must look at how he leveraged the Old Testament and the New Covenant to do the things he says Scripture should do.

I teach from the Old Testament on a regular basis. That's why the folks in my churches were not confused by my "Unhitch" statement. They knew exactly what I was talking about. I'm not in any way saying we should abandon the teachings of the Old Testament. That would be foolish. In fact, the first third of *Irresistible* is a journey through the Old Testament. All I'm saying is that we should take our cue from the apostle Paul in how we leverage the Old Covenant as New Covenant people.

REGGIE: As we talked about the value of the Old Testament, you mentioned that you preach in the Old Testament. Do you believe the Old Testament Scriptures play a role in discipleship today?

ANDY: Absolutely, because it's God-breathed, it's Scripture, and it's the back story for the main story. In *Irresistible*, I dedicate a whole chapter to explain how we should view and interact with the Old Testament as Christians. But again, I'm taking my cue from the apostle Paul, who is very explicit in how he leveraged—but didn't *apply*—Old Covenant commands.

The Gospel writers say, and the apostle Paul reiterates in 1 Corinthians, that on the night of his arrest, Jesus established a New Covenant that fulfilled and replaced God's covenant with the nation of Israel. I understand there are different theological systems that see this differently, but I think the apostle Paul is extraordinarily clear on this. The Old Covenant leads us to the New. The history of the ancient Israelites is a bloody, gritty, violent, exciting, story-driven history. It is the story of God wading into the mess that humankind made in order to redeem the world. And in the Old Testament, we find God playing by the rules of the kingdoms of this world in order to establish a kingdom that was nothing like this world.

The two covenants go together, since it's one enormous epic story. But for those of us who grew up in the church like I did, we were handed a Bible, told it's all God's Word, and then we just mixed and matched from one covenant to the next. We picked a story here and a phrase there and a promise here or there. I think it's easy for us to miss the overarching epic narrative that connects the Old Testament narratives with the New.

The Old Testament, even though it's at the beginning of our Bibles, comes at the back of our apologetic approach. The front of our apologetic approach needs to return to the apologetic of the first century, and that was an empty tomb. It all starts there.

REGGIE: I love that you talk about the back story and the front story. I think sometimes these disagreements are a matter of semantics. In light of this, if you're speaking to leaders who have to take doctrinal positions on what they believe about the Bible, what would be something you would hand to them?

ANDY: When I was in seminary, the brilliant Dr. Charles Ryrie, editor of the Ryrie Study Bible, was one of my professors. In one of our classes, we were talking about inerrancy, and I'll never forget what he said: "What the Bible says is true, is true." That's it. What the Bible says is true, is true. If you're trying to help children or middle schoolers or high schoolers or even adults who are not going to read a four-hundred-page book on inerrancy, you can tell them that through the ages, Christians have believed that what the Bible affirms as true *is* true. Clearly, you can tease that out and get as complicated as you want from there. But that's the starting point.

REGGIE: Let's come back to your point about sequence and context, the idea of a slippery slope. I think one question leaders have is how far we should elevate the Bible and what does it mean if we have elevated it beyond Jesus, beyond who Jesus is, and beyond what Jesus says. In some cases, perhaps, we've made it our guidebook and we've put something in front of Jesus that shouldn't have been there.

ANDY: I think this is an important question, one that I get pretty often. One of the pushbacks I get from academic circles is, "Andy, you are splitting the Word of God, the Bible, from the incarnate Word, the historical Jesus." When I get pushback like this, I say, "Look, the people I'm trying to talk to have no idea what you're talking about. What you're asking me is an important question, and I would love to dialogue with you. But that's not the group I'm talking to."

Again, I just want to take people to the empty tomb to acknowledge that *something* happened in history, and that God has done *something* in history on their behalf. I want them to see that Peter and the disciples stared into an actual, physical, literal empty tomb, and these men who had lost their courage in the garden of Gethsemane found their courage, went to the streets of Jerusalem, and faced down the high priest, the very one who had Jesus crucified. I want people to go there and re-embrace faith in Jesus. Once they do, you can talk to them for the rest of their lives about how they sort out 1 John, John 1:1, and all of these fascinating, wonderful, complex things we all love to talk about.

REGGIE: I get that. Sometimes we bury the lead story. If I'm sitting down with a college student or a friend who has prejudged what I believe about the Bible, I'm not leading with a complicated theological point in my conversation with them. I think the essence of what you're saying is "Don't bury the lead. Make sure you're leading with the right story—the resurrection."

ANDY: Remember, when Luke wrote his Gospel, he said, "Many people have sat down to try to document what has happened here among us." Many. What were they documenting? They weren't simply documenting the life of Jesus. If Jesus had died on a Roman cross, there would be nothing to document. The reason Luke decided something needed to be documented (along with John and Mark and Matthew and, apparently, many more) is because something unusual happened—*Jesus rose from the dead*. The resurrection is why we have the Bible. The resurrection is why we have a New Testament, and the resurrection is why you and I, as non-Hebrew Gentiles, have an Old Testament. If there was no resurrection, there would just be the Hebrew Bible. And you and I would know virtually nothing about it because what we know about it, we learned in church. But if there was no resurrection, there is no church, and there is no Bible. You and I wouldn't even know those stories. Again, I am trying to draw people's attention back to this moment in time. Once they get there and get this one point, bring on the theological systems. You can have them. I'm just going to stand on this point for the rest of my life, because I believe it's that important.

REGGIE: It sounds like you are saying that if we go back to the resurrection, someone doesn't have to believe exactly what I believe about the Bible to be a Christian. They just have to believe in Jesus and what Jesus did. But let's talk more about that. If I'm having a conversation with someone who's drifted from the faith, is there any evidence of the resurrection I can share with them that is outside of the Bible itself?

ANDY: That is a great question, because it's a question skeptics ask and that's where they want to locate the argument. But let's focus on the idea of evidence outside *the Bible*. I would point out there's no evidence inside *the Bible* either because there would not be *a Bible* if there wasn't first a resurrection. Let me tease that out. We don't begin by cross-examining *the Bible* (as a collection of books). Who you need to cross-examine is Matthew. And when you're finished with Matthew, then you have to cross-examine Mark's testimony (which came from Peter). Then you have to go to Luke, who said he thoroughly investigated all of these things. Then you have to go to John. Then you have to go to Peter's letters, because apparently Peter believed in the resurrection.

And then you get to James. James was the brother of Jesus, and James doesn't show up in the narrative until *after* the resurrection. James believed his own brother was his Lord. No one doubts that James lived; he was known as James the Just and is referenced outside of New Testament documents. Josephus documents James' death. He was stoned illegally, yet he died believing his brother was his Lord. So you have to explain the existence of all these testimonies: Matthew, Mark, Luke,

John, James, and Peter. And then you have to explain away the apostle Paul. Specifically, you have to explain away 1 Corinthians. This is a letter no one disputes he wrote, and it was written around AD 55, after he had been to Corinth in AD 53, after he'd been to Cyprus in AD 47, and after he had been to Jerusalem in AD 43. Paul became a Christian about three to five years after the resurrection.

Bart Ehrman acknowledges that the apostle Paul probably became a believer, a Jesus follower, three to five years after the resurrection. The apostle Paul is the fly in the ointment, because he tells us that the Christians in Jerusalem *already* believed in the resurrection when he became a Christian. In fact, the Christians in Jerusalem had already transitioned Passover from a celebration of what had happened in ancient Israel to a new celebration based on Jesus establishing a New Covenant.

There is indisputable evidence that Jewish Christians in Jerusalem already believed in the resurrection just a few years after the event. My point is that you can't be intellectually honest and push belief in the resurrection of Jesus outside the time frame of the eyewitnesses. There wasn't enough time for a myth of that magnitude to have emerged. So, you asked, "Is there evidence outside the Bible?" My first response is that the Bible is the evidence itself—because *without the resurrection, we would have no Bible*. But secondly, you just can't dismiss the Bible all at once. You can't say, "Well, there's the Bible, but are there other sources?" That's somebody who doesn't understand what the Bible *is*. The Bible is a collection of different sources. So you'd need to say, "Other than Matthew and Mark and Luke and John and Peter and James and Paul, is there any other evidence?" That's the question no one asks, but I want this generation and future generations to ask it. I want to tether their faith not to the Bible as a collection of letters and books but to the event that created the Bible.

REGGIE: I want to shift to another question—the difference between the New Covenant and the Old Covenant. In *Irresistible*, you bring it all down to a very clear and succinct idea about the New Covenant versus the Old Covenant—the concept of love.

ANDY: The New Covenant simplifies everything—it's far less complicated, but it is far more demanding. I'm a parent. If you give your kids 10 rules or 8 rules or 4 rules, you know they will find space in the middle, the work-around, the loophole: "You said 8:00, but you didn't say 8:00 p.m." So if you have a rule for every eventuality, you're going to need endless rules.

Jesus, in his brilliance, says to his disciples, "I'm establishing a New Covenant, and now I'm about to give you the terms and conditions." There were 613 terms and conditions for the Old Covenant, divided into civil, moral, and ethical obligations. Israel had her 613 laws, which covered everything and made perfect sense, and we can go back to that in just a minute. The Old Covenant was brilliant—light-years ahead of everything in ancient times. But it had a time limit. Jesus comes along and says there's a New Covenant and there are terms and conditions for this covenant as well. Actually, just one: "You are to love the way your heavenly Father through me has loved you. You're to love as I have loved you."

Now when he said that, they immediately had illustrations of how he had loved them in their time together. But the next day, he would put on a demonstration of love that would take their breath away— because it took his breath away. On the other side of the resurrection, they understood this. By the time the apostle Paul became a Christian, the Christian community around Jerusalem had already created a creed. This may be the oldest Christian creed, a creed that Paul includes in his letter to the church in Corinth. The creed stated: *Christ died for our sins and was buried; he rose from the dead and was seen.* The early Christian Jewish community understood the significance of both the death and the resurrection of Christ and married it to his one command. That one commandment covered every eventuality, because we usually know what love requires of us. We know what honor demands. When you realize that you are face to face with men and women for whom Jesus died, any excuse you have for mistreating them goes away. I don't need chapter and verse. I just have that one, all-encompassing command.

One of the tragedies of our current version of Christianity is that we have taken Jesus' new commandment and put it in a bucket with all the other biblical commands. Then we've shaken them up and given them all equal authority. I believe that on the night of Passover, Jesus was giving us a new command that replaced and informed all the rest.

One of the questions I get sometimes is, "Aren't you afraid people are just going to use love as an excuse to sin?" I suppose they might, but let's be honest. Christians have found excuses to sin whether they have the 10 Commandments, the 613 commandments, or the 613 plus all of Paul's commandments. People are going to do what people are going to do. Personally, I don't think there is a loophole in the love that Jesus demanded that night, and it's not soft. Remember, the next day, he died covered in his own body fluids as a demonstration of the kind of love he calls us to. So, no, this is not soft or permissive. It's extraordinarily demanding. It demands that I put others ahead of myself. So, no, we don't need to fear it.

REGGIE: I think some of the confusion, as I read through the questions we get about *Irresistible*, has to do with the value of the New Testament instruction, the epistles, Jesus preaching the Beatitudes, etc. If it was really that clear that love was the one thing necessary, then what about the rest of the teachings in the New Testament? Why do we need that?

ANDY: This is a great question. I go back to Bible Study Methods 101. Paul said Jesus was born of a woman, born under the law, which means that throughout his entire ministry Jesus operated under the Old Covenant. He was born under the law. But he was born under the law to redeem those under the law *out from under the law*. There's a tension in Jesus' teaching and preaching in which he is operating as a Jewish man under the law. He is dropping breadcrumbs to people and sending signals that something *new* is coming; something *new* is coming; something *new* is coming. He reduces 613 commandments to two, and then he redefines what we understand by "neighbor." Then, on the last night before he is killed, he brings it all together and says, "I'm replacing all of the commandments with the one new commandment."

The apostle Paul had extraordinary clarity about this. In the course of a single day, he pivoted from being an Old Covenant-keeping, law-abiding Pharisee—who, by his own admission, was really good at keeping the law—to a Jesus follower. When the scales fell from his eyes, he not only gained clarity with his physical sight, he gained perspective that no one else has had because he was on *both sides* of the covenant. He had been to the dark side of where the Old Covenant takes you, where he was able to justify violence against Christians in order to serve God. But as a Christian, he never leveraged violence again. He saw the implications of the New Covenant with unmistakable clarity.

What we find in Paul's letters are not new rules to live by. What we find in his letters are applications of Jesus' one new commandment. If you'll read what he says through this filter, you'll notice he connects all of his imperatives to "just as in Christ," meaning have the same attitude as Christ Jesus. He does not connect his moral commands to the Old Covenant to motivate Christians. Sure, he will reference the Old Covenant, but if you look carefully, you will notice these are references to historical details that are fulfilled in Jesus, not platforms that he leverages for authority. In other words, he's not saying that since Moses said, "Do this or don't do that," you should do this or don't do that." Instead, he leverages the New Covenant. He points us to what God has done in Jesus.

There is this little phrase that he repeats over and over: "in Christ, in Christ, in Christ." That's his code word, his way of saying that there is something new and different in this New Covenant. The New Testament imperatives are not new rules for us. They are applications to address ethical and moral questions that he felt Gentiles needed to understand for them to live out this New Covenant command. For example, Ephesians 5 says, "Submit to one another out of reverence for Christ." That's the banner statement: "Submit to one another out of reverence for Christ." We almost don't need anything else. But then in the next sentence, he says, "Wives, here's what it looks like. You submit to your husbands. Husbands, here's what it looks like. You love your wife like Christ loved the church."

REGGIE: That's a great way to think about it. Let's say I'm a pastor sitting here listening to you talk about this, and I'm thinking, *What does that mean for me on Sunday? I mean, I've got to preach from something; I've got to speak about something. So how does that affect how I communicate and preach?*

ANDY: Here's what I've found, and I've been doing this intentionally for the past nine years. Understanding the New Covenant makes it easier and simpler to preach and communicate. There are Old Testament narratives and stories that every preacher and every curriculum writer feels compelled to either skip or to sand off the rough edges. With the approach I'm suggesting, you no longer have to sand off the rough edges. You let David rant all he wants about the wicked and how he hopes God will kill his enemies, and you don't have to apologize or say, "But I think what he meant was . . ." or "Let's skip that one because it doesn't line up with the Sermon on the Mount." David does not line up with the Sermon on the Mount, because David was a warrior who emerged from battle covered in his enemy's blood. In that day, you didn't shoot and kill people from a distance. If you were a warrior, you could smell the breath of your enemy. David was a violent man familiar with violence.

But what would we expect from a warrior who had faced people trying to kill him over and over and over and over? We understand his anger and his frustration and his question about why the wicked prosper. Within the context of a covenant that says, "If you obey, you will be blessed, and if you disobey and worship other gods, you're going in time-out," it makes perfect sense. David's Old Covenant context makes perfect sense of his rants and his prayers, as it does the actions and the behaviors of the prophets and the actions and behaviors of God in his interactions with people and nations.

I've been accused of being a Marcionite. Marcion was a second-century Christian leader and writer who was so frustrated with God's Old Testament behavior, he decided it must be a different God. I would argue that Marcion was a pagan, because he believed in more than one god. Well, I don't believe anything of the sort. I think there is one God and that God's Old Covenant behavior makes perfect sense in light of the fact that at this point in the plan of redemption, God is the founder of a nation who takes a group of slaves, with no civil law, whose entire self-esteem has been wrapped around the fact that as long as they can remember, they have served Egyptians and their gods. And now they're taken out of slavery, and Moses is an apologist attempting to convince them who Yahweh is and who they are. It's a gritty, ancient culture we can't even begin to understand today. To manifest his goodness and glory, God redeemed this group of people as a means of redeeming the world.

When you embrace the Old Covenant for what it is in relationship to the New Covenant, you no longer need to sand off the rough edges. We can let those narratives be exactly what they are in context. Of course, there's always a way to tie them back into what God is doing in our generation and in our world, and that's what opens up the Bible to preaching today. I don't think this limits what we can say, because (again) the pressure's off to make the Old Testament and how God relates to Israel sound like the New Testament and how he relates to the church.

REGGIE: If I understand you correctly, what you're highlighting is that everything we speak about on a Sunday should come from a point of reference in the New Covenant. We're coming at the Old Testament from a new motive, a new basis of relationship.

ANDY: Yes, a new relationship with God, one possible thanks to the Jewish people and God's faithfulness to them. Because of that faithfulness, we're reminded of God's faithfulness to us, even though it is expressed to us in a different way. Under Old Covenant terms and conditions, Jesus lost because he died. If you died, you lost. And if you died young, you were not blessed. In the Old Covenant, the evidence of God's blessing was that you lived a long time. But consider that not many of Jesus' followers, those in the early church, lived a long time. Many things in the Old Covenant are now reversed.

In the Old Covenant, you lay down your life for the king, but under the New Covenant, the king lays down his life for his subjects. Again, throughout the Gospels, Jesus dropped hints that something new was coming—all the way up to the end. They're on the way to Jerusalem, and his disciples think he's about to rip off his rabbi robe and proclaim himself Messiah. And what are they doing? They're arguing about who gets to sit on the left and right in his kingdom. So he sits them all down and he says, "Look, you know how it is with the Gentiles. If you're at the top of the heap, you leverage your power for your own sake. But not so with you. *Not so with you.* In my kingdom, it is different. It's reversed. Everything is upside down. I'm the King who has come to lay down his life for his subjects." So, there's this overarching epic story that has continuity from the Old to the New, but there is also contrast. Again, I think the person who saw with the greatest clarity—this contrast between the Old and the New—was the apostle Paul. In the book, I encourage readers to stay close to the apostle Paul in terms of how we understand the believer's relationship with the Old Covenant.

REGGIE: When you get into the New Testament with letters from James and some of the other writers, they refer to love as the royal law. But this isn't going "soft," right? This isn't an attempt to avoid offending people or an easy approach that avoids hard things, is it?

ANDY: Every parent knows that when you love someone, trying to avoid making them upset is a recipe for terrible rebellion later. Permissive parenting is not love. Avoiding conflict is not love. The New Testament reminds us that God disciplines those he loves. This is not something "soft" or an attempt to avoid offense. In fact, while it's less complicated than the Old Covenant laws, it's far more demanding.

REGGIE: One of the things we love about this tour and getting people to read *Irresistible* is our hope they'll do it in groups and as teams. This allows them to have a conversation process. What would you say to the person thinking, *Okay, how do we get elders and other leaders on board with this way of thinking and this way of presenting? How do you lead up?*

ANDY: When we started North Point twenty-three years ago, one of the things we did from the very beginning was read books together. Every Monday. And we would let the author teach us their content and then we would ask: How does this fit with our context? We would finish a book, go to another book. For over two decades, I've bought the staff books and we've processed the content of the author.

So let me be the bad guy. Buy your team a copy of *Irresistible* and read it together. Discuss a chapter every time you meet. Start a conversation. Here's what you'll discover: At the beginning of the book, I make it very clear I'm not trying to make a theological point, but I'm trying to re-reach a generation and make sure we don't lose another one. If you're a pastor or a church leader, I know you're concerned about this generation. You may not like my response. But if you don't agree, you still need to do something. Don't fear what you *may* lose. Fear what you *are* losing.

If you don't like my approach, find another approach. Maybe this book will start a conversation that leads you to a better approach. The goal is the same . . . to make sure we don't lose another generation of kids who grew up in our churches.

REGGIE: I think what you're doing is pushing the status quo. At the end of the day, we can't keep doing things the way we've been doing them, and we all know that change happens when the gain associated with change becomes greater than the pain associated with the status quo. I hear you saying, "You've got to sit around a table and push at this. You've got to change some things. So, start here in a conversation."

ANDY: Or start somewhere, because the church has not responded to this. The church preaches and teaches like we've always preached and taught. We make the church more modern; we make it louder; we make it softer; we make it brighter; we have more screens. And I'm all for all these things. I love creating fabulous environments, but this generation isn't impressed with my new sermon series or the fact that we've got a new building or we repainted the building or we have brighter projectors. All that stuff that was so new and novel twenty or thirty years ago isn't new or novel now. Today, they're asking different questions and they're leaving for different reasons. They're not leaving the church because they're bored. They're leaving the church because they don't believe the Bible anymore.

REGGIE: Many of the questions we've had in our tour stops are about what this looks like practically. For example, how does it change how we do small groups in our church? Does this mean we should rethink the kinds of studies our groups are doing?

ANDY: Bible studies are great. Any curriculum that's written around a Bible study or a topic that's handled in Scripture doesn't need to change or go away. If you have a group of married adults or single adults in a Bible study, you've won. That's the goal. I'm trying to communicate to the group who has done all those Bible studies, they've got the camp T-shirts, but for whatever reason they don't believe it's true anymore. I want to get them re-engaged with Scripture or maybe just have conversations around Scripture. However we do that, that's a win.

REGGIE: But it still seems like before they're in a Bible study, they've got to understand a premise or have a perspective for how this fits together, or they could end up being disillusioned again.

ANDY: Right. And the question is, "Where do we start?" What's the beginning? What's the initial conversation? I think the initial conversation is this: "In the first century, there was a Greek named Luke who sat down to document the events that had happened in his area and in his generation. Many people had tried to document them. Here's what he came up with and why." Just start at the beginning with the Gospel of Luke. That's the beginning of our story.

REGGIE: Right. We all know that if we run into someone who is trying to understand what Christianity is, we don't start with Leviticus or Deuteronomy. We start with a Gospel, right?

ANDY: Exactly. In fact, this past Sunday, I was doing a series called *The Bible for Grown-Ups*. I made the point that John, near the end of his Gospel, says, "If this is all you ever get, this is all you need." He is saying that if this is the only document you run into, it's all here for you.

REGGIE: That sounds like what I was taught twenty years ago by Campus Crusade. Start with the Gospel of John. Give them the Gospel of John.

So, how do you apply this to children and teenagers? Let's talk about that before we wrap up. Do you teach children the Old Testament? How much of it do you teach? And how do you incorporate this apologetic approach to teenagers?

ANDY: Yes, we teach everybody the entire thing; we teach children the entire Bible. As you know, you teach kids the age-appropriate portions of Scripture, but at some point you cover it all. The last thing we want is to further fragment the way our children understand and interact with the Bible. They've hopped, skipped, and jumped around our favorite passages and narratives, and they have skipped over passages. Then when they turn eighteen or go to college, they go on the internet and they find out *what else* the Bible says.

Today, it is incumbent upon us to make sure when kids leave our churches, there aren't any surprises waiting for them. They need to know about the invasion of Canaan before a college professor asks about God-sponsored genocide. They need to hear that and be ready to say, "Oh, no, you don't understand, professor, there was no genocide. I can prove it. Members of the nations that Israel supposedly exterminated show up throughout the history of Israel. So clearly, they didn't exterminate these people. Sir, you don't understand what the Old Testament is saying there."

There have been books and articles written about these things. We need to make sure that our children leave our student ministries understanding how the big pieces of Scripture fit together, especially the Old Testament and the New Testament.

REGGIE: So, we're positioning them to understand this in a defensible way?

ANDY: Yes. And it begins with the approach we see in the Gospel of Luke. The only reason anyone knows the stories from the Old Testament is because they went to church. But if there was no resurrection, there would be no church. Apart from the resurrection, Old Testament narratives would not matter to us today. Nor would we believe any of them were true. We'd treat them like the Babylonian creation myths.

The only reason Christians take any of the Old Testament seriously is because there was a resurrection. I learned this from Dr. Norm Geisler almost forty years ago. Since the Gospels are historically reliable documents, we believe Jesus rose from the dead. If he rose from the dead, we believe he's who he claimed to be and that whatever he said is true—including what he said about the Law and the Prophets, our Old Testament. We take the Old Testament seriously because Jesus did, not because it's in a book called the Bible.

REGGIE: It seems to me that's an important distinction. It's so easy to flip that and argue the Bible gives credibility to Jesus instead of saying Jesus gives credibility to the Bible.

ANDY: Yes. The Bible did not create Christianity. Christians created the Bible. And let me put it another way. If we ask the average student in our student ministries, "Do you believe there was a little boy named David who slew a giant named Goliath?" I think our children and students would say yes. If you asked, "Why do you believe it?" they'd say, "Because the Bible tells me so." But what I'm saying is that's the wrong answer. Because you can also say, "Do you believe Jesus died on the cross for your sin?" Yes. "Why?" Because the Bible tells me so. Wrong answer.

The Bible is not the reason we believe Jesus died on the cross for our sin. Paul believed Jesus died for his sin 380 years before the Bible was assembled. We believe it because Matthew told us; Mark told us; Luke told us; John told us; and Peter and James told us. And the reason we believe the story of David and Goliath is because Jesus affirmed the Law and the Prophets. It all starts with Jesus and with the resurrection.

REGGIE: One last question. What about those individuals who are apathetic; they don't care about any of this? How can we evangelize somebody who, for whatever reason, has just decided, "You know what, I'm done"?

ANDY: Jesus answered that. He said, "By this, all men will know that you're my disciples, if you have answers to all their hard questions."

Seriously, for the person who has a brother-in-law, a sister-in-law, a husband or wife, or a twenty-five-year-old son or daughter who says, "You know what, that's good for you; it's just not good for me." Here is what I tell them: "You cannot argue people into the kingdom of God, and you can't make anyone believe anything. Your best bet is to make sure the relationship ties are as strong as they can possibly be." And here's the good news and the bad news. Most adults come to faith or come back to faith because of tragedy. Most adults come to faith or come back to faith when they realize their lives are out of control or that they've never been in control.

Most adults only look up when they're *forced* to look up. As a parent, as a mom or dad, or as a grandparent, your best bet is to make sure the relationship is strong so when they begin to crack and when they have questions, they will come back to you and not feel like they will be chastised or judged.

REGGIE: Because the one thing they will want when the world crashes around them is hope, and I think that's what is meant when we're told to be ready to give an answer for the hope we have.

ANDY: That's exactly right. Peter said that, and if you were to say, "Peter, let me ask you another question, a follow-up question. Where do you find your hope?" he would not have said, "The Bible." He would have said, "I'll tell you where I found my hope. When I saw my master and my rabbi die, I gave up hope. I was planning to go back to fishing. When John and I stared into an empty tomb, I was afraid to hope. But when I saw him alive, my hope flared back to life." His hope was anchored in the resurrection, and I think his statement in that letter is an invitation for us to anchor our hope there as well.

NOTES

Chapter 1: The New Standard American Version

1. Karen Armstrong, *Fields of Blood: Religion and the History of Violence* (New York: Anchor, 2015 reprint edition), 149.
2. Luke 23:4.
3. See Matthew 27:18.
4. John 11:47–48.
5. Acts 17:24.
6. Acts 17:30.
7. Mark 2.22.

Chapter 2: Going Global

1. Interestingly, Eugene Peterson translates Genesis 12:2 (MSG): "I'll make you famous."
2. Genesis 12:2–3.
3. Exodus 20:2.
4. Exodus 20:3.
5. Exodus 24:3: "When Moses went and told the people all the Lord's words and laws, they responded with one voice, 'Everything the Lord has said we will do.'"
6. Exodus 20:4–5.
7. Exodus 24:3.
8. Exodus 32:1.
9. Exodus 32:2–4.
10. Exodus 40:34–35.
11. Exodus 34:27.
12. Exodus 19:4–6.
13. For an excellent treatment of the moral and ethical dilemma associated with Israel's conquest of Canaan, I recommend Paul Copan's book *Is God a Moral Monster?* (Baker, 2011).
14. 1 Samuel 8:20.
15. See Deuteronomy 17:14–20 where Moses anticipates the nation's eventual desire for a king as well as the potential pitfalls of a monarchy.
16. 1 Samuel 8:7–9.
17. 1 Samuel 8:19
18. 1 Samuel 8:20.

Chapter 3: Temple Tantrum

1. As translated by the prophet Eugene H. Peterson, 2 Samuel 7:2, The Message.
2. 2 Samuel 7:3.
3. 2 Samuel 7:6–7.
4. 2 Samuel 7:8–17.
5. 2 Samuel 7:9.
6. 1 Kings 9:8.
7. By this time, everything traditionally housed in the holy of holies had either been stolen, hidden, or had diminished with time.
8. 1 Kings 8:6.
9. 1 Kings 8:10–11.
10. 1 Kings 11:3.
11. 1 Kings 11:5.
12. 1 Kings 9:8.

Chapter 4: Splittin' Up

1. Isaiah 49:6.
2. Isaiah 49:6.
3. Ezra 3.
4. Ezra 3:12.
5. Haggai 2:3–7.
6. Haggai 2:9.
7. In the Hebrew Bible, Malachi is the final text in the second division, titled *Neviim*, which means Prophets.
8. Malachi 1:10.
9. Malachi 3:1.
10. Galatians 4:4–5.
11. Matthew 1:20–23.

Chapter 5: Recentering the Universe

1. Matthew 12:6.
2. Josephus claims tens of thousands gathered to protest the desecration of the temple.
3. Josephus, *Antiquities of the Jews*, 389.
4. Matthew 23.
5. Matthew 23:33.
6. Dora Askowith, *The Toleration and Persecution of the Jews in the Roman Empire: Part 1* (Andesite Press, Nabu Public Domain Reprints, 2017), 52–53.
7. Josephus, *Antiquities* 18.313.
8. Apparently, the sacrilege of this decision was lost on temple treasurers. The Tyrian shekel was imprinted with the head of a pagan deity on one side and an eagle—a graven image—on the other. In spite of this, the Tyrian shekel was the only currency allowed.
9. Mark 13:1.
10. Matthew 24:2.
11. Matthew 24:3.
12. Luke 21:20–21.

13. Luke 21:20–21.
14. Luke 21:20–21.
15. Luke 21:23.
16. Josephus, *Jewish Wars.*
17. Luke 21:24.
18. Matthew 24:2.

Section 2 Introduction

1. John 1:29–31.
2. Matthew 4:12–13: "When Jesus heard that John had been put in prison, he withdrew to Galilee. Leaving Nazareth, he went and lived in Capernaum, which was by the lake ... "

Chapter 6: Brand-New Movement

1. Matthew 16:13.
2. Matthew 16:14.
3. Matthew 16:15–16.
4. Matthew 16:17–18.
5. Acts 19:28–29.
6. Acts 19:32 NASB.
7. Acts 19:32 NASB.
8. The term *ekklesia* appears in the Septuagint, the Greek translation of the Hebrew Scriptures; our Old Testament. There it is used to describe the assembly of ancient Israelites. Jews who lived outside Judea worshipped at local synagogues. These gatherings were referred to as *ekklesias.*
9. It is widely accepted Jesus spoke Aramaic. The Greek *ekklesia* is assumed to be the equivalent of the Aramaic term Jesus used in his original pronouncement.
10. Acts 24:14.
11. Geoffrey W. Bromiley, *The International Standard Bible Encyclopedia, Revised,* vol. 2 (Grand Rapids: Eerdmans, 1988, 2002), 85.
12. *The Sacred Writings of Tertullian*; An Answer to the Jews, Chapter VII: The Question of Whether Christ Be Come Taken Up.

Chapter 7: Brand-New Agreement

1. John 8:59; 10:31.
2. Luke 22:14–19.
3. Luke 22:20.
4. Jeremiah 31:31–32.
5. Jeremiah 31:34.
6. Deuteronomy 13:6–10.
7. Acts 15.
8. 1 Corinthians 9:19–23.

Chapter 8: Your First Look at the Good Book

1. See Malachi 4:1–5.
2. s.v. διαθηκη, *A Greek-English Lexicon of the New Testament,* 3rd edition (Chicago: University of Chicago Press, 2000).

3. s.v., בְּרִית, *Brown-Driver-Briggs Hebrew and English Lexicon* (Peabody, Mass.: Hendrickson, 1996 reprint edition).
4. 2 Chronicles 7:14.
5. See Deuteronomy 21:18–21.
6. Claus Westermann, *Genesis 12–36: A Commentary* (Minneapolis: Augsburg, 1981), 225.
7. Genesis 15:9–10.
8. Genesis 15:17.
9. Luke 22:20.
10. Hebrews 7:22.
11. Hebrews 8:6.

Chapter 9: The Bible According to Jesus

1. Galatians 4:4–5.
2. Matthew 5:38.
3. Deuteronomy 19:21.
4. Matthew 5:39–41.
5. Matthew 5:43–45a.
6. Matthew 5:27–28.
7. Matthew 5:17.
8. Matthew 5:18.
9. Luke 4:20–21.
10. πληρόω, *A Greek-English Lexicon of the New Testament*, 3rd edition.
11. John Piper, *A Peculiar Glory: How the Christian Scriptures Reveal Their Complete Truthfulness* (Wheaton, Ill.: Crossway, 2016), np.
12. Piper, *A Peculiar Glory*.
13. See Matthew 24; Mark 13; Luke 21.
14. τελέω: to complete an activity or process, bring to an end, finish, complete, *A Greek-English Lexicon of the New Testament*, 3rd edition.

Chapter 10: Homebodies

1. Matthew 28:18–20.
2. Acts 9:15.
3. Acts 9:20–22.
4. Peter's conversion is usually dated sometime between 35 and 40. It could have been as late as 45.
5. 2 Maccabees 7.
6. Acts 10:14.
7. Acts 10:28.
8. Acts 10:34–35.
9. Acts 10:45.
10. Acts 11:2–3.
11. Acts 11:17.
12. Acts 11:18.
13. Acts 15:1.
14. Acts 15:2.
15. Acts 15:5–6.
16. Acts 15:4.

17. Acts 15:7–8.
18. Acts 15:10.
19. Acts 15:11.
20. Acts 15:19.
21. Acts 15:20.
22. Acts 15:21.
23. Exodus 20:13.
24. Exodus 20:15.
25. Acts 15:23–29.
26. Acts 15:30–31.
27. See Leviticus 17–18.
28. Leviticus 17:10.
29. Some commentators believe "sexual immorality" was a reference to the moral prohibitions listed in Leviticus 18:6–24. But most of these prohibited behaviors were already prohibited in first-century Roman culture. (See 1 Corinthians 5:1 and Leviticus 18:8.) Besides, the Levitical prohibitions assume polygamy, which was frowned upon in first-century Roman culture. For the Jerusalem Council to insist Gentiles adhere to this portion of Levitical law was unnecessary and potentially insulting. Paul, taking his cue from Jesus, raised the bar regarding sexual behavior. See Craig S. Keener's treatment of *porneia* in *Acts: An Exegetical Commentary*, Volume 3 (Grand Rapids: Baker Academic, 2015), 2271.
30. Acts 15:35.
31. See John 17.
32. Matthew 5:19.
33. Matthew 5:17.
34. Mark 13:2.

Chapter 11: *The Apoplectic Apostle*

1. Ephesians 3:6.
2. Romans 7:4.
3. Exodus 20:14.
4. Romans 7:6.
5. 1 Corinthians 6:19.
6. Romans 7:6.
7. παλαιότης, *A Greek-English Lexicon of the New Testament*, 3rd edition.
8. 2 Corinthians 3:14.
9. Galatians 1:6–7.
10. Galatians 1:8.
11. Galatians 1:9.
12. Galatians 3:7–9.
13. Galatians 3:19.
14. Galatians 3:24–25.
15. Galatians 5:2–3.
16. Galatians 5:9.
17. Galatians 5:12.
18. ἀποκόπτω: to cut so as to make a separation, cut off, *A Greek-English Lexicon of the New Testament*, 3rd edition.

19. Acts 9:1–2.
20. 1 Samuel 27:8–9.
21. 2 Corinthians 3:6.

Chapter 12: Obsolete-r Than Ever

1. Hebrews 8:6.
2. Hebrews 8:7.
3. Hebrews 8:13.
4. Acts 9:2.
5. Modern-day Turkey.

Chapter 13: Our Old Friend

1. See Galatians 5:4.
2. Philippians 2:6.
3. Philippians 2:7–8.
4. See Hebrews 8:6.
5. NIV 2011 translates *Sheol* as "realm of the dead." See Deuteronomy 32:22.
6. 2 Samuel 12:23.
7. 1 Corinthians 10:11
8. Romans 15:4–5.
9. 2 Timothy 3:16.
10. See Matthew 5:19.
11. N. T. Wright, *The Climax of the Covenant* (Minneapolis: Fortress, 1991), 181.

Section 3 Introduction

1. Exodus 20:2–6.
2. Joshua 1:8.

Chapter 14: Trending Horizontal

1. Matthew 5:23–24.
2. Matthew 22:15.
3. Matthew 22:29.
4. Matthew 22:33.
5. Matthew 22:34–35.
6. Matthew 22:36.
7. Matthew 22:37–38; see also Deuteronomy 6:5.
8. Matthew 22:39.
9. Leviticus 19:18.
10. Matthew 22:40.
11. κρεμάννυμι, *A Greek-English Lexicon of the New Testament*, 3rd edition.
12. Matthew 22:40, *Zondervan Exegetical Commentary*.
13. Leviticus 19:18.
14. Luke 10:25.
15. Luke 10:26.
16. Luke 10:27.
17. Luke 10:28.
18. Luke 10:29.

19. Luke 10:29.
20. Luke 10:30.
21. Luke 10:33.
22. Luke 10:34.
23. Luke 10:35.
24. Scot McKnight, *Few and Far Between: The Life of a Creed* (Brill Online Books and Journals).
25. Luke 10:36.
26. Luke 10:37.

Chapter 15: A New Command

1. John 13:33.
2. John 13:34.
3. Matthew 22:37–40.
4. See Luke 7:48–49 and Luke 5:21–22.
5. John 13:34.
6. John 13:34.
7. John 13:34.
8. John 13:35.
9. See John 13:15.
10. Philippians 2:5–8.
11. John 13:35.
12. John 13:36.

Chapter 16: Paul and the Irresistible Ethic

1. See 1 Corinthians 7:12.
2. Ephesians 4:31–32.
3. Ephesians 5:1–2.
4. Ephesians 5:3.
5. Ephesians 5:8.
6. Galatians 5:12.
7. Galatians 5:13.
8. Galatians 5:14.
9. Galatians 5:6.
10. Galatians 5:6, *Zondervan Exegetical Commentary*.
11. See James 2:14–17.
12. Philippians 3:4–6.
13. Philippians 3:7.
14. Philippians 3:8.
15. Philippians 3:9.
16. Philippians 2:3–4.
17. Philippians 2:5.
18. Philippians 2:5.

Chapter 17: It's Mutual

1. Ephesians 5:22.
2. Ephesians 5:21.

3. Ephesians 5:25.
4. Matthew 19:3.
5. 1 Peter 3:7.
6. John 15:12 NASB.
7. Galatians 5:6.

Chapter 18: Don't Even Think about It

1. 1 John 1:1.
2. 1 John 1:2.
3. 1 John 1:3.
4. 1 John 4:8.
5. 1 John 4:16.
6. John 14:9.
7. 1 John 2:3.
8. 1 John 2:4.
9. 1 John 2:5.
10. 1 John 2:7.
11. 1 John 2:7.
12. 1 John 2:8.
13. 1 John 2:9.
14. 1 John 2:10.
15. 1 John 2:11.
16. 1 John 2:2.
17. 1 John 4:11.
18. John 1:14.
19. 1 John 4:20.
20. 1 John 3:16, 18.
21. 1 John 4:20.

Chapter 19: A Better Question

1. See 1 John 2:7.
2. Exodus 20:12.
3. See Galatians 5:22–23.
4. 1 Corinthians 13:1.
5. See 1 John 2:20, 27.
6. 1 Corinthians 13:2.
7. 1 Corinthians 13:3.

Chapter 20: What Love Required of Me

1. 1 Corinthians 6:19 NASB.
2. C. S. Lewis, *The Weight of Glory and Other Addresses* (New York: HarperCollins, 2001, first paperback edition).
3. Galatians 6:1.
4. "Which of these three do you think was a neighbor to the man who fell into the hands of robbers?"
5. Romans 5:6–8.
6. 1 Corinthians 13:9–10.

7. 1 Corinthians 13:12.
8. 1 Corinthians 13:8.
9. 1 Corinthians 13:13.

Section 4 Introduction

1. 1 Peter 3:15.
2. 1 Peter 3:15.
3. 1 Peter 3:16.

Chapter 21: Dorothy Was Right

1. "The Unaffiliated," *2014 Religious Landscape Study*, May 12, 2015, http://
   www.pewforum.org/religious-landscape-study/religious-tradition/unaffiliated
   -religious-nones/.
2. John O'Sullivan, "Christianity, post-Christianity, and the future of the West,"
   National Review, December 14, 2013, http://www.nationalreview.com/article/
   366263/our-post-christian-society-john-osullivan.
3. Barna Group, "State of the Church 2016," *Barna*, September 15, 2016, https://
   www.barna.com/research/state-church-2016/#.V9y4z5MrKRt.
4. Steve Green and Todd Hilliard, *The Bible in America* (Oklahoma City:
   DustJacket Press, 2013), 8.
5. *The Bible in America*, 56–58.
6. *The Bible in America*, 89.
7. Acts 4:29–30.

Chapter 22: Name Callers

1. "Why America's 'nones' left religion behind," Michael Lipka, *Factank*, August
   24, 2016.
2. 1 Corinthians 1:22–23.
3. 1 Corinthians 2:2.
4. See Matthew 5:17; 11:13; 22:40.
5. Acts 24:14.
6. There was a threefold designation in use at the time as well. Luke 24:44:
   "Everything must be fulfilled that is written about me in the law of Moses, the
   Prophets and the Psalms."
7. See Romans 7:6; 2 Corinthians 3:14; Hebrews 8:6.
8. τῆς παλαιᾶς διαθήκης βιβλία.
9. From the apology addressed to Marcus Aurelius Antoninus. http://www.early
   christianwritings.com/text/melito.html.
10. Around AD 180.
11. Luke 1:1–5 NASB.
12. 1 Peter 3:15.
13. Richard Dawkins, *The God Delusion* (New York: Bantam, 2006), 51.
14. Sam Harris, *Letter to a Christian Nation* (New York: Bantam, 2007), 67.
15. Dawkins, *The God Delusion*, 268.
16. Harris, *Letter to a Christian Nation*, 4.
17. See Acts 4:13.

Chapter 23: First Things First

1. John 6:66.
2. John 6:68–69.
3. "Death Was Arrested" (Atlanta: North Point Publishing, 2015).

Chapter 24: The Bible Says

1. The biblical scholar F. F. Bruce notes that Chrysostom appears to be the first writer (in his *Homilies on Matthew*, delivered between 386 and 388) to use the Greek phrase *ta biblia* ("the books") to describe both the Old and New Testaments together. *The Canon of Scripture* (Downers Grove, Ill.: IVP Academic, 1988), 214.
2. 2 Timothy 3:16.
3. 2 Peter 1:21.
4. 2 Timothy 3:16. By "Scripture," Paul was in all likelihood referring to the Jewish Scriptures.
5. Athanasius, Letter 39.
6. Bob Seger, "Against the Wind."
7. Deuteronomy 24:1–3.
8. Deuteronomy 24:16.
9. Yes, the Bible contains more than two covenants, but since our English Bibles are organized around two, I thought it best to leave it there for now. But good catch!
10. Leviticus 20:10.
11. Deuteronomy 22:20–21.
12. 1 Corinthians 9:19.
13. 1 Corinthians 9:20–23.
14. Acts 13:23.
15. Acts 13:30–31.
16. Acts 13:32–33.
17. Acts 13:38–39.
18. Acts 17:18.
19. Acts 17:22.
20. Exodus 20:4.
21. Matthew 10:16.
22. Acts 17:31.
23. Acts 17:32–33.

Conclusion

1. Also spelled Colosseum.
2. Some estimates put the total number of animals killed at over 10,000.
3. Circus in the ancient sense. This was usually an oval-shaped, roofless arena surrounded by tiers of seats. It was used primarily for competitive events such as horse races and chariot races.
4. Tacitus, *The Annals*, Book 15, chapter 44.
5. Ephesians 3:20–21.

Irresistible Video Study

Reclaiming the New that Jesus Unleashed for the World

Andy Stanley

Once upon a time there existed a version of our faith worth living and dying for, something the world found irresistible. Men and women pursued it at the risk of persecution, job loss, and eviction from their homes, temples, and society.

What if we actually followed their lead? Perhaps it would change how we read the Bible. Perhaps it would help us understand our own faith and what we believe. Perhaps we would change the world again.

In this six-session video study (DVD/video downloads sold separately), pastor and author Andy Stanley shows how Jesus' arrival signaled that the Old Testament was fulfilled and its laws reduced to a single verb—love—to be applied to God, neighbor, and enemy. So, what is required if we want to follow Jesus' example and radically love the people around us? We almost always know the answer. The hard part is actually doing what love requires.

Rather than working harder to make Christianity more interesting, we need to recover what once made faith in Jesus irresistible to the world.

Sessions include:

1. Simply Resistible
2. Brand-New Agreement
3. The Bible According to Jesus
4. The Irresistible Ethic
5. What Love Requires of Me
6. A New Approach

Available in stores and online!

Deep & Wide

Andy Stanley

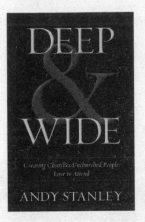

Andy Stanley's bestselling and award-winning vision for the local church is now available in softcover. New bonus content includes a study guide, church staff helps, and an interview with Andy on the most frequently asked questions about *Deep and Wide*.

With surprising candor and transparency, pastor Andy Stanley explains how one of America's largest churches began with a high-profile divorce and a church split.

But that's just the beginning...

Deep and Wide provides church leaders with an in-depth look into North Point Community Church and its strategy for creating churches unchurched people absolutely love to attend.

Available in stores and online!